A BLESSING TO EACH OTHER

A BLESSING TO EACH OTHER

Cardinal Joseph Bernardin and Jewish-Catholic Dialogue

LITURGY TRAINING PUBLICATIONS

ACKNOWLEDGMENTS

The following persons contributed not only their written words but their thoughts and zeal to this book:

Reverend Thomas A. Baima is director of the Office for Ecumenical and Interreligious Affairs of the archdiocese of Chicago.

Edward Cardinal Cassidy is president of the Pontifical Commission for Religious Relations with the Jews.

Sister Mary Ellen Coombe, NDS, is director of the Institute for Catholic-Jewish Education in Chicago.

Reverend Daniel F. Montalbano is associate director of the Office for Ecumenical and Interreligious Affairs of the archdiocese of Chicago.

Ms. Sharon Morton is director of Religious Education at Am Shalom Congregation, Glencoe, Illinois.

Reverend Doctor John T. Pawlikowski, OSM, is professor of Social Ethics at Catholic Theological Union of Chicago.

Rabbi Herman Schaalman is Rabbi Emeritus of the Emmanuel Congregation, Chicago, and is past president of the Council of Religious Leaders.

In addition, thanks are due to Reverend Michael Place for assistance in preparing the manuscript; to Ms. Barbara Feldt, executive secretary of the Office for Ecumenical and Interreligious Affairs; and to Ms. Mary Laur, who prepared the index. This book was edited by Gabe Huck with assistance from Pedro A. Vélez and Theresa Houston. The design is by Jill Smith. The cover photo is by Joel Fishman. Other photos are acknowledged in place. The production artist was Mark Hollopeter. Joe Conlon assisted in production of the cover. The typefaces are Veljovic and Trajan. This book was printed by Thiessen Graphics in Chicago, Illinois.

The cover: Cardinal Bernardin in the Valley of the Destroyed Communities, a special memorial within Yad Vashem in Jerusalem. It commemorates the many centers of Jewish culture in Europe that were lost during the Holocaust. The names of cities and towns with sizable Jewish populations before the war are engraved on the walls.

Guidelines for Catholic-Jewish Relations © 1985 United States Catholic Conference (USCC) Washington, D.C., and *God's Mercy Endures Forever: Guidelines on the Presentation of Jews and Judaism in Catholic Preaching* © 1988 *USCC* are used with permission.

Excerpts from *Vatican Council II: The Conciliar and Post Conciliar Documents, New Revised Edition,* edited by Austin Flannery, OP, © 1996, Costello Publishing Company, Inc., Northport, New York are used by permission of the publisher, all rights reserved.

"Reconciling Church and Synagogues" and "A September Prayer" reprinted with permission of *The New World,* Chicago.

00 99 98 97 96   10 9 8 7 6 5 4 3 2 1

Library of Congress Catalog Card Number 96-79340

ISBN 1-56854-104-X

BERNAR

TABLE OF CONTENTS

❖

ADDRESSES BY CARDINAL BERNARDIN

Cardinal Bernardin's addresses are usually without title. These are identified in this book by the audience or group to whom they were given. Some are called "addresses" to indicate a longer talk. Others are called "remarks" to indicate the talk was part of a larger program. There are some few texts called "invocations" or "prayers." Even when a text has a title, the description of the audience is included here as part of the subtitle.

※

Cardinal Edward Cassidy

A BISHOP TEACHES ABOUT "NOSTRA AETATE"

I am pleased to have the opportunity of welcoming, through this foreword, the publication of *A Blessing to Each Other: Cardinal Joseph Bernardin and Jewish-Catholic Dialogue.*

Not long after my appointment by Pope John Paul II as president of the Pontifical Commission for Religious Relations with the Jews, I was able to spend a little time in the archdiocese of Chicago and to experience firsthand the fine work that has been done there at the local level in the field both of Christian unity and of interreligious dialogue.

During my visit I was honored to take part in a memorial service for Yom Hashoah, which took place in the context of a meeting of the archdiocese of Chicago with its ecumenical and interfaith partners. I met not only Catholics and Jews but also Christians of other ecclesial communities. All spoke of the leadership of Cardinal Bernardin in both the ecumenical and interreligious fields. I was grateful for and encouraged by the sensitivity that had obviously developed among these leaders and was then being expressed as they jointly commemorated the victims of the Shoah.

But as you will find in reading the pages that follow, interfaith dialogue is much more than ceremonial observances, as important as these are. True dialogue involves a kind of cooperation that extends to and touches many aspects of a community's life. I am reminded of the remark made by Pope John Paul II in his address to the American Jewish Committee in 1995 when he said:

As we look to the future, there is an urgent need for us to continue building on the foundations already laid. One of our greatest mutual challenges remains at the level of education and information, where the results of our cooperation must ultimately be implemented. If it is to be fruitful, dialogue between Christians and Jews must find eloquent expression in the life of both our communities.

The archbishop of Chicago and his partners in the Catholic and Jewish communities of Chicago have taken up this challenge. Cardinal Bernardin has shown leadership both as a teacher of the Second Vatican Council's *Nostra Aetate* and as a pastor to the wider community. The Chicago dialogue is organically part of the wider relationship of Jews and Catholics on the international scene. Before you begin to read this study of one local bishop's efforts to teach *Nostra Aetate,* I would like to share with you the global perspective of Catholic-Jewish relations. I do this to highlight just how important it is to the international dialogue to have quality local efforts, such as that of Chicago. Each fosters and enriches the other. Each also proves the effectiveness of the other.

The International Liaison Committee is the principal and official place of Catholic-Jewish dialogue at the global level. In 1990, in Prague, the members of this Committee emphasized the new spirit of relations that had developed and by which the past spirit of distrust and suspicion was replaced by reconciliation, mutual understanding and finally, cooperation between Jews and Catholics. In Baltimore in 1992, this Committee faced the deep wounds of history and the real possibility of a new anti-Semitism in the modern period. And in 1994, in Jerusalem, the International Liaison Committee asked itself how Catholics and Jews could together respond to the challenges of the day as members of faith communities with a common root in Abraham and a shared tradition based in the revelation of the scriptures.

The Chicago dialogue has followed this path of reconciliation, mutual understanding and cooperation. From the early beginnings in the Chicago Conference on Religion and Race to the present joint program efforts for clergy and laity, we see a steady progress toward the goals of reconciliation, understanding and cooperation.

I was reminded again of what Pope John Paul II said in his message to Poland in 1993 on the anniversary of the Warsaw Ghetto Uprising, which I quoted in Jerusalem, and share again here:

> As Christians and Jews, following the example of the faith of Abraham, we are called to be a blessing for the world (cf. Genesis 12:2 ff.). This is the common task awaiting us. It is therefore necessary for us, Christians and Jews, to be first a blessing to each other.

This could just as well be the motto of Cardinal Bernardin and the Catholic-Jewish dialogue in Chicago. It is my hope that this book is a blessing to Christians and Jews as both communities continue the journey together toward understanding and harmony.

Vatican City
June 1996

3

Rabbi Herman Schaalman

TO HERALD AND CREATE A NEW DAY

WE are approaching the end of the second millennium and are beginning to speculate about the third, which lies beneath the horizon waiting to be called into being. We are in this millennial twilight between the dusk and the eventual dawn because Christendom has succeeded in organizing the flow of time not only for itself but, practically and realistically, for the entire world. This slowly waning flow of the second and the anticipated birth of the third millennium inescapably leads to reflection.

What has happened since Christendom used an arbitrary year one in the relentless unfolding of nearly 2,000 years? Surely, torrents of words and thoughts will burst forth to assess the status of the earth, of culture and cultures, of nations, of life both in the abstract and the often painful concrete. We are beginning, and will undoubtedly intensify, an in-depth review of the human experience both as it relates to ourselves, to each other and to God. Everything will be placed under the high-powered microscope of the human mind and imagination. Nothing, it is likely, will escape and be left uncovered.

In such a time the Jewish people, though living liturgically by their own and older calendar, and counting traditionally this year to be 5756 putatively from creation, also will engage in this review occasioned by the millennial moment. This last century, this twentieth, dare not be left out, because in every sense and cumulatively it has become the bloodiest and most painful in a long history all too well acquainted with pain, horror and death. In all the generations of a Jewish presence on earth, perhaps only the first and second centuries in their futile, bloody struggle against Rome can match the horrendous record of the twentieth century.

Endless attempts have been, and most likely will continue to be made to understand this unique, strange, stressed, often deadly history of the Jewish people. Many wise and erudite theories have been proposed to explain this most uncommon story. None of these can escape the powerful, fate-laden impact of Christendom on the life and destiny of the Jew.

Beginning in the second half of the first century, the small, formerly all Jewish community of those who believed in the messiahship of Jesus and the main body of the then-living Jews split asunder. Tensions grew and issued quite quickly into outright enmity. Buttressed by the Constantinian elevation of young Christianity to be the sole, licit religion of the Roman Empire, and increasingly fortified by subsequent civil and religious edicts and legislation, a dehumanization and demonization of the Jewish people began that all too frequently led to degradation, segregation and often wholesale slaughter. As the dean of American Jewish historians, Salo Baron, put it, Jewish life and history became "lachrymose."

Without a doubt, these centuries-long defamations and persecutions deeply stained the record of Western civilization at whose center lay Christianity. There were, of course, exceptions to this predominant attitude here or there, and they are worth remembering, but overwhelmingly and effectively Christian-oriented and dominated European and related Western culture was usually ferociously hostile to Jews and Judaism.

While there are other factors, ultimately the Shoah of the forties of this century is unthinkable without this background. It is this deep, long-standing anti-Jewish stain that made possible the unprecedented and unspeakable horrors of the "Endlösung" that issued in the death camps and their millions of Jewish victims — men, women and children.

When the Second World War was over, the world began to hear and to grasp, gradually and often reluctantly, the depth of this deadly catastrophe that had been inflicted primarily on the Jewish people. Two-thirds of the Jews living in Europe had been wiped out in systematic, government-inspired and supervised mass murder. Many people, surely not all, realized how profoundly past history and behavior had contributed to the possibility and actuality of this horror, the Shoah.

Some searched their conscience and scrutinized their cultures and beliefs. They concluded that wittingly and unwittingly they had a part in the atrocity of the Shoah. Some came forward courageously confessing their own insights and repudiating the teachings of supercessionism and triumphalism. They called for a radical reshaping of the understanding of Judaism and of the relation between Jews and Christians, between church and synagogue.

Nostra Aetate, the breakthrough document adopted by the Second Vatican Council in 1965, signaled forcefully and unmistakably this radical turn from the past and proclaimed a new beginning.

The spirit and concrete implication of this breakthrough proclamation has been confirmed and elaborated on by subsequent statements by popes and other church leaders. None has done so more forthrightly than Cardinal Joseph Bernardin, the archbishop of Chicago.

These pages contain a part of his courageous, scholarly and sensitive treatment of the church's relationship to the Jewish people and Judaism and of its involvement through its past attitudes and teachings in the horrendous events of the early forties. He has thrown a penetrating light on this murky scene and raised that most welcome hope of a totally different, mutually respectful and understanding relationship. Basing himself on official statements by occupants of the throne of Saint Peter, notably Pope John Paul II, and on documents explicating further the meaning and practical intent of *Nostra Aetate,* the cardinal has not only fully understood the risk implicit in all genuine dialogue but has been publicly willing to take it. He can, thereby, assume a leading role in this most necessary, promising and healing undertaking of replacing centuries-old hostile modes by daringly fresh and open ones. He has become an inspiring model for all those who, deeply desirous of reversing the past, seek a radically new way of understanding Judaism and Jews. Cardinal Bernardin is a most respected and effective voice proclaiming this new way in which Judaism and Christianity, Jews and Christians, can meet, listen to each other and learn to live side by side in friendship and peace.

The essays contained in this volume are a partial record of this great religious leader's convictions. They contain thorough, honest and often unsparing analyses of the past and call for religious renewal and practical steps to achieve greater understanding. Again and again Cardinal Bernardin calls on the church and all Christians to reverse the trends and positions of the past. He asks all to enter on a path of understanding, teaching and utterance. Such genuine dialogue will open an entirely new and wholesome chapter in the relations of all Christians — but especially Catholics — and Jews.

May God bless this work.

Reverend Thomas A. Baima

CATHOLIC-JEWISH RELATIONS IN CHICAGO

CATHOLICS and Jews have lived side by side in Chicago for many years. One hundred years ago, both Jews and Catholics were seen as strangers in Protestant America. And it was as strangers, followers of foreign religions, that they both came to Chicago in the summer of 1893 to enter the first World's Parliament of Religions.

While it was widely believed that the Parliament would show the superiority of Protestant Christianity, the actual effect was for Judaism and Catholic Christianity to be accepted as mainstream American religions. Gradually, from 1893 on, popular consciousness shifted from seeing the United States as a Protestant Christian country to thinking of America as a country of Protestants, Catholics and Jews.

It would be more than 50 years before further dialogue took place between the faith communities.

After the Holocaust and the founding of the State of Israel, nothing in Christian-Jewish relations would be the same again. The spirit of self-reliance that was a permanent quality of the Jewish community moved from a passive stance to one of activism. New expressions of this self-reliance, particularly in the form of protective and defensive organizations, gave a new meaning to the byword: "No one will care for the needs of Jews as much as Jews." By the late 1950s Jews were well-organized for entering the public scene in many more direct ways.

These mediation institutions are critically important in the history of interfaith relations. As they became involved in social and community affairs, they came into contact with the social and communal organizations of the Catholic Church. Here the recent story of interreligious affairs in Chicago begins.

The archdiocese of Chicago's Office for Urban Affairs, under the direction of Monsignor John J. Egan, began in 1958 to create a network of relationships between the archdiocese and socially concerned organizations in many other religious communities. These many individual contacts led to the formal, organizational relationships that began in the Civil Rights movement. In an effort to confront racism, the archdiocese of Chicago, the Episcopal diocese of Chicago, the Chicago Board of Rabbis and the Church Federation of Greater Chicago, in 1963, established the Chicago Conference on Religion and Race (CCRR). The CCRR brought the religious communities into the Civil Rights movement as it promoted understanding through deeds.

At these same times, in Rome, the Catholic bishops of the world were meeting in general council. Vatican Council II was charting a new course for the church in the modern world. Four of its major documents dealt with ecumenical or interreligious matters and so marked the entrance of the Catholic Church into the ecumenical and interreligious movements. In 1965, the Council promulgated the document that would become the basis of Cardinal Bernardin's teaching. *Nostra Aetate* ("In This Age of Ours"), the *Declaration on the Relationship of the Church to Non-Christian Religions,* reclaimed the theological connection of the church to Judaism. It condemned anti-Semitism and called for repentance by Christians for the hatred, the persecutions and the prejudice directed at any time against the Jews.

In this same year, in response to the decrees of Vatican Council II, the archbishop of Chicago, John Cardinal Cody, established the Commission for Human Relations and Ecumenism. Under the direction of Monsignor Edward M. Egan, the Commission educated Chicago's Catholics about ecumenism. Its lasting contribution were the policies that guided the archdiocese's entrance into Chicago's interchurch activities and dialogue. Cardinal Cody gave this Commission a central importance in the structure of the archdiocese, a sign for the Catholic Church that these activities were bound to the office of the archbishop. This stance has been constantly maintained since 1965.

The Reverend William Lion succeeded Monsignor Egan. He was also the executive director of the Catholic Conference of Illinois and therefore in a position to cooperate with the Jewish Federation in public policy matters. During this period, CCRR remained the main institutional expression of Catholic-Jewish relations.

In 1982, the new archbishop of Chicago, Joseph L. Bernardin, moved the archdiocese another step forward in its institutional commitment to dialogue. He established a separate, fully staffed agency as part of the diocesan administration. Cardinal Bernardin invited Monsignor John J. Egan to become the director of the archdiocesan Office for Human Relations and Ecumenism. The archdiocese now expanded its dialogue with the Jewish community beyond the multilateral venue of CCRR to the organization of specific bilateral programs.

At Mundelein College in October of 1985, Cardinal Bernardin presided over a convocation of Jewish and Catholic leaders to mark the twentieth anniversary of *Nostra Aetate*. In that event, the cardinal prayed that the commemoration would begin a new phase in the history of Catholic-Jewish relations in Chicago. Rabbi Louis Jacobs, professor of Talmud from Leo Baeck College in London, gave the main address and joined in the cardinal's prayer.

That same year the American Jewish Committee and the archdiocesan Office for Human Relations and Ecumenism organized and supported several lay dialogue groups that paired neighborhood parish churches and synagogues. The project's goals were to break down stereotypes, reduce tension between religious communities and develop new perspectives on interfaith relations at the grassroots level. At one time there were as many as 15 groups meeting in Chicago and the suburbs. Dialogue groups continue today. Some groups meet for a specific time; others are ongoing. New groups are formed each year.

An annual priest-rabbi retreat, also organized by the American Jewish Committee in cooperation with the archdiocese, has allowed priests and rabbis from the Chicago area to attend lectures, engage in small group discussions, share prayer services and join in friendship. Each retreat is focused on a single topic. These have included: prayer, public worship and private reflection, marriage and intermarriage, abortion, the concept of land in Judaism and Christianity. These two-day retreats have provided a unique opportunity for participants to engage in true inter-faith dialogue. In recent years the retreat has included Christian clergy from the Episcopal, Lutheran and Greek Orthodox churches as well.

In the meantime, the CCRR began to show signs of weakness. Recognizing the changed circumstances of the early 1980s, Monsignor Egan moved to reorganize the CCRR into a broad-based, high-level, interfaith structure. He called on key judicatory executives, led by Cardinal Bernardin, to form a roundtable. In 1984 the CCRR was restructured into the Council of Religious Leaders of Metropolitan Chicago (CRLMC). For the first time, all the heads of judicatories, not their representatives, were at the same table. To maintain this new level of relationship, the organization adopted a rule that no substitutes were permitted.

The Council of Religious Leaders works mainly in the area of public witness. It has issued pastoral letters on racism and gambling, as well as education. It is currently studying pastoral issues related to childhood.

Another project now more than a decade old is the Scholars' Dialogue Group. Founded under the direction of Sister Joan M. McGuire, OP, this group is based in study, an activity honored in both traditions. Study becomes the vehicle for relationship. Sponsored by the archdiocese, the Chicago Board of Rabbis, and the Jewish Community Relations Council, this scholars' dialogue examines topics of theological and social concern.

A major effort in dialogue is the Institute for Catholic-Jewish Education established in 1982 by Sister Anna Marie Erst and the American Jewish Committee. Under the leadership of Sister Mary Ellen Coombe, the Institution has become a unique partnership between the Sisters of Sion, the archdiocese of Chicago and the American Jewish Committee. This partnership has allowed the Institute to initiate and develop a variety of "Partnering Programs," which include outreach to both Catholic and Jewish schools, educators, and neighborhood parish and synagogue communities. This allows Jews to hear about Christianity from practicing Catholic Christians. And it allows Catholic students to learn about Judaism from practicing Jews. This principle of "self-description" is at the center of everything the Institute does.

Another unique project has been the Joseph Cardinal Bernardin Center for the Study of Eastern European Jewry. This scholarly institute is a project of the Spertus Institute of Jewish Studies, in cooperation with the archdiocese of Chicago. With an initial focus on Poland, the Center has hosted exchanges of professors between Chicago and Poland. One major success was a seven-week institute for professors of the major seminaries of Poland. These scholars were able to study Judaism in the midst of the vibrant Jewish community in Chicago. In addition to this international program, the center works in cooperation with the archdiocesan Office for Ethnic Ministries to offer programs for the local Polish-American community to enhance Polish-Jewish relations.

A dialogue among women has developed as well. Under the joint sponsorship of the American Jewish Committee and the archdiocese, the Women's Dialogue Group recently became a trialogue as Muslim women joined the conversations. Like the Jewish-Catholic dialogue groups, the trialogue bases discussion on experiences of life-cycle events, holidays, central beliefs and social concerns in the three communities.

Interfaith marriage has been an important concern for both the archdiocese and the Jewish community. Reverend John Cusick, director of the archdiocesan Office for Young Adults Ministry, and Reverend Daniel F. Montalbano, associate director of the archdiocesan Office for Human Relations and Ecumenism, have provided pastoral care to many couples entering Catholic-Jewish marriages. Seeing the problems an interfaith marriage poses, these couples with Cusick and Montalbano brought together ten other couples in 1988. From this came the Jewish-Catholic Couples Dialogue Group in Chicago. Today the mailing list includes about 400 couples in various stages of their relationship. Some are just dating, others are planning their wedding and many have begun establishing their families. The group meets once a month with an average of 40 – 60 people in attendance. In addition to the Dialogue Group, two other groups have developed. The Wedding Group meets three to four times a year specifically to discuss all aspects of an interfaith wedding ceremony. The Family School is a parent-taught, twice-monthly program for children five years of age and older.

In addition to these bilateral relations, new multilateral efforts have developed since the time of the CCRR. The Chicago Board of Rabbis is the main representative in these. Working with the archdiocese of Chicago, the Reformed Church in America, the Greek Orthodox diocese and the Evangelical Lutheran Church in America, the Chicago Board of Rabbis sponsors the O'Hare Airport Chapel. The O'Hare Interfaith Chapel Corporation operates the most extensive airport chapel program in the nation. Open 24 hours each day, the chapel provides everything the major religions need for prayer. The Chicago Board of Rabbis has provided the Jewish prayer books to the chapel for this purpose. The chapel offers Catholic, Protestant and Islamic worship services each week. It offers referrals to Jewish rabbis in emergency situations, thereby providing an important link between the traveling public and the local religious community.

The National Conference of Christians and Jews is the facilitator of other contacts between Catholics and Jews. Two of its programs are contributed to by both the Chicago Board of Rabbis and the archdiocese. These are the interfaith calendar and the Thanksgiving service. The interfaith calendar is now a nationally acclaimed product. Using the principle stated above of "self description," 14 religious communities describe on the yearly calendar their teachings and practices, and explain the major feasts and commemorations on their calendar. The same group also sponsors the annual Metropolitan Chicago Thanksgiving service.

A final area of archdiocesan dialogue efforts lies in its publishing house, Liturgy Training Publications. Over the years, LTP has distinguished itself as a promoter of the interfaith attitude through such titles as: *The Passover Celebration: A Haggadah for the Seder; Songs of the Seder Meal; From Desolation to Hope: An Interreligious Holocaust Memorial Service; Thank God: Prayers of Jews and Christians Together; Jews and Christians: A Dialogue Service about Prayer; Teaching Christian Children about Judaism; When Catholics Speak about Jews: Notes for Homilists and Catechists.* This is one of the enduring contributions of the church of Chicago to the dialogue throughout the English-speaking world.

Because it all started with the 1893 Parliament in Chicago, the 1993 Parliament of the World's Religions was a historic gathering for the religions in Chicago. Virtually all aspects of the Jewish and Catholic communities were involved. While four Jewish organizations withdrew their cosponsorship over previous anti-Semitic remarks by one of the plenary speakers, Jewish participation in the event and its follow-up remained high. In this event, the Catholic and Jewish communities were able to do for others what was done for them in 1893: welcome minority religions to the American mainstream. As a result of the 1993 Parliament, Muslims, Hindus, Buddhists, Jains, Zoroastrians, Baha'is and others are taking their place with Catholics, Protestants and Jews in the minds of people as American religions. The continuations of the Parliament, especially the Metropolitan Interreligious Initiative, are further developing the network of relationships that fosters the multilateral interreligious dialogue in this city.

All of this set the stage for the largest dialogue undertaking of the two communities, Cardinal Bernardin's 1995 visit to Israel.

From the start, Cardinal Bernardin wanted his first visit to the Holy Land to be a spiritual visit. It is, however, impossible to visit the Middle East without encountering politics. And this is all the more true for the senior prelate in the United States. As a way of balancing this, Cardinal Bernardin decided to make the trip a dialogue visit. He would go to the Holy Land but in the company of the leadership of the Catholic-Jewish Dialogue Group in Chicago. The delegation would try to understand both the shrines and the living Christian community, the religion of Judaism in its place of origin, and the living reality of the State of Israel. And he would try to listen to the struggles of the peoples not only in Israel but in the West Bank and Gaza. He would try to hear and see directly. Finally, he would try to make a contribution to Catholic-Jewish dialogue by delivering a major academic address on anti-Semitism at the Hebrew University of Jerusalem.

All this was possible only because of the more than 25 years of dialogue in Chicago. Because of the depth of the relationship brought about by those 25 years, this dialogue visit could, in the words of one delegate, "pull no punches." The very hard questions could be voiced and heard. The Holy Land, good and bad, was shared together.

Fourteen men and women set out on March 20, 1995, from O'Hare International Airport for the land of Abraham, Isaac and Jacob, for the land of Jesus, Mary and the 12 apostles. Together they journeyed to Yad Vashem and walked the Via Dolorosa. Together they went to Bethlehem University and to the Old City to hear of the struggle of Palestinians living under the Israeli occupation of the West Bank. They met with Prime Minister Rabin and Foreign Minister Peres to hear about their hopes for the peace process. And they went to Gaza City to meet with President Arafat to hear directly the perspective of the Palestinian authority on the obstacles to peace.

The delegation met with the religious leadership of both the church and synagogue. And they returned home, changed by the journey that they had made together.

To continue what Cardinal Bernardin began in the Middle East, the archdiocese of Chicago established an annual address to be known as the Jerusalem Lecture. This permanent program will examine a topic in the religious relationship of Catholics and Jews in a two-year cycle. For each topic, a Catholic and then a Jewish scholar will study the theme and offer a theological reflection in a public lecture. The first theme was anti-Semitism. Cardinal Bernardin's talk on Mount Scopus began the conversation. In 1996, Professor Emil Fackenheim delivered a second reflection on "Jewish-Catholic Relations after the Holocaust." The next two-year cycle will study Jewish-Catholic relations in the first century.

The Catholic-Jewish dialogue in Chicago then comprises many different relationships. It reaches many segments of the two communities, clergy and lay, professional and popular, religious and secular. It is a tribute to Cardinal Bernardin that under his leadership such creative expressions of the Second Vatican Council's teaching on dialogue could flourish. We thank God for his leadership and for all the distance our two communities have traveled.

❈

Reverend John T. Pawlikowski, OSM

COVENANTAL PARTNERSHIP—CARDINAL BERNARDIN'S THEOLOGICAL APPROACH TO CHRISTIAN-JEWISH RELATIONS

IN his several addresses that focus directly on the theological dimensions of the church's relationship with the Jewish people, Cardinal Bernardin exhibits full awareness of Christianity's strongly negative outlook toward Jews and Judaism. This tradition, sometimes referred to by its Latin name *adversus Judaeos* ("against the Jews") permeated much of patristic theology. Its impact continued throughout the medieval era. While the cardinal is aware that it has been somewhat muted in tone in the twentieth century, especially since the Second Vatican Council's *Declaration of the Relation of the Church to Non-Christian Religions,* he also is fully conscious that a substrata of this theology remains with us today in many circles. His statements show a willingness to challenge this negative theology of Judaism head-on.

In his Hebrew University address (1995), he staunchly maintains that we cannot fully grasp how Jews fared in much of Western history without some understanding of this adversus Judaeos theology. Such theology had a definite impact on social legislation in many places as well as on the stance of the Holy See and a number of "Christian" nations toward the idea of a Jewish homeland. And in his Saint Thomas University address (1988), he welcomes the change now underway in Catholicism as the result of studies by scholars and statements by church leaders. These are rapidly eroding the impact of this centuries-long negative portrayal of Jews and Judaism in Christian theology.

Cardinal Bernardin also recognizes that while theological cleansing remains paramount for the church, it alone will not heal the pain and suffering that has resulted from this adversus Judaeos teaching. Hence in his Hebrew University address he joins Pope John Paul II in calling the church to engage in public repentance, echoing the pope's call to make such repentance an integral part of the preparation for the celebration of the third millennium of Christianity in the year 2000.

But Cardinal Bernardin is quite aware that removing the negative view of Jews and Judaism and repenting for the devastation anti-Semitism has brought on the Jewish community will not end Christian responsibility. We are called to build a new constructive theology of the Christian-Jewish relationship. This theology must be rooted in the sense of profound Jewish-Christian bondedness that Pope John Paul II has emphasized so often in his writings. Such a renewed theology must be anchored in an understanding of scripture based on recent scholarship.

In both his address to the American Jewish Committee (1984) and his major lecture at the University of Saint Thomas (1988), the cardinal stresses the significant rethinking that has occurred in recent biblical scholarship regarding both the Old Testament (Hebrew Scriptures) and the New Testament. In the case of the Hebrew Scriptures, Cardinal Bernardin emphasizes the positive contribution these writings made to the spirituality of Jesus and the apostolic church. For Jesus and the early Christian community the Hebrew Scriptures provided a wellspring of religious meaning. We cannot fully appreciate, or emulate today, the spirituality of Jesus and his followers without deep appreciation of the positive impact the Hebrew Scriptures had on this spirituality. The Hebrew Scriptures can no longer be regarded as merely prelude or foil for the teachings of the New Testament.

In his University of Saint Thomas address, the cardinal speaks of "a genuine revolution in the New Testament scholarship" that is beginning to transform our entire understanding of Jesus' relationship to the Judaism of his day. He underlines the teaching of the 1985 Vatican *Notes* on speaking about Jews in catechetics and preaching, which stress Jesus' profound Jewishness and the proximity of his thought to Pharisaism. The cardinal joins the ranks of those Christian and Jewish scholars who increasingly are presenting the separation between Jews and Christians as a very gradual process that did not begin in earnest until the end of the

Jewish war with Rome in 70 CE and that continued in some places for several centuries.

It is the cardinal's judgment that this scriptural revolution will have to extend to all areas of church life, not merely the interpretation of scripture. The new positive approach to the Hebrew Scriptures and the profound sense of Jesus' Jewishness must be incorporated into our catechetical material and our liturgy. He acknowledges the important steps that have already been undertaken in terms of educational materials, a process that must go forth unabated. And there is need to begin the effort with the liturgy with deliberate urgency.

The scriptural revolution now underway will necessarily be, according to the cardinal, seed for a new theology of the Christian-Jewish relationship. He began exploring this issue early on, in his address to the American Jewish Committee (1984), where he underlined that "Christian doctrine needs to be stated in such a way as to acknowledge authentic theological space for Judaism."

His most developed ideas on this theme are to be found in his University of Saint Thomas presentation. Following the direction taken by Pope John Paul II, the cardinal stresses three ideas that are central to any authentic theology of the relationship of the church and the Jewish people in light of *Nostra Aetate* and recent scriptural scholarship. The first notion is that there continues to exist a deep spiritual bond between the church and the people Israel, a link that is unique to the Christian-Jewish relationship. The resurrection of Jesus has not eroded the original covenant with the Jewish people.

The second idea focuses on the "living heritage" of Judaism that Christianity shares in light of its intimate bond with the Jewish people. This "living heritage" includes not only the Hebrew Scriptures but the teachings of rabbinic, medieval and modern Judaism as well. This latter point is underscored by the cardinal. As he sees it, present-day Jewish perspectives on theology, ethics and spirituality must be regarded as *integral* to the development of Christian self-understanding, not merely outside resources from a parallel faith community to be included in a peripheral way. In light of the spiritual bonding between Christians and Jews proclaimed by Pope John Paul II, the religious resources of Judaism become a matter of central concern for faith identity in the church as such, not merely something we draw on only when in direct dialogue with the Jewish community.

The cardinal is likewise aware of the impact of the Holocaust on Christian theology. This is the third important theme of his writings on the Christian-Jewish relationship. Certainly, as the cardinal has made abundantly clear in his Hebrew University address, the Holocaust demands mourning and repentance on the part of the Christian community. But Christian responsibility in terms of the Holocaust does not stop there. There is need to renew Christian theology in several important ways in light of the Shoah. First of all, the experience of the Holocaust calls for an immediate end to any remaining vestiges of the adversus Judaeos theology of the past. Beyond that, there is the need to pursue the issue of how to understand God's relationship to the world after the Holocaust. This is a question that the church might profitably pursue in dialogue with Jewish scholars and religious leaders.

Cardinal Bernardin also sees the Holocaust raising important ethical questions for Catholics and people of all faith traditions in our time. Given the ultimate aim of the Nazis to transform totally the basis of human values, how do we ground ethical values in a public society so affected by technology and bureaucracy, a society in which sensitivity to human life seems to be rapidly receding? How do we employ power for the promotion of good rather than to support a campaign of mass human destruction, as Nazism did? How do we recover a sense of the importance of history in terms of human salvation and make theology more "subject-centered." These are the questions the cardinal posed in his University of Saint Thomas address in particular. While he realizes that an adequate response will require continued deliberation by Christian theologians in partnership with their Jewish colleagues, he has tried to state the basic agenda for their deliberations in view of the Shoah.

In his keynote address to the May 1992 meeting of the Jewish-Catholic International Liaison Committee, Cardinal Bernardin deepens his reflections on the basic significance of the Holocaust for Christian theology. In this address he also raises three specific issues that do not appear in his other presentations in the context of the Christian-Jewish dialogue. The first is the growing importance of ecological concern in our day. The cardinal believes that Catholics can gain important perspective on this issue through an understanding of the misuse of technological capacity during the Holocaust as well as from reflection on the notion of human co-creatorship found in the Jewish biblical and mystical traditions.

The cardinal also believes that the Holocaust is important for an understanding of contemporary issues of war and peace, an area of special concern for him given his role as chairman of the bishops' committee that wrote the pastoral letter on peace as well as the 1993 update statement. The cardinal recognizes that one of the most difficult areas in the dialogue concerns issues of war and peace in the Middle East today. He regards an understanding of the Holocaust and its lingering impact as critical for a full grasp of this question.

Finally, the cardinal raises the issue of protecting human life at all levels in light of the Holocaust. He has especially been concerned about the worldwide abuse of children, something he notes in his Baltimore address, and the problem of abortion. In light of the mass murder of innocent children during the Holocaust, and manipulation of medical science by the Nazi doctors, it becomes imperative in the cardinal's view to work for the protection of all human life. It is his hope that the dialogue can address such issues.

Cardinal Bernardin also has acknowledged the crucial significance of the Holocaust for understanding the use of power and the role of religion in the public sphere in our time. He devotes the major part of his address to the Twelfth National Workshop on Christian-Jewish Relations in Chicago (November 1990) to these matters. Following up on the remarks of Romano Guardini made soon after World War ii to the effect that the challenge before humanity after the Holocaust is to integrate power into life in a way that does not prove destructive, the cardinal makes several important affirmations. First of all, he insists that in light of the Second Vatican Council's historic *Declaration on Religious Liberty* no religious group ought to set out to impose its will on the body politic. But the Holocaust has reminded us of the importance of public culture. The Nazis were masters at shaping public culture toward their perverse policies. Hence the post-Holocaust social situation does require religious groups to turn their attention to the state of public culture. The exit of religion from the process of shaping public culture could easily result in the emergence of what some scholars have termed "naked state sovereignty." Surely this was the reality at the height of Nazi power in Germany.

Religion's primary thrust in terms of impacting public culture ought to be dialogue and persuasion. Yet Cardinal Bernardin acknowledges that at certain times religious groups, ideally in coalition and not on their own, may have to move beyond persuasion and dialogue into what he terms a "power mode" for the sake of preserving certain fundamental moral values in a given society. He cites a number of previous examples in American history when religious groups successfully put together coalitions that had sufficient power to influence national legislation. Two outstanding examples are the joint Catholic-Protestant-Jewish support for labor legislation in the 1930s and 1940s, especially the legislation connected with the New Deal, and the massive civil rights legislation in the 1960s passed by Congress in part due to the social protests in which churches played an important organizing role.

Cardinal Bernardin's theological writings reveal a religious leader fully aware of the human suffering and destruction caused by the displacement theologies of Jews and Judaism that dominated Catholic thinking and preaching for centuries. They show a church leader fully committed to the generation and implementation of a far more constructive theology of Christian-Jewish bonds. This new theology must rely on the contemporary understanding of the portrayal of Jews and Judaism in the scriptures as well as the solid teaching provided by the statements of Vatican II and John Paul II. But the cardinal is likewise conscious that our new theological journey has only begun. We are "partners in waiting," as Professor Clark Williamson has described the Christian-Jewish relationship, as we continue to probe further our respective visions of the salvific road ahead.

Reverend Daniel F. Montalbano

RESPECTFUL DIALOGUE WITH THE WORLD

I was in the college seminary during the years of the Second Vatican Council (1962–1965), and I remember clearly the rector telling us that we could spend our whole priestly lives implementing the directions and decisions of the Council. In my youthful naiveté, I thought surely we could accomplish these goals in a few years and then move on to something else.

Thirty years have passed, and I've long appreciated the difficulty of understanding the original meaning of the Council's work and of interpreting that meaning and putting it to work throughout the worldwide church and, especially, here in the archdiocese of Chicago.

Cardinal Joseph Bernardin has embraced a bishop's work: to listen and to teach and to lead the people to a vision of what the Council means today, for us, in our particular situation. These texts are just one facet of the many-faceted work of a person committed not only to the content but also to the style of Vatican II.

Some today would assert the truth of the faith by fiat and declaration. Others, while not diminishing the treasure of faith, seek its understanding and acceptance through listening and the honest conversation we call dialogue. Cardinal Bernardin has taken the latter path. He is well rooted in the Council's teaching about the search for truth:

> The search for truth, however, must be carried out in a
> manner that is appropriate to the dignity and social
> nature of the human person: that is, by free enquiry with

the help of teaching or instruction, communication and dialogue. It is by these means that people share with each other the truth they have discovered, or think they have discovered, in such a way that they help one another in the search for the truth. Moreover, it is by personal assent that they must adhere to the truth they have discovered. (Vatican II, *Dignitatis Humanae, Declaration on Religious Liberty,* 3)

The Second Vatican Council represented a sea change in many areas of church life. Catholicism is a historic tradition with deep roots and a wide variety of theologies, cultures and peoples as part of its reality. The Council chose an openness to the world and its goodness, too long neglected.

The church at Vatican II decided to engage the world in a positive, dialogical fashion — but with eyes wide open. *Gaudium et Spes,* the *Pastoral Constitution on the Church in the Modern World,* was the primary document outlining this hope and approach. The Extraordinary Synod of Bishops of 1985 concluded with this affirmation and charge to church leadership:

> The church as communion is a sacrament for the salvation of the world. Therefore, the authorities in the church have been placed there by Christ for the salvation of the world. In this context we affirm the great importance and timelessness of the *Pastoral Constitution, Gaudium et Spes.* At the same time, however, we perceive that the signs of the times are in part different from those of the time of the Council, with greater problems and anguish. Today, in fact, everywhere in the world we witness an increase in hunger, oppression, injustice and war, terrorism and other forms of violence of every sort. This requires a new and more profound theological reflection in order to interpret these signs in the light of the gospel. (*Origins,* 1985, 449)

Cardinal Bernardin, through his leadership in writing the American bishops' pastoral letter, *The Challenge of Peace,* showed forceful leadership in applying Catholic teaching to the contemporary issues of war and peace. In his development of a consistent ethic of life he has offered a compelling vision of the sacredness of life from the unborn to the aged, for the condemned and the marginalized. In his support for and participation in the Religious Alliance Against Pornography, he has worked against the degradation of human sexuality. He has offered clear and decisive leadership in his pastoral letter on healthcare, struggling to assert the place of religiously based healthcare in a milieu that increasingly focuses on profits while often ignoring the medical needs of the poor. And in many forums he has challenged both this city and the nation to recognize, examine and heal the racial prejudice that prevents a just and compassionate American society from being fully realized.

Consistently, courageously and competently, Cardinal Bernardin has taken the opportunities available to him to offer solid teaching and practical help to people of good will. His vision and work have been both local and global.

Two of the shortest documents of Vatican II were perhaps the most innovative: *Dignitatis Humanae* (cited above) and *Nostra Aetate.* While the former commits the Catholic Church to a recognition of the dignity and autonomy of the human person in his or her search for the truth, the latter begins an official recognition of the reality and truth of non-Christian religions, especially Judaism.

> Since Christians and Jews have such a common spiritual heritage, this sacred Council wishes to encourage and further mutual understanding and appreciation. This can be achieved, especially, by way of biblical and theological enquiry and through friendly discussions. (*Nostra Aetate,* 4)

As important and significant as this official declaration was in 1965, it would have languished without serious work to explore its meaning and implement that meaning. Pope John Paul II has been eloquent in word and deed in interpreting and witnessing to the relationship between Christian and Jew. This collection of talks demonstrates that throughout his service as bishop, Cardinal Bernardin has made this relationship a substantive pastoral concern.

Everyone involved knows how difficult it is to build this relationship. On the Christian side, some do not see the point of such dialogue and others have no hope for it. There are those who quote John's gospel: "I am the way, the truth and the life. No one comes to the Father except through me" (14:6). They interpret this in an exclusive manner, precluding any real dialogue. Others would read from the Acts of the Apostles: "At this Peter opened his mouth and said: 'For a certainty I perceive that God shows no partiality, but in every nation the person that fears God and does what is right is acceptable to God'" (10:34). They see here the charge to respect and to dialogue as foundational to Christian faith.

On the Jewish side there are comparable difficulties and challenges. From a Jewish perspective Christianity can be viewed as unnecessary, suspect and idolatrous.

But we live in the same world, now largely free of the ghettos both Jews and Catholics once inhabited. How shall we, both pastorally and theologically, recognize each other? That has been the challenge since the Council and the work we are engaged in up to the present moment. And very much has been accomplished.

One thing has become clear: Exaggerated and unnuanced claims to truth by either side of this relationship destroy dialogue, while the serious, thoughtful and loving efforts by Christians and Jews make a future together possible. In words that break new ground even by their temperance, in reflections that are both accessible and profound, Cardinal Bernardin has been a leader in this effort.

THE CHICAGO BOARD OF RABBIS
AND THE JEWISH FEDERATION OF METROPOLITAN CHICAGO

JOSEPH L. BERNARDIN WAS APPOINTED ARCHBISHOP OF CHICAGO ON JULY 10, 1982.
THE FOLLOWING FEBRUARY, HE WAS CREATED CARDINAL BY POPE JOHN PAUL II.
HIS FIRST ADDRESS TO CHICAGO'S JEWISH COMMUNITY OCCURRED JUST ONE MONTH AFTER
HIS RETURN FROM ROME.

My dear brothers and sisters of the Chicago Board of Rabbis and the Jewish Federation of Chicago!

I am grateful for your kind and thoughtful invitation. I am very happy to be with you this afternoon. From the very first moment that you invited me, I have looked forward to this encounter. My only regret is that because of the extraordinarily heavy schedule of my first six months in the city of Chicago, it has taken so long to get together with you.

I wish first to address you very personally. I wish to greet you in the same way that I greeted my fellow priests of the archdiocese on the evening before my official installation. I come to you as your brother, Joseph. I come to you as a friend, seeking the warmth, understanding and support of your friendship. I ask you to accept my presence among you as a sign of the great respect and affection I have for you, and as a pledge of my continued prayers and support for you in your future.

It is significant, I believe, that our first meeting should take place during the year marking the twentieth anniversary of the beginning of the Second Vatican Council. From the Catholic perspective, the Council was the turning point in Catholic-Jewish relations, because from the Council came *Nostra Aetate.* In that historic document, the Council fathers reviewed the elements of our common heritage, called for a mutual understanding of and respect for our respective religious traditions, univocally stated that in no way could the Jewish people be held accountable for the death of Christ, and deplored "the hatred, persecutions and displays of anti-Semitism directed against the Jews at any time and from any source" (4). The Council gave impetus to a dialogue that has taken place at the local, national and international levels. In the United States, Catholics and Jews have worked together more than in any other country. There exists today a network of close, cooperative contacts between Jewish and Catholic representatives who can be called on in moments of crisis and need on both sides. Admittedly, this dialogue has not eliminated all tensions. Yet, there have been continuing positive developments in Christian-Jewish relations and in the Catholic Church's appreciation of the Jewish tradition.

In November 1980, Pope John Paul II stressed the need for this dialogue in a talk he gave to the Jewish community at Mainz, Germany. "The depth and richness of our common heritage," he said, "are revealed to us particularly in our friendly dialogue and trusting collaboration. . . . It is not just a question of correcting a false religious view of the Jewish people, which in the course of history was one of the causes that contributed to misunderstanding and persecution, but above all of the dialogue between the two religions that — with Islam — gave the world faith in the one, ineffable God who speaks to us, and a desire to serve him on behalf of the whole world."

A year and a half later — in March 1982 — he returned to this theme when he addressed delegates of episcopal conferences and other experts who were meeting in Rome concerning the Catholic Church's relations with Judaism. On this occasion he also stressed the need for quality in our ongoing exchanges. "I am happy to know," he said, "that you are making many efforts, by studying and praying together, to grasp better and to formulate more clearly the often difficult biblical and theological problems raised by the progress of Judeo-Christian dialogue. Imprecision and mediocrity in this field do enormous harm to such a dialogue. May God grant that Christians and Jews may hold more in-depth exchanges based on their own identities, without allowing either one or the other side to be obscured but always seeking truly for the will of the God who revealed himself."

I wish to personally endorse the efforts to promote better Jewish-Christian relations, and I pray that there might be a greater level of interaction here in the Chicago area. In line with the holy father's emphasis on the need for greater mutual understanding, I will encourage our educational institutions and programs of the archdiocese to enhance their treatment of Judaism and of Christian-Jewish relations as a way of removing any remaining vestiges of anti-Semitism and helping Catholics acquire a better understanding of religious values of the Jewish tradition that were so central to the ministry and teaching of Jesus himself. In this connection, I am pleased to inform you that our Office for Divine Worship recently asked Father John Pawlikowski of Catholic Theological Union to write a series of articles in *Liturgy 80* on how Judaism might be presented during our key liturgical seasons.

I would like now to address briefly several areas of particular concern to the Jewish community.

The first is Israel and its relationship to all the Middle East. The volatile situation in the Middle East, constantly shifting and perennially complex, has created tensions for everyone. On this particular issue, we are united in many of our perspectives, but we also differ on some of them.

We both agree on the overriding need for peace. The National Conference of Catholic Bishops (NCCB) in its 1973 statement on the Middle East and again in November 1978, called unequivocally for the recognition of the State of Israel within secure and recognized boundaries as a basic element of any lasting and just peace. I believe that Catholics generally support Israel and have positive attitudes toward it. Catholics relate sympathetically to Israel as a democracy in an increasingly totalitarian world.

Moreover, Catholics are beginning to understand the religious and cultural factors that tie all Jews to the land of Israel. Whatever difficulties we as Christians may experience in sharing this view, we must understand this link between land and people that has been a central element in the writings and worship of Jews for two millennia. In a 1975 statement commemorating the tenth anniversary of *Nostra Aetate,* the American bishops affirmed the need for Catholics to be sensitive to this point, adding: "Appreciation of this link is not to give assent to any particular religious interpretation of this bond. Nor is this affirmation meant to deny the legitimate rights of other parties in the region, or to adopt any political stance in the controversies over the Middle East."

In this connection, I would like to allude to the fact that some members of the Jewish community seem to be making the kind of support of Judaism and Israel found among certain Evangelical groups the barometer for Jewish relations with mainline Christian churches, including the Catholic Church. This could create a problem for Catholic-Jewish relations. While Catholic theology has come to recognize clearly the permanence of the Jewish covenant, and while Catholics have grown in their appreciation of the Jewish land tradition as a result of Christian biblical scholarship, Israel will never play the kind of role in our theology that it does for some of these Evangelical groups. Hence, while Catholics may retain a strong commitment to Israel, we cannot be expected to speak about this commitment in the same theological language as they.

It was because of this sensitivity to the link between land and people that we quickly expressed disapproval of the 1975 United Nations vote that sought to equate Zionism with racism. Speaking as the president of the NCCB, I stated at the time: "The resolution is unjust. Because of its substantive inadequacy it both retards the necessary struggle against racism in the world and opens the door to harassment, discrimination and denial of basic rights to members of the Jewish community throughout the world."

While there is agreement on many elements of the Middle East situation, nonetheless there also exist significant differences. This is why there is a great necessity for dialogue on the Middle East and on U.S. policy in the Middle East. We enter this dialogue not only as major religious traditions but also as citizens of the country with the most significant impact on the Middle East. The Catholic participation in this dialogue is based on the 1973 and 1978 statements to which I have alluded, as well as a series of statements dealing with Lebanon. Those statements call not only for a settlement in the Middle East based on the recognition of the right of Israel's secure existence but also the right of Palestinians to a homeland. That is not all of our position because the issues themselves are so complex, but I am highlighting these two points to indicate that there are significant differences between us.

Other issues, for example, would include Israeli and other forces in Lebanon, as well as the status of other occupied territories and this, of course, includes discussion of the question of Jerusalem. Obviously, the American bishops are much influenced on the position of this latter point by the position of the Holy See. We have to discuss our differences among ourselves and at the same time cooperate to shape U.S. policy in the direction of a long-term, stable and just resolution of the Middle East situation. This dialogue will test both our religious vision and the moral vision we bring to the public debate in the U.S., but I am convinced that we serve religion and society best by actively participating in the public dialogue.

I take this occasion to commend the quality and sincerity of the official Israeli report on the Beirut camp massacres. In this connection, I cannot fail to mention that there was also Christian involvement in this tragedy since members of our faith community were the actual killers.

I am also sensitive to the displeasure of the Jewish community over the holy father's meeting with Yasser Arafat. We are faced here with differing perspectives on this visit in the Catholic and Jewish communities. The Catholic community generally sees such visits as pastoral efforts at reconciliation. The papacy has a tradition of talking with various world leaders. The popes have met with leaders of the Soviet Union and Poland; in recent days Pope John Paul II met with those of Nicaragua, El Salvador and Guatemala. Certainly such meetings in no way constitute an endorsement of their fundamental policies. Moreover, I have reason to believe that when the pope did meet with Arafat he urged him to recognize Israel and to abandon terrorism.

I can understand, however, how Jews in light of the PLO's past record of terrorism, might fear that this visit would be perceived as a toleration, if not acceptance, of terrorism even though this was not the Holy See's intention. As a matter of fact, a number of Catholics communicated their reservations about the visit. At the same time, candor also prompts me to express some wonderment about statements made by a few Jewish leaders at the time of the visit. These statements, made at a time of great emotion, seemed to imply church involvement in the Holocaust and were perceived by many as a personal attack on the pope. Such comments deeply offended many Catholics and were not conducive to genuine dialogue.

Another area of concern of special importance to the Jewish community is proselytism. The many unjust practices, such as forced baptism, associated with the spread of the gospel throughout Christian history, have made this a particularly sensitive issue in our relations. Today, the church is clearly committed to the principles of religious liberty, a commitment that of itself necessitates the rejection of all unfair proselytizing that might have taken place in the past.

In a paper delivered in Venice at the 1977 meeting of the International Catholic-Jewish Liaison Committee, Professor Tomaso Federici, professor of biblical theology at Saint Anselmo in Rome, set down clearly the principles to be followed in Christian evangelization. The mission to witness, he points out, is a vital necessity to the Christian; indeed, it is an essential aspect of Christian life. This is appropriate even in dialogue, for dialogue presumes that each side will articulate frankly and honestly what it believes in, and will respect the other's right to do so. We believe in Christ as the Risen Lord and quite naturally invite all persons to join us in our community of faith. To deny or to hide this would destroy our integrity as committed Christians. As Professor Federici states:

> [witness] is constitutive of the church's very mission to the world and its peoples and is in accord with the concern which is to be heard in the very first days of the church itself (cf. I Corinthians 9:16: "Woe to me if I do not preach the gospel!") and has never disappeared and has now been clearly restated by the Second Vatican Council. ("Mission and Witness of the Church," *Origins,* October 19, 1978)

Witness, however, is to be distinguished from proselytism and is to be guided by the rules of justice and love. Federici thus excludes "any sort of witness which in any way constitutes a physical, moral, psychological or cultural constraint on the Jews, both individuals and communities, such as might in any way destroy or even simply reduce their personal judgment, free will or full autonomy of decision" (ibid.).

Rather clear guidelines can be drawn from such principles that are particularly appropriate to a society such as ours in which one religion, Christianity, tends to dominate by sheer force of numbers.

A third area of concern is Soviet Jewry. In the past there have been many examples of close cooperation on this issue. Unfortunately the situation has been rather bleak during the past year. I am familiar with the work of the National Interreligious Task Force on Soviet Jewry, which is based here in Chicago, and I recognize the role it fulfills. In this connection, I would like to voice my support for Anatoly Scharansky. I know his case has had special significance for the Jewish community.

I would like, at this time, to repeat a suggestion I have made several times in the past. Where possible, the protest should be broadened to include all people whose human rights are being violated, not only in Russia but elsewhere. I am thinking, for example, of the people of Lithuania who have suffered greatly because of their religious convictions since their annexation to Russia in the

1940s. There are also other groups in Russia and many other parts of the world as well whose human rights have been violated for religious and political reasons. We must remember all our brothers and sisters who need our help. Those of us who enjoy freedom must speak with one voice in condemnation of all persecution and oppression. Let it not be said that one segment of the human family suffered while another segment stood idly by, doing or saying nothing. Both the Hebrew and Christian Scriptures condemn this failure to stand up and be counted when the occasion demands forceful action.

So far, I have spoken about Jewish concerns and Catholic responses to them. There are also Catholic concerns about which we ask for more dialogue and understanding. The first is aid to children who attend church-related schools. This has long been a sore spot among American Catholics, especially parents. I suggest that, in the spirit that has marked our dialogue in other areas, we now sit down together to discuss this topic. The anguish and hurt felt by Catholics at the systematic economic discrimination against them in their efforts to maintain what they consider their right to "free" exercise of religion is very real and very deep. While there is still considerable opposition from the Jewish community, I am encouraged that some Jewish leaders have begun to call for a reassessment of the traditional line of opposition to any form of relief for parents who use their God-given and constitutional right to send their children to the school of their choice. I know, too, that the Union of Orthodox Jewish Congregations has dissented from the position of opposition assumed by other Jewish groups.

A second area of concern is respect for life and, in particular, abortion. Some maintain that this is simply a sectarian issue, but I reject that contention. While, admittedly, the Catholic Church is more concerned about it than any other institution, abortion — in my view — is basically a question of human rights, the right of an unborn infant to live. Because of the great debate about abortion, there is need for more dialogue so that we can avoid the misconceptions and stereotypes that plague us, so that we can develop greater understanding and sensitivity to deeply held convictions.

Happily, there exists an example of what can be done when our two communities commit themselves to authentic dialogue, even on such emotion-laden issues as abortion. In September 1977, the Los Angeles priest-rabbi group (sponsored by the Los Angeles chapter of the American Jewish Committee, the Board of Rabbis of Southern California and the Roman Catholic archdiocese of Los Angeles) issued a joint statement on "Respect for Life — Jewish and Roman Catholic Reflections on Abortion and Related Issues." The differing Catholic and Jewish viewpoints were presented separately, along with an indication of the areas of considerable mutual concern and convergence. While no consensus was reached on certain points, ground rules for future dialogues and cooperation were set forth in a concluding "Joint Expression of Goals." After stating what might be done to reduce tensions in the abortion controversy, to encourage religious groups to teach respect for life in their individual communities in accordance with their sacred traditions, to eliminate coercion by government agencies, to advocate positive alternatives to abortion and to promote social situations that will encourage the responsible bearing and rearing of children, the group concluded: "While Roman Catholics and Jews may not agree to make prohibitions of all abortions American law, nonetheless we should work together to make respect for life, and particularly the joyful celebration of new life, an American ideal." This significant effort in Los Angeles proves that even the most volatile subject matter can be faced positively and creatively if properly approached in dialogue.

I would like now to conclude with an appeal for a greater degree of interreligious cooperation on various social issues that are affecting both our nation and our city. The current economic crisis is playing havoc with so many of our people. Even though there are signs of an impending recovery, it will be a long time before the present crisis, with all its human suffering, is resolved. While we are not economists, we do have the obligation, I believe, to make sure that the voices of the poor and disadvantaged are heard in the national debate about the allocation of resources and the development of policies that affect the well-being of our society.

There is another concern that we must address in some way. The political changes presently underway in our city have given rise to many fears and prejudices. Our united voice should be heard on behalf of justice, decency and fairness. We already have a structure, of course, that makes it possible for us to come together, as Jews, Protestants, Orthodox and Catholics, to address the important social issues of our day. I am referring to the Chicago Conference on Religion and Race. Let us use this and other structures to full advantage.

I also invite you to join us Catholic bishops in our search for peace. As you know, the bishops of this country are involved in the development of a major document (called a pastoral letter) on war and peace, with special emphasis on the nuclear arms race and the need to find alternatives to warfare, both nuclear and conventional. This pastoral has two purposes: to help form the consciences of our own constituents on war and peace issues, and to make our contribution to the public debate on these topics. As expected, the document has been both praised and damned. The important thing, however, is that it has been noticed and, indeed, taken seriously, both in our own country and abroad. The document we are preparing, when completed, will not be the last word. It is really only the beginning of our reflection on the necessity of turning the ever upward spiral of the arms race downward and how we might go about that. I invite you to join us in this reflection. I know, of course, that the organized Jewish community has also been concerned about peace, as evidenced by the fact that the General Assembly of the Council of Jewish Federations endorsed the nuclear freeze. I recognize and understand, too, certain Jewish difficulties in this area because of their deep concern for Israel's security. Still it would be useful to have you join us in our reflection on the use of power and circumstances under which that use is legitimate. It would also be useful to get your perspective of war and peace in the Hebrew Scriptures as we develop a theology of peace, based on both the Hebrew and the Christian Scriptures.

As Pope John Paul II told the Jewish community at Mainz:

Jews and Christians, as children of Abraham, are called to be a blessing for the world (cf. Genesis 12:2ff.), committing themselves for justice among all men and peoples, with the fullness and depth that God himself intended us to have, and with all the readiness for sacrifice that this high goal may demand. The more our meeting is imprinted with this sacred duty, the more it becomes a blessing also for ourselves.

My dear brothers and sisters, dialogue and collaboration are not options for us. They are a necessity. Never again can we permit ourselves to be alienated from each other; never again can we let our minds and our hearts be misshaped by the prejudices and hatreds of the past. Never again can we allow a climate that could produce another Holocaust.

We have so much in common. But ultimately it is our faith in God, who created us in his image and likeness, that unites us. So may we always celebrate that unity, while respecting the different traditions, and working with each other, in love, for the betterment of ourselves and the entire human family.

Today, I pledge to you my love, my support, my determination to work with you on all the matters that concern us as Jews and Catholics, as citizens, but most of all, as caring friends.

JEWISH COMMUNITY CENTERS OF CHICAGO

ONE MONTH BEFORE THIS TALK, CARDINAL BERNARDIN MADE A PASTORAL VISIT TO THE CATHOLIC CHURCH IN POLAND. DURING THAT TRIP, THE CARDINAL VISITED AUSCHWITZ.

My dear brothers and sisters, thank you for your kind, thoughtful invitation to be with you and to address you this evening. I am very happy to be here! As I told the Chicago Board of Rabbis and the Jewish Federation of Chicago 18 months ago, "I come to you as your brother, Joseph." I hope that you will understand that I have come here as a friend — someone who respects you, who wants to know you better, who also wants you to know him better. My presence here this evening is a mere token of my affection for you all.

This evening I would like to offer my reflections on some aspects of the current Jewish-Christian relations. It has been 19 years since the Second Vatican Council issued a document entitled *Nostra Aetate,* marking a turning point in Jewish-Christian relations. That historic document reviewed the elements of our common heritage, called for a mutual understanding of and respect for our respective religious traditions, and deplored "the hatred, persecutions and displays of anti-Semitism directed against the Jews at any time and from any source" (4).

Much has happened in the nearly two decades since the Second Vatican Council, much of it encouraging. Frequent contacts and dialogues between Catholics and Jews have established a healthy climate of mutual trust and respect that has enabled us to define more clearly what we have in common and to identify more precisely where we have differences. Although this dialogue is taking place on an international level as well, it is in the United States that Catholics and Jews have worked together more than anywhere else in the world. For example, I met with a Jewish-Roman Catholic dialogue group that has been meeting faithfully for 15 years.

There exists today a network of close, cooperative contacts between Jewish and Catholic representatives who can be called on in moments of crisis and need on both sides. Admittedly, this dialogue has not eliminated all tensions. Yet there have been continuing positive developments in Christian-Jewish relations and in the Catholic Church's appreciation of the Jewish tradition.

I personally endorse the efforts to promote better Jewish-Christian relations, and I continue to pray that there may continue to be substantial interaction here in the Chicago area. I am encouraging our archdiocesan educational institutions and programs to enhance their treatment of Judaism and of Jewish-Christian relations as a way of eliminating any remaining vestiges of anti-Semitism and helping Catholics acquire a better understanding of the religious values of the Jewish tradition that were so central to the ministry and teaching of Jesus and the early church.

In reflecting on current Jewish-Catholic relations, I will address two Jewish and then two Catholic concerns. The Jewish concerns are the Holocaust (and its aftermath) and Israel.

A month ago yesterday I visited Auschwitz during my trip to Poland. It was my second visit to this terrible place, but the impact on me was as strong as the first time. I reflected that one cannot merely *visit* a place like this. There, in a powerful way, we are challenged to face squarely what humanity is capable of perpetrating. We find that there is no alternative but to take a firm stand against such irrational prejudice directed against people who are of a different race or religion or political outlook. We dare not forget the Holocaust or pretend that it did not happen. To forget would be tantamount to opening ourselves to its being repeated. We must ensure that never happens!

Ensuring that it does not happen implies opposing anyone who exhibits or disseminates prejudice against any person or any people. During the past several months we read and heard remarks against the Jewish community attributed to Louis Farrakhan, leader of the Black Muslim sect known as the Nation of Islam. On June 28, I wrote a public letter to Rabbi Herbert Bronstein denouncing such prejudicial characterizations of Judaism. I assured him, and, through him, the entire Jewish community not only of my prayers but also of my pledge to promote "mutual respect for all religious traditions." I concluded by offering him "my cooperation in healing the wounds inflicted by religious prejudice and disrespect."

Opposition to the rhetoric of prejudice includes rejection of *any* rhetoric of racial or religious superiority. We live in a pluralistic society. There is nothing more detrimental to the common good than such rhetoric. *All* such inflammatory language must be opposed. This means opposing not only the words of Minister Louis Farrakhan but also, frankly, those of Rabbi Meir Kahane. I must advise you that Catholics are watching closely the role of Rabbi Kahane in the development of public policies in the State of Israel.

I know that Israel is a fundamental concern of the entire Jewish community. The volatile situation in the Middle East, constantly shifting and perennially complex, has created such great tensions. On this particular issue, we are united in many of our perspectives, but we also differ on some of them.

We both agree on the overriding need for peace. Moreover, Catholics are beginning to understand the religious and cultural factors that create bonds between all Jews and the land of Israel.

There are also some differences. In 1973 and 1978 the National Conference of Catholic Bishops issued statements calling for a settlement in the Middle East based on the recognition of the right of Israel's secure existence but also the right of Palestinians to a homeland. That is not the whole of our position, but I highlight these two points to indicate that there are some significant differences among us.

On May 24, Pope John Paul II issued an apostolic letter on Jerusalem. I would like to review some of its basic components because there has been some misunderstanding about it. The holy father points out the fact that this historic city is considered holy by Jews, Christians and Muslims. He states that "Jerusalem stands out as a [potential] symbol of coming together, of union and of universal peace for the human family." Today, however, "Jerusalem continues to be the cause of daily conflict, violence and partisan reprisals."

The popes of this century have repeatedly called for an adequate solution to the problem of Jerusalem because the Catholic Church has been "concerned for peace among peoples no less than for spiritual, historical and cultural reasons of an eminently religious nature." Pope John Paul II does not call for the internationalization of Jerusalem, as sometimes alleged, but for doing "everything possible to preserve the unique and sacred character of the city." This implies not only protecting and preserving the monuments or sacred places but the very existence of religious communities who reside there, and continued access to the pilgrims.

Having addressed what I perceive to be the two major concerns for the Jewish community and our Catholic response to the issues, I will now present two basic concerns of the Catholic community for your consideration: building a peaceful world and working together to protect and foster human life.

As you know, the Catholic bishops of the United States have developed a major document (called a pastoral letter) on war and peace, with special emphasis on the nuclear arms race and the need to find alternatives to warfare, both nuclear and conventional. This pastoral has two purposes: to help form the consciences of our own constituents on war and peace issues, and to make our contribution to the public debate on these topics. As expected, the document has been both praised and damned. The important thing is that it has been noticed and, indeed, taken seriously, both in our country and abroad.

This document was not meant to be the last word. It is the beginning of what we hope will be a fruitful dialogue. I invite you to join us in our reflections and deliberations, in our search for peace. I am well aware that the Jewish community has also been concerned about peace, as evidenced by the fact that the General Assembly of the Council of Jewish Federations has endorsed the nuclear freeze. I know also of some Jewish difficulties in this area because of their deep concern for Israel's security. Still, it would be useful to have you join us in our reflection on the use of power and the circumstances under which that use is legitimate.

In the latter part of this pastoral letter on war and peace, the United States bishops provide an outline of our response to the challenge of building a peaceful world. We note that peace is impossible "without a full awareness of the worth and dignity of every human person, and of the sacredness of all human life." Violence against the human person, against human life, runs counter to our fundamental religious beliefs and erodes our respect for life itself.

Such violence has many faces. Among the many life-threatening issues that confront us in our contemporary world are genetics, abortion, capital punishment and euthanasia alongside modern warfare itself. There are also life-diminishing issues such as racism, sexism, prostitution and pornography.

The United States bishops have expressed views on many public policy issues relating to these threats and diminishments of human life. Bishop Malone, the current president of the National Conference of Catholic Bishops, has stated:

> These range from protecting human life from the attack of abortion, to safeguarding human life from the devastation of nuclear war; they extend to the enhancement of life through promoting human rights and satisfying human needs like nutrition, education, housing and health care for the poor.

During the past year, I have emphasized the linkage of this broad range of concern in my call for a consistent ethic of life. I am not ignoring the fact that each of these issues constitutes a distinct problem, enormously complicated, and deserving individual treatment.

My purpose in proposing a consistent ethic of life is to argue that success on any one of these issues threatening life requires a concern for the broader attitude in society about respect for human life. Attitude is the place to root an ethic of life. Change of attitude in turn can lead to change of policies and practices in our society.

When human life under any circumstances is not held as sacred in a society, *all* human life in that society is threatened. When it is held as sacred in all circumstances, all human life is protected. Every social system — east or west, north or south — should be judged by the way in which it reverences, or fails to reverence, the unique and equal dignity of every person.

I invite you to consider with us the question of a consistent ethic. I realize that there is not a consensus among Catholics and Jews on many issues I include under the umbrella of a consistent ethic. Frankly, there is not a full consensus on some of them or on the need for a consistent ethic within the Catholic community itself.

Some maintain that abortion is simply a sectarian issue, but I reject that contention. While, admittedly, the Catholic Church is more concerned about it than any other institution, abortion — in my view — is basically a question of human rights, the right of an unborn infant to live. I know that some have doubts about when human life begins and therefore question whether there is an obligation to protect the rights of an unborn child, especially in the early stages of development. In the Catholic view, however, there is no doubt that the life process begins at the moment of conception, and so we are concerned that it be protected.

I have singled out the example of abortion because it is very important for us Catholics in the present context. But we are not a one-issue community. We place equal importance on preventing nuclear war and reversing the arms race as well as on programs that meet the needs of the poor.

We have seen what can be done when our two communities commit themselves to authentic dialogue, even on such emotion-laden issues as abortion. In September 1977, a priest-rabbi group in Los Angeles issued a joint statement on "Respect for Life — Jewish and Roman Catholic Reflections on Abortion and Related Issues." The differing points of view were presented separately along with an indication of the areas of considerable mutual concern and convergence. Ground rules were set forth for future dialogues and cooperation. The group concluded: "While Roman Catholics and Jews may not agree to make the prohibition of all abortions American law, nonetheless we should work together to make respect for life, and particularly the joyful celebration of new life, an American ideal."

My dear brothers and sisters, dialogue and collaboration are not options for us. They are a necessity. Never again can we commit ourselves to be alienated from each other; never again can we let our minds and our hearts be misshaped by the prejudices and hatreds of the past. Never again can we allow a climate that could produce another Holocaust. We must pray, reflect and work together.

We have so much in common. But ultimately it is our faith in the God whose image and likeness we bear, that unites us. We need to celebrate that unity always even while we respect our different traditions. We can work with each other, in love, for the betterment of ourselves and the entire human family.

I have spoken with you frankly and honestly this evening because I believe we are brothers and sisters. I pledge to you my love, my support and my determination to work with you on all the matters that concern us as Jews and Catholics, as citizens, but most of all, as caring friends.

NATIONAL EXECUTIVE COUNCIL MEETING
AMERICAN JEWISH COMMITTEE

IN ADDITION TO HIS MINISTRY AS A DIOCESAN BISHOP, CARDINAL BERNARDIN
HAS HELD SEVERAL NATIONAL POSITIONS IN THE CHURCH. FROM 1974 TO 1977
HE WAS PRESIDENT OF THE NATIONAL CONFERENCE OF CATHOLIC BISHOPS. HE IS PERHAPS
BEST KNOWN FOR HIS WORK AS CHAIRMAN OF THE COMMITTEE THAT DRAFTED THE
AMERICAN BISHOPS' PASTORAL LETTER ON PEACE IN 1983. THIS TALK IS AN EXAMPLE OF THE
CARDINAL'S WIDER MINISTRY ON THE NATIONAL SCENE.

My brothers and sisters, I greet you this evening in a spirit of *shalom.* Peace be with you! I was very honored to receive an invitation to address you a second time. I sincerely admire the ongoing commitment that the American Jewish Committee has made to improve interreligious relations and to join in action on behalf of civil and human rights. You have truly been pioneers in both areas, each of which remains of profound concern to me.

Rabbi Marc Tanenbaum has rendered an inestimable service to all of us through his efforts during and since the Second Vatican Council. While I know his work in interreligious affairs has been largely assumed in most able fashion by Rabbi James Rudin, we continue to look forward to Rabbi Tanenbaum's prophetic comments on international affairs. I also wish to acknowledge publicly the quiet, persistent work of Mrs. Judith Banki, who has labored so effectively over many years in bringing to our attention continuing problems concerning religious education and Christian Passion plays.

As I stand before you this evening, I wish to pledge the continued cooperation of the Catholic Church in the United States and in particular, the archdiocese of Chicago with Rabbi Rudin and his colleagues. Currently in Chicago there are four major Catholic-Jewish dialogue groups, and we are actively planning to expand this effort.

I strongly identify with your current national priorities in Christian-Jewish relations. For example, I agree that we need to celebrate the twentieth anniversary of *Nostra Aetate* during 1985. This historic declaration of the Second Vatican Council on the church's relationship with the Jewish people set us on a new constructive course after centuries of persecution and mutual antagonism. These celebrations will provide a way of promoting greater consciousness of our respective traditions, forging new bonds of social cohesion, and enhancing Christianity's appreciation of the Jewish tradition, which provides such an important context for Jesus' teachings. We hope to cooperate in all this with the Committee and other Jewish groups here in Chicago.

The persistent effort to free Christian and Jewish textbooks of all racial and religious stereotypes must continue in earnest. Though we have made great strides in this since the sixties, the work is not yet completed. We need further careful analysis of our current texts to measure our progress more accurately and identify the remaining problematic areas.

I welcome your recent efforts to prod the conscience of Christian churches regarding persistent prejudicial and stereotyped aspects of some Passion plays in this country and abroad. *Nostra Aetate* committed the entire Catholic community to remove every vestige of anti-Semitic teaching from our presentation of the gospel in any form. The primary emphasis of any Passion play must be on the love and mercy Jesus preached to all, a love and mercy firmly rooted in the teachings of the Torah. Hence, we need to listen when you raise questions about alleged gospel representations that fail to portray the profound and positive influence of Jewish tradition on the formation of Jesus' teaching and on the spirit of the early church.

In regard to another of your priorities, let me highlight the work of the National Interreligious Task Force on Soviet Jewry, headquartered in Chicago and ably directed by Sister Ann Gillen. Without the support of the American Jewish Committee, this task force would not have seen the light of day. Its efforts on behalf of Soviet Christians and Jews, whose situation at the moment seems as perilous as at any time in recent memory, merits our wholehearted backing. I am pleased that the task force has also focused attention on other groups whose human rights are being violated. Lithuanian and Ukrainian Catholics, in particular, are appreciative of its interventions.

There is one other matter I would like to raise before moving to the heart of my address. The persistence, even the escalation, of anti-Semitic outbreaks in several parts of the world has troubled me greatly. I was profoundly affected by my return visit to Auschwitz this past summer. One cannot simply *visit* Auschwitz. Standing there, we are strongly challenged to face squarely the capacity of humanity for organized mass destruction. We recognize that we have no alternative but to take a firm stand against such irrational prejudice directed against anyone or any group that differs from us in race, religion, sexual orientation or political outlook.

My experiences at Auschwitz have deepened my commitment to take very seriously any and all manifestations of anti-Semitism — no matter how inconsequential they may appear at first glance. The rapid rise of Nazism showed us how quickly an apparently insignificant movement can assume control over a society. For this reason I have spoken with determined voice against the prejudicial statements of Louis Farrakhan. I especially repudiate his "theological" attacks on the integrity of Judaism.

I commend the leadership of American Judaism as well as Israeli political leaders for the manner in which they have unqualifiedly condemned a similar form of racist attack by Rabbi Meir Kahane against Israeli Arabs. This posture must firmly continue. Christian religious leaders of every denomination must show the same courage in repudiating anyone who utters anti-Semitic statements against Jews.

I wish to focus my major reflections this evening on three sensitive dimensions of our current relationship: (1) the theological expression of the bond between us, (2) the State of Israel, and (3) current church-state relations in our nation.

THE THEOLOGICAL EXPRESSION OF THE BOND BETWEEN US

Let me begin with the story of the Crucifixion. Throughout the centuries the accounts of Jesus' death unfortunately served as a source of deep conflict between our communities. Many Christians held Jews collectively responsible for Jesus' death, calling them "Christ killers." The Second Vatican Council laid to rest this charge of deicide that contemporary biblical scholarship has shown to be without foundation.

However, this development at the level of official Catholic teaching has not ended all problems at the popular level in regard to the narration of Christ's death. Popular culture frequently reinforces the stereotype of Jewish collective responsibility for Jesus' death.

Besides removing any lingering anti-Judaism in our presentations of the crucifixion, we must help our people to recognize its potential for bringing Jews and Christians closer together. Until this more positive side of the crucifixion story relative to Judaism touches Christian consciousness, the anti-Semitic interpretation long associated with it will not be finally excised.

Let me be more specific about what I mean. In relating the story of Jesus' death, we need to stress that the religious ideals, which Jesus preached and tried to implement in the social structure of his day, were shared by the most creative and forward-looking forces in Judaism of that period. Actually, Jesus and his followers stood in concert with a significant part of the Jewish community in opposing the unjust structure that existed at that time. His death bore witness to many of the same ideals proclaimed by other rabbis.

Another important element in the restoration of the Jewish context of Christianity is a deeper appreciation within the church of the first part of the

Bible — the Hebrew Scriptures, or the "First Testament" as it is called in a recent statement by the Pontifical Biblical Commission. Too often Christians have looked on the Old or First Testament as a mere prelude to the spiritual insights found in the New Testament. We need to increase our appreciation for the First Testament as a source of ongoing religious meaning for us in its own right. It is part of our heritage, not merely a backdrop for the teachings of Jesus.

The final theological area I want to raise briefly is how our understanding of Jesus, as Messiah, affects our relationship with Judaism. This is a very difficult and sensitive area, for it touches on the central expression of our Christian faith. Hence Jews must appreciate the fact that Christians will reflect on this relationship with appropriate caution.

Traditionally Christians have sometimes thought that Jews are no longer favored or loved by God because they failed to acknowledge the Messiah. This is simply not true. Christian doctrine needs to be stated in such a way as to acknowledge authentic theological space for Judaism. I am pleased to see an increasing number of theologians devoting themselves to this task, and I urge Christian theologians to give this work a high priority. The restatement that emerges may never be in complete harmony with Jewish self-expression, but, of course, Jews do not need Christian validation for their religious expression! Nevertheless, especially in light of the Holocaust, we have an obligation as Christians to search for ways to express in a positive way — one that is more in accord with the actual scriptures — the close bond between Judaism and Christianity.

THE STATE OF ISRAEL

I now wish to address a topic that I know is of central concern to you and the rest of the Jewish community: the continued security of the State of Israel. I know that, despite wide diversity of opinion within your community about its ultimate significance, Israel is pivotal in Jewish self-understanding. However its meaning is expressed, nearly all Jews view Israel as central to their identity as a people.

On the particular question of Israel, we are united in many of our perspectives, but we also differ on some of them.

We both agree on the overriding need for stability and peace. The National Conference of Catholic Bishops in its 1973 statement on the Middle East and again in November 1978, called unequivocally for the recognition of the State of Israel within secure and recognized boundaries as a basic element of any lasting and just peace. Since those official statements, I have personally and consistently given support to this position in many ways. I understand and am most sensitive to your continued concern about Israel's vulnerability. The history of the state has been shaped by the experience of the Holocaust and the documented discrimination that Jews have historically faced in the East and the West. A resident of a Kibbutz, a survivor of Auschwitz, poignantly captured this reality for me when he remarked, "This land is our resurrection!"

The complex political realities of the Middle East have been an obstacle standing in the way of full diplomatic recognition of the State of Israel by the Holy See, even though this has been urged by many Catholics and Jews, including leaders of your organization. However, it is important to note that the relationship between the Holy See and Israel has improved significantly over the last decade, a fact not always clearly acknowledged in some discussions of the matter. The Holy See recognizes the State of Israel and receives its representatives.

I would be remiss as a Christian religious leader if I did not share with you some uneasiness about certain aspects of the current Middle East situation and its implications for our dialogue.

First of all, I repeat the note of caution I sounded when addressing the Chicago Board of Rabbis and the Jewish Federation of Metropolitan Chicago soon after my arrival in Chicago. Theological statements of support for Israel by some fundamentalist Christian groups are not a valid barometer for evaluating responses from mainline Christians, including the Catholic community.

We simply do not share the same theological tradition with them. We also see a danger in a theological approach that remains isolated from the complexity of Middle East politics: It may too easily lead to a suspension of all concrete moral evaluation. Our tradition of justice and peace requires that we look not only at the theological dimensions of Israel but also at the state of actual relations between Jews and Arabs in that land.

With regard to the present situation in Israel, I would like very briefly to raise two points that need discussion in our dialogue. The first is the seemingly intensified marginalization of the Arab population in Israel proper. Since many of these Arab citizens of Israel are Christians, we cannot ignore their situation. Frankly, no democratic society can truly hope to prosper with such a large, frustrated minority.

The situation on the West Bank is my other concern. I support the positions taken by the National Conference of Catholic Bishops and the Holy See that call for a political solution to this problem. Any attempt by Israel to absorb totally the West Bank through direct or *de facto* annexation will cause immense tension in the Jewish-Christian relationship. Justice demands that we recognize the necessity for a Palestinian homeland mutually agreed on by the key actors in the region.

As many of you know, the bishops' conference has for many years been part of the public debate about U.S. policy in the Middle East. We have tried to take the concerns of Israel about security and safety with utmost seriousness; we have also tried to be equally concerned about the legitimate interests of the Palestinian people and the Arab nations.

I want to emphasize that my sharing these concerns is not meant to be contentious. My point quite simply is that these and other related issues merit serious consideration in our dialogue. Our discussions will reach full maturity if we are able to discuss such concerns in a frank but respectful manner.

RELIGION AND POLITICS IN A PLURALISTIC SOCIETY

My final topic for consideration this evening is one that has occupied a great deal of my attention in recent months. It is the intricate, often emotional, issue of religion and politics in a pluralistic society. I recently spoke on this issue at the Woodstock Theological Center at Georgetown University. It was a long, complex talk, and I will not try to summarize it this evening. I merely want to highlight a few points that are relevant to this presentation.

At the outset, I wish to reaffirm in the strongest terms possible my continued commitment to the principles articulated by the Second Vatican Council in the historic statement on religious liberty. In many ways, that document, along with *Nostra Aetate,* was the most unique contribution of American Catholic experience to the work of the Council.

In this spirit I would like to offer some observations regarding the role religion and religious leaders ought to play in the public life of our nation. This question has engendered strong feelings during the current presidential campaign, and the discussion will continue. The proper role of religious groups in the shaping of public policy is one of the most challenging issues facing the American public in these last years of the twentieth century. Our future as a moral voice in the world may depend on how it is resolved.

This is not a new theme in our history as a nation. From Washington's first inaugural to Lincoln's second inaugural, from the Declaration of Independence to the decisive issues of this election, the themes of religion, morality and politics are woven through the American experience. Intellectually and politically, the key question in every stage of the American civil experiment has not been *whether* these themes should be discussed but how to structure the debate for the welfare of the church and the state.

Let me hasten to add that there is a legitimate secularity of the political process just as there is a legitimate role for religious and moral discourse in our nation's life. The dialogue that keeps both alive must be careful conversation that seeks neither to transform secularity into secularism nor to change the religious role into religiously dominated public discourse. At the same time, this discourse is structured by religious pluralism.

Some mistakenly try to limit morality to personal matters. Religion cannot be so constricted. The founding principle of our society is the dignity and worth of every individual. Religious values include recognition of the dignity and worth of all people under God *and* the responsibilities of a social morality that flow from this belief.

Catholic social doctrine is based on two truths about the human person: Human life is both sacred and social. Because we esteem human life as sacred, we have a duty to protect and foster it at all stages of development from conception to death and in all circumstances. Because we acknowledge it as social, we must develop the kind of societal environment that protects and fosters its development. All the interventions of the United States Catholic Bishops on a spectrum of social issues are based on this belief.

Some assume that the development of public policy is a purely secular and political endeavor, or merely economic and technical in scope. If this were the case, then the church and religious leaders would have no specific role in the development of such policy. However, as a society, we are increasingly confronted with a range of issues that have undeniable moral dimensions. It is not possible to define, debate or decide these policy issues without addressing explicitly their moral character. The issues span the whole spectrum of life from conception to death, and they bear on major segments of our domestic and foreign policy.

Two characteristics of American society that intensify the moral urgency of this range of issues are the global impact of our policies and the technological character of our culture. The role of human rights in U.S. foreign policy, for example, has specific consequences each day for people from Eastern Europe through Southern Africa, from South America to Asia. But the formulation of a human rights policy is not a purely political or technical question. It requires sustained moral analysis from case to case.

I realize that not all of you may agree with the framework I have just outlined. The discussion of religion and politics will continue in earnest after the election. I truly encourage this. I hope that it will take place in a context permeated by the spirit of our common religious heritage: "Blessed indeed is it when brothers and sisters dwell together as one."

My dear friends, this evening I have come to you as your brother. I have spoken honestly and frankly as is appropriate among brothers and sisters. We have so much in common. But ultimately it is our faith in God, who created us in his image and likeness, that unites us more than anything else. So may we always celebrate that unity, while respecting our different traditions, and working with each other, in love, for the betterment of ourselves and the entire human family. Please accept my presence among you this evening as a sign of the great respect and affection I have for you, as well as a reaffirmation of my commitment to dialogue with you and walk with you.

May the Lord bless you and keep you.

May God's face shine upon you, and be gracious to you.

May God look upon you with kindness, and give you peace. Amen.

HYDE PARK-KENWOOD INTERFAITH COUNCIL
CONGREGATION RODFEI ZEDEK

❖

FOR a group that has been meeting for 74 years — with Catholics participating for about 40 years — this gathering is not a particularly extraordinary affair! On the other hand, many people in this room probably still remember vividly the favorable impression that Cardinal Suenens made when he delivered an address at the University of Chicago nearly 20 years ago. His presence and message were considered extraordinary at the time, giving impetus, for example, to the establishment of the Catholic Theological Union in this neighborhood and ushering in a more intensive and comprehensive era of ecumenism in this neighborhood and city.

I feel that I'm just about the right age to appreciate the significance of our gathering in this particular place this evening. I'm old enough to realize that 30 years ago a Catholic archbishop could hardly be invited — or have accepted such an invitation — to give an address in a Jewish temple! I'm also young enough to feel fully at home here greatly enjoying your warm hospitality!

This evening I'd like to do three things: (1) briefly review the current status of ecumenism, (2) explore the present challenge of ecumenical collaboration and (3) briefly describe a specific level of local collaboration — the Council of Religious Leaders of Metropolitan Chicago.

THE CURRENT STATUS OF ECUMENISM
Last November we celebrated the twentieth anniversary of the Second Vatican Council's *Decree on Ecumenism,* and next October we will celebrate the twentieth

anniversary of the decree *Nostra Aetate,* which has provided Catholics with the basis for the most significant improvement in Catholic-Jewish relations since the first century of the Christian era!

Many of us undoubtedly have fond memories of the early days of ecumenical dialogue. There was excitement in the air, and we were rightly convinced that God was guiding our efforts. It may not be misleading to suggest that, when we began these processes with the hope that they would lead, on the one hand, to deeper Christian unity, and, on the other hand, to closer Jewish-Christian relations, we did not have a clear set of directions. We were not yet aware of the paths we would have to walk. We didn't know the time frame to which we were committing ourselves or the eventual scope of the needed dialogue.

As the dialogue has matured through the years, we have become more sober and realistic about the journey on which we have embarked. It is clearer today that all these processes are long-range. There is, perhaps, less excitement today but more openness and general concern for one another. We have moved closer to one another, even though we may not as yet walk side by side.

The complexity of the process becomes clear when one examines the kinds and numbers of ecumenical dialogues taking place on the local, national and international levels. For example, the Catholic Church alone is engaged in formal dialogues with the Orthodox churches, the Anglicans, the Lutherans, the Methodists, the Presbyterian-Reformed churches, the Southern Baptists and the Disciples of Christ, among others. Likewise, as I intimated earlier, there are many efforts at the local, national and international levels that are improving Jewish-Catholic relations. One such effort, for example, has addressed the portrayal of Jews and Judaism in religious textbooks.

While discussions at the international and national levels continue among various groups, official approval of the studies and recommendations of these groups has not been forthcoming. This is not surprising, given some of the complexities encountered. At the same time, ecumenism is taken for granted in the seminary environment today, even if it does not always receive the same emphasis that it did a decade ago.

One of the problems that we face in the U.S. in regard to long-term ecumenical endeavors is our cultural preoccupation with quick results from our efforts. It's much more difficult for us to sustain interest in processes that necessarily extend over decades. However, the stakes are so high and the need for harmony among the churches and synagogues so great that we must transcend our cultural bias and commit ourselves to a long-term process.

I'm not referring merely to theological discussions on the international and national levels or to ecumenical sharing among scholars and seminarians. The real test of ecumenism will take place in the hearts and minds of the members of our local churches and synagogues. We have made some progress in learning to pray together and for one another. We have begun to regard one another as brothers and sisters, to recognize that, despite our differences, we are all children of the one God.

Nevertheless, it's not enough that we pray for or with one another, that we dialogue about theological issues or that we learn to live in peace and harmony with one another. We must also collaborate, whenever feasible, to build a better world. I would like to address this collaboration in more detail.

THE CHALLENGE OF COLLABORATION

The world in which we live is challenged by the chilling specter of nuclear war and blemished by the numbing effects of widespread poverty and other social ills. Our brothers and sisters are dying of hunger in Africa and warring against one another in Asia and Central America. The North, to a large extent, controls the economics of the South, while the West and the East spar with competing ideologies.

In our own country — and in this very city — we face critical issues that affect the health and well-being of all our people: our families, our youth, our elderly. Unemployment, underemployment, crime, poor and inadequate health services, the deterioration of family life, decreasing federal social services, violence in our streets and on our playgrounds: Each of these enormously complex problems seriously impacts human life and demands our common concern, the combined use of our resources and our full collaboration.

Confronting them alone will often prove inadequate. But we need not stand alone or walk single file into the next millennium; indeed, we must not!

One way of collaborating is joint participation in the national public policy debate on crucial issues. The premise of the U.S. Catholic bishops' pastoral letter on war and peace — and also the proposed letter on the economy, which is still in draft form — is that every major policy decision has a moral dimension. There is no such thing as an "amoral" policy.

By opening space in the public debate for the moral dimensions of public issues, we have tried to establish the principle that, in every forum where issues are addressed, decisions made and policies shaped, there should be explicit public consideration of their moral implications. This means that many groups and individuals should participate in the analysis of the ethical and empirical dimensions of the issues.

Today we face a series of questions ranging from medical care to international relations, from equity and employment to budget priorities and national purpose — issues whose moral implications are as important to our future as the technical calculations that absorb most of our public debates.

Religious groups should not expect or be given special treatment in this regard. We should earn a hearing in the public debate by the quality of our analysis and argumentation. If we can demonstrate how a moral vision shapes and enriches the choices and the challenges that confront us as a nation or as an urban community, then consideration will be given to the moral factor in policy discussions.

Such participation in the public arena would benefit from a more extensive ecumenical exchange among the churches and synagogues. On the war and peace question we share a common vision on a whole range of topics. This is not true, of course, on every moral issue in the political and social spectrum. Nonetheless, we are sufficiently well-grounded in our ecumenical relationships at this point in our history that we need not fear facing our differences candidly as well as our shared concerns.

Moreover, our ecumenical experience of the past 20 years — your experience of the past 74 years! — provides us with an opportunity in our fragile and explosive world to model the processes, attitudes and beliefs that can lead to reconciliation, justice and peace. The interfaith movement has demonstrated that people with widely divergent views and convictions can come together, that they can discuss the issues dividing them and look forward to solutions, and that they can join hands and celebrate what they have in common.

Let me make this more concrete by applying this model to Chicago and the metropolitan area. We have reason to be proud of the broad range of ethnic, racial and religious backgrounds within our community. Each wave of immigrants has enriched our life and broadened our experience of the wider world. We have a marvelous opportunity to demonstrate to the world that people of diverse backgrounds *can* live together in harmony and peace.

However, our diversity is not simply an opportunity — it is a serious challenge because this *diversity* all too easily translates into ethnic, racial and religious *division.* This great city has painfully witnessed the cancer of racism at work in a community. The Catholic Church has joined others in condemning racism as a sin and heresy because it is directly opposed to the most basic doctrines of Judaism and Christianity. We believe that all peoples are made in the image and likeness of the Creator and that all share an essential equality.

Apart from our social diversity, economic change is seriously affecting our quality of life. As a community, we face critical issues that affect the health and well-being of all our people — our families, our youth, our elderly.

In recent months I have visited various neighborhoods of Chicago and the suburbs. I have come to realize that Chicago is not *one* city but *two*: the prosperous city, full of hope and potential, which we see reflected in the impressive skyscrapers downtown, along the magnificent lakeshore — including the east side of Hyde Park and Kenwood — and in the beautiful residential areas of the outer city and suburbs. And the other city of bone-crushing poverty and spirit-eroding unemployment, of decaying housing and fleeing business and industry, the city of fear and near despair that lies between the two sections of the prosperous city, the city where children go to bed hungry on a regular basis.

Last Sunday's *New York Times* carried a special feature on hunger in America, demonstrating that, while it is difficult to define "hunger" as such, there are millions of people in the United States who are hungry! These are not mere statistics. These are people like you and me, people with individual names and faces.

A story in Monday's *Sun-Times* described such a person, an eight-year-old boy named Terrence who frets that his mother can't pay the family's bills. He explains, "I ran away from home once so my Mommy would have one less [child] to worry about." But then he adds that he doesn't consider himself poor because "poor people are sad all the time. I'm happy!" He's a brave, sensitive young man. He retains his sense of dignity, but, still, he's often hungry. Unfortunately, we all know that his plight is not unique. There are so many others like him in this metropolitan area.

I'm aware of the wonderful work you do running a food pantry and soup kitchen. Any organization whose soup kitchen serves about 40,000 meals in 20 months knows the extent of hunger in this city. I fully support your efforts and encourage you to continue to provide these necessary services for the most vulnerable in our midst.

Nevertheless, we all must admit that no single person, institution or co-operative organization can solve these enormous problems alone. It will take all of us, working together, to effectively cope with the enormous challenge facing Chicago today.

But, to unite this city in the face of serious social, economic and political problems means that we must take down the fences that separate people from one another. In response to a neighbor who annually repeated the axiom "Good fences make good neighbors," the poet Robert Frost retorted:

> Something there is that doesn't love a wall. . .
> ". . . Before I built a wall, I'd ask to know
> What I was walling in or walling out,
> And to whom I was like to give offense.
> Something there is that doesn't love a wall,
> That wants it down."

Today it's not a question of loving or not loving a wall. Today we have no choice — if we want to survive as a human community — but to tear down the walls that divide us. If ever they made for good neighbors, that time is past!

I'm aware that the Hyde Park-Kenwood community has been multiracial and multicultural for nearly three decades. Your successes have provided models for other areas of the metropolitan area and, indeed, for the entire nation. You will need to stay alert to ensure that you do not erect walls between yourselves and your brothers and sisters who live to the north, west and south of you, some of whom are the most vulnerable in our larger community.

Perhaps a more direct way of stating the challenge that lies before you is this: Will new developments along 47th Street and 63rd Street provide contrast or continuity with your community? Are you going to erect bridges or walls?

THE COUNCIL OF RELIGIOUS LEADERS OF METROPOLITAN CHICAGO

I'd like to turn to a particular kind of ecumenical collaboration, recently established in the metropolitan area: the Council of Religious Leaders of Metropolitan Chicago.

In May, 1984, I invited 19 Chicago religious leaders to a meeting at Holy Name Cathedral. They represented the top administrative and pastoral positions for their respective religious bodies. Fifteen were able to join me for that first in a series of meetings.

The concerns that motivated me to set up the meeting were the social divisions in our city — especially along racial lines — that were hindering us from facing effectively the crucial social, economic and political issues that I have mentioned earlier. These leaders — representing, besides the Catholic Church, the Orthodox Church, various Protestant and Evangelical churches, and the Chicago Board of Rabbis — agreed to issue a statement about Chicago's current status and specifically what we should do to erase the racism from our midst. This statement, as you know, was issued last September.

One of its provisions that caught public attention was our offer to provide "neutral space" where key politicians could meet to discuss opposing views without the pressures of the media and public. Principal figures of Chicago government responded, and some of us religious leaders met on two occasions with them. Afterward we assessed that the sessions had been moderately successful. While all the problems were not resolved, the candid dialogue we facilitated was helpful.

Last February we organized ourselves more formally as the Council of Religious Leaders of Metropolitan Chicago, a group that will meet four times a year with two purposes in mind: (1) "to know one another well [and] to explore together the meaning of church and synagogue in our metropolitan area, and (2) to study and act together on those significant issues affecting our people and the community we are privileged to serve." As of May, we have 25 members, representing a spectrum of religious bodies in the metropolitan area.

To enable us to move more quickly when the need arises, we formed an executive committee consisting of Rabbi Herbert Bornstein, president of the Chicago Board of Rabbis; Reverend Sterling Cary, Illinois Conference, United Church of Christ; Bishop Paul Erickson, president of the Illinois Synod of the Lutheran Church in America; His Grace Iakovos, bishop of the Greek Orthodox diocese of Chicago; Dr. James P. Tillman, president of the Chicago Baptist Institute; and myself.

While we do not view the Council as programmatic in nature, we do intend to speak out on issues of major concern to the citizens of Chicago. We hope to help provide both the vision and motivation needed among the members of our synagogues and churches — and, indeed, all people of good will — to address the important social and moral issues facing us today. In addition to the statement on racism, we have issued a joint statement on the need for an ethics ordinance for Chicago, calling for public hearings on the rival proposals currently before the City Council. Our other concerns include jobs, housing, health and hunger.

We also realize that a major reason for much of the distrust and discomfort between various racial and ethnic groups is the fact that their members simply don't know each other as people. We tend to stereotype one another in ways that range from bigotry to romanticism. We've decided that we can and must do something about this.

Hence, one of our current ecumenical projects is the development of guidelines for churches and synagogues that want to enter into pairing relationships with one another through such means as exchange of pulpits and choirs, regular visitations and exchange of programs. We are considering facilitating the pairings of diverse congregations with one another so that they may pledge to plan ways to work together over the course of a year. We will probably limit the number of pairings during the first year of the program to assess more readily the program's feasibility and effectiveness. I mention this particular project as an example of the efforts we hope to make to bring about greater understanding and unity in our community.

The Council of Religious Leaders of Metropolitan Chicago has considerable potential. Our collaboration is not meant to substitute for the essential work you are doing in your own neighborhood. At the same time, we need your support and cooperation just as we continue to support your efforts. It all comes down to this: Together, we can do so much more than any of us can do on his or her own. We really have no choice given the comprehensive, complex nature of the problems that face our community.

More than that, working together as brothers and sisters, as children of the same God, is what the Creator has always intended that we do — live and work in peace, harmony, justice and unity with one another for the building up of God's new creation.

My dear friends, this evening I have come to you as your brother. We have so much in common. But, ultimately, it is our faith in God, who created us in his image and likeness, that unites us more than anything else. So may we always celebrate that unity, while respecting our different traditions and working with each other, in love, for the betterment of ourselves and the entire human family. Please accept my presence among you as a sign of my commitment to ecumenical and interfaith understanding and collaboration.

NOSTRA AETATE CELEBRATION

IN 1965, THE SECOND VATICAN COUNCIL ISSUED ITS HISTORIC DOCUMENT, "NOSTRA AETATE" (IN OUR TIME), THE DECLARATION ON THE RELATIONSHIP OF THE CHURCH TO NON-CHRISTIAN RELIGIONS. THIS DOCUMENT WAS SEEN BY MANY AS THE ENTRANCE OF THE CATHOLIC CHURCH INTO THE INTERFAITH MOVEMENT. TWENTY YEARS LATER, THE ARCHDIOCESE SPONSORED THIS CELEBRATION. RABBI LOUIS JACOBS, PROFESSOR OF TALMUD, LEO BAECK COLLEGE IN LONDON, DELIVERED THE KEYNOTE ADDRESS. CARDINAL BERNARDIN ALSO ADDRESSED THE ASSEMBLY.

❈

My brothers and sisters, I greet you today in the spirit of *shalom,* for "peace" captures very well the theme of our celebration of the twentieth anniversary of *Nostra Aetate.* This Vatican II declaration on the church and the Jewish people marked a turning point in Jewish-Christian relations. It called for a mutual understanding of and respect for our respective religious traditions, and deplored "the hatred, persecutions and displays of anti-Semitism directed at Jews at any time and from any source" (4).

This evening we give thanks to the God of Abraham and Sarah, of Jesus and Mary, for the two decades of enhanced understanding and reconciliation that have marked the relationship between our two religious communities since the Council.

Peace, *shalom,* is increasingly becoming characteristic of our encounters after centuries of mutual hostility caused in large part by some Christians' misguided belief that it was permissible to punish Jews as so-called "Christ killers." The Second Vatican Council made it clear that such actions cannot be considered as consonant with the teachings of the New Testament.

On a number of occasions in the past three years, I have had the opportunity to address the Jewish community on the subject of Christian-Jewish relations. This evening I welcome the opportunity to address my remarks on this important topic primarily to the Catholic community of the archdiocese.

Nostra Aetate has given Catholics a threefold responsibility. Our first task is to ensure that all vestiges of anti-Semitism are removed from our teaching, liturgy and preaching. For this goal to be fully realized, we must begin to acknowledge and proclaim — far more extensively than we have thus far — the profoundly positive impact that the Old or First Testament and Second Temple Judaism had on the religious perspective and values of Jesus and the early church. The Gospel of Matthew states clearly that Jesus came not to reject or abolish the law and the prophets but to fulfill them.

In recently released catechetical *Notes* on the proper presentation of Judaism by Catholics, the Holy See has emphasized:

> Because of the unique relations that exist between Christianity and Judaism — "linked together at the very level of their identity" (Pope John Paul II, March 6, 1982) — the Jews and Judaism should not occupy an occasional and marginal place in catechesis: Their presence there is essential and should be organically integrated (I:2).

I urge archdiocesan educators, preachers and liturgists to make this ecclesial perspective their own in their ministry. Any presentation of Jesus' message that fails to note its indebtedness to the Jewish biblical heritage and the Judaism of his time fails to present the gospel in its fullness and integrity. Jewish tradition was integral to the piety, preaching and ministry of the Lord.

Our second responsibility in light of *Nostra Aetate* is authentic dialogue with members of the Jewish community. While study of the Jewish tradition is vital, it can never be a substitute for face-to-face encounters with our Jewish sisters and brothers. I'm very pleased that a number of local dialogue groups already exist in the archdiocese, one going back as far as 1969. I encourage our pastors and people to cooperate with our Office of Human Relations and Ecumenism in supporting the efforts of existing groups and in establishing additional dialogues.

In these groups Catholics and Jews have the opportunity to share their religious and moral perspectives. They come to understand better the varieties of Jewish and Catholic expression, the ways in which we define our existence as religious communities. In doing this we will move beyond dealing with one another as caricatures, as has too often been the case in the past. In this regard, the Holy See's 1975 guidelines for the implementation of *Nostra Aetate* specifically remind Catholics that coming to know the Jewish people "as they define themselves" is indispensable for authentic dialogue.

My experience has been that Catholics who enter into dialogue with other Jewish friends come away with a new appreciation not only of the richness of the Jewish tradition but also of how much it has contributed to the development of the Christian faith. They also learn how pivotal both the experience of the Nazi Holocaust and the rebirth of the State of Israel are to Jewish self-identity in our day. I have, as you know, spoken about this on a number of occasions and will continue to listen and to reflect on these and other matters that are so central to Jewish contemporary identity.

Interfaith dialogue is essential if we are to experience *shalom,* but dialogue is not an easy process. It requires mutual respect and trust. Each party must strive to understand the ideas and feelings, the dreams and values of the other. Dialogue, in other words, is a two-way street. Eventually, we must be able to discuss our differences, no matter how painful that may be, no matter how sensitive the issues might be. As we grow in the awareness that we are brothers and sisters, children of the same God, we will find both the wisdom and the courage to deepen our commitment to the dialogical process.

Through dialogue Catholics and Jews also will come to experience a new sense of bondedness, a new spirit of *shalom,* which is so necessary for the cooperative efforts we need to transform our national ethos from a proclivity for war to a burning passion for peace.

This brings us to the third responsibility that *Nostra Aetate* outlines for Catholics: the pursuit of peace with justice. If our study and dialogue fail to develop within us a new commitment to work with one another toward the elimination of economic and political injustice, it will ultimately have failed.

I welcome the Jewish input into the U.S. Catholic bishops' pastoral letter on the economy. I also welcome the joint publication by the Union of American Hebrew Congregations and the National Conference of Catholic Bishops of a common study guide on the bishops' pastoral letter on war and peace: *The Challenge of Shalom for Catholics and Jews* (edited by Annette Daum and Eugene Fisher). I urge archdiocesan educators to use this valuable resource. We also need to intensify our combined efforts on behalf of freedom and dignity for Catholics and Jews in the Soviet Union and other parts of Eastern Europe.

Closer to home, we are all residents of this metropolitan area where human suffering is on the increase. In my address to the annual meeting of the Jewish Community Centers of Chicago last year, I spoke of the impressions of human suffering that I received as I visited a West Side housing project. If the spirit of *shalom,* generated by our dialogue, is to meet the full text of both Torah and gospel, we must reconcile ourselves with those in our midst who increasingly lack the basic requirements of food and shelter.

Before closing, I would like to mention a project that is presently being considered here in Chicago. This project, I am convinced, will have special meaning for Chicago, which is home to so many Eastern Europeans.

We believe that a deeper understanding of the past will help us to understand better the present. In particular, we believe that a deepened study — by scholars, clergy and teachers — of the past 800 years of Eastern European Judaism and Catholicism will greatly enhance our understanding of this important period and ambiance in our history. But even more important, such a study will contribute to a greater appreciation for the bonds that have united our two religious communities both in the past and at the present.

It is with that conviction that Chicago's Spertus College of Judaica has announced its intention to establish a center for the study of Polish and Eastern European Jewry. My name will be associated with the center. I consider this a great honor and will do all I can to make what is presently a dream become a reality.

My prayer is that this weekend of commemoration and celebration will begin a new phase in the history of Catholic-Jewish relations in Chicago. We have the opportunity to become a shining example to the nation of interreligious reconciliation that results in deep social commitment.

We will probably never agree on all the theological issues that lie before us, nor are we likely to achieve consensus on every public policy question. But we can seek and find a unity of heart whose enriching power will sustain us despite our differences until God's reign appears in its full glory. May God strengthen us in this resolve.

EMMANUEL CONGREGATION

YOM HASHOAH IS HOLOCAUST MEMORIAL DAY, A SPECIAL REMEMBRANCE ON
THE JEWISH CALENDAR. IT COMMEMORATES THE SHOAH, THE HOLOCAUST.
ON THIS DAY, CARDINAL BERNARDIN WAS INVITED TO ADDRESS THE PARTICIPANTS IN
THE MEMORIAL SERVICE AT EMMANUEL CONGREGATION IN CHICAGO.

I have never visited Yad Vashem in Jerusalem, but a friend of mine brought back a book of photographs that he bought there. Its title is *The Holocaust.* The caption of the first photo describes a "Nazi mass rally in Berlin (August 15, 1936) at which they saw a Germany 'cleansed' of Jews. The chief slogan in this picture reads: 'The Jews are our misfortune.'"

The final photo in the book bears this caption: "Children — prisoners of Auschwitz concentration camp — after liberation (January 1945)." Those ten years, 1935 to 1945, encompass one of the most horrible events of human history, the systematic annihilation of more than six million human beings, not by a natural disaster or by an epidemic but by the cruelty, hatred and prejudice of other human beings. The Holocaust.

The chapter headings of that book from Yad Vashem chronicle the awful progression: Anti-Jewish policy and persecutions in Germany. The period of restrictions and internment of Jews, 1939–1941. The final solution, 1941–1945. The reaction of the free world. Armed resistance and the struggle for survival.

This evening I would like to share with you some reflections based on one photo from that book. It is not the most horrible picture, nor is it the most famous. Let me describe it for you and then share some of my own reactions and reflections.

Two men face one another. One is a Nazi soldier. The other a Jewish civilian. The Nazi wears a steel helmet with the straps secured tightly under his prominent chin. The civilian wears a cloth cap with a billed visor. The soldier's mouth looks as if it is just about to break into a grin. He seems to be enjoying what he is doing. By contrast, the Jewish civilian's face is contorted, twisted, as if he is about to weep. There is great pain, grief, agony, embarrassment in his countenance. In his right hand the soldier has a pair of scissors — not a weapon. He is cutting off the beard and earlocks of the Jewish believer.

The caption reads, "Shearing off or plucking out the beard and earlocks of Orthodox Jews in front of jeering crowds was a favorite pastime in occupied Poland."

Why does that picture remain in my mind? On the surface, it is far more benign than the pictures of emaciated bodies lying strewn in a huge mass grave in the Nordhausen concentration camp. It is not as confronting as the 18 faces staring from the wooden bunks at Buchenwald. It is not as gruesome as the skeletal remains outside the crematorium furnaces at Majdanek. It is not as outrageous as the picture of the long lines of new arrivals at Auschwitz as they wait their turn to appear before the platform. There the "selection" process takes place, determining who will go to the barracks and who will go to the gas chambers.

Why then does it stand out? Because it is so close to being ordinary. Because it is not so horrendous as to be totally alien to our own experience. Because it is within the realm of our own possibilities for cruelty.

Commentators on the Holocaust have talked about the banality of evil. So many of the perpetrators of the horrors of the Holocaust were banal, petty, mean-spirited, envious, cruel people. They were bullies who had an extraordinary opportunity to act out their prejudices, their hatreds.

That is what we see in the picture that I just described: A bully who has power over another human being. A person who can transform a simple act that barbers perform daily into an act of humiliation and desecration. How simple it is to cut someone's hair! And yet, what a violation of one's dignity it can be. What a violation of a sacred way of life, a faith, a tradition, a commitment! A smirk on one face. Depth of pain, loss, humiliation on the other.

As we gaze on that picture, we realize that we are seeing the seeds of the Holocaust before our very eyes. The desire to strike out at what is sacred. The desire to trivialize that which gives meaning to another's life. The meanness of spirit that strikes deeply into the soul of another individual human being. How can one person do that to another? What worm of hatred eats away at the human heart? What gain is there from such outrage?

It was the repetition of such individual acts of cruelty that accumulated in the despicable event we know as the Holocaust. Individual against individual. Group against group. Perpetrators. Onlookers. Collaborators in evil.

As we look at this scene, we realize that we are, at our worst moments, capable of similar actions. No, we could not starve people to death. No, we would not turn on a gas oven or crematorium. No, we would not shoot children in cold blood. But yes, we could humiliate another human person. Yes, we could smirk in enjoyment at someone else's embarrassment. Yes, we could mock someone else's cherished symbols of belief.

The child who taunts a classmate beyond endurance. The adult who tells jokes with racial, religious or ethnic mockery. The superior who publicly berates an employee. These commonplace instances are not entirely alien to the banality, the petty cruelty, the meanness of spirit in that photograph.

We say of the Holocaust, and rightly so, "Never again!" It is important for us to remember to memorialize. And you and I must react strongly when we see neo-Nazis in uniform, when we see a monument to the Holocaust defaced, when we see racist or anti-Semitic graffiti on a synagogue or church, when we see the first signs of prejudice.

Let me assure you, when I say this, I do not wish in any way to minimize the tremendous horror of the Holocaust. Rather, I want to alert all of us — all people of good will — to the need to root out the seeds of hatred or cruelty wherever they spring up. Why? Because, just as giant plants grow from tiny seeds, so the Holocaust did come full blown into our world. It started gradually and grew. "Never again" means nipping it in the bud, eradicating its roots before they develop further.

It is for that that you and I pray together on this sacred day, Yom Hashoah.

I have no idea as to what happened to those two men in that photograph — the Nazi soldier with the scissors and the Jewish civilian whose beard and earlocks were sheared away. The photography froze one moment in time in both their lives. Did either of them survive the Holocaust and the war? One can only speculate.

For me, the Jewish man is a symbol not only of the six million that died but also of the survivors and their children and grandchildren — the struggles within their spirits, their struggles to be true to themselves, true to their tradition, true to God in the face of such cruelty, such horror, such crushing grief. What was going on within their minds, their hearts, their spirits during those horrendous days, months, years?

I searched the scriptures for some clue, for some echo of their laments, and I would like to share with you what I found. For me, and perhaps also for you, they capture the struggle and the faith that marked so many of the victims and the survivors of the Holocaust. I will read some excerpts from chapter three of 'Eykah, the Book of Lamentations:

> He has led me and made me walk in darkness
>> and not light.
> He has wasted my flesh and my skin;
>> he has broken my bones.
> He has fenced me in,
>> and encompassed me with bitterness and hardship.
> Whenever I have cried, and called for help,
>> he has ignored my prayer.

He has been a lurking bear to me,
     a lion in ambush.
He has waylaid me and mangled me.
He has made me desolate.
I have become the butt of all peoples,
     their taunt song all the time.
He has filled me with bitterness;
     he has sated me with anguish.
So I said,
     "Gone is my strength, and
     my hope is in the Lord."
I am crushed in spirit.
But this I call to mind and so I have hope,
     that the gracious deeds of the Lord never cease,
     his compassion never fails.
     They are fresh every morning.
     Great is his faithfulness.
I said, "The Lord is my heritage.
     Therefore, I will hope in him."

Two men face to face. One with a pair of scissors and a smug grin. He is in command. The other with shorn locks and deep pain. That is what we see on the surface of things.

But the words of the Book of Lamentations help us see beneath the surface. The magnificence of faith and goodness stands triumphant over the banality of evil and malice. The Holocaust recalls, at one and the same time, the depths to which humanity can fall and the heights to which human beings can rise. In the final analysis, love is stronger than death. Faith is stronger than hatred. Compassion will outlast cruelty. My dear brothers and sisters, may we always remember these profound lessons of the Holocaust.

CENTER FOR JEWISH AND CHRISTIAN LEARNING

EACH YEAR THE COLLEGE OF SAINT THOMAS, THROUGH ITS CENTER FOR JEWISH
AND CHRISTIAN LEARNING, SPONSORS A SYMPOSIUM AT WHICH SCHOLARS AND LEADERS
FROM BOTH COMMUNITIES ARE INVITED TO SPEAK ABOUT TOPICS AFFECTING
THE RELATIONSHIP BETWEEN JEWS AND CHRISTIANS.

I am very grateful for your kind invitation to address this ongoing forum on Christian-Jewish relations. I commend the College of Saint Thomas for its long-standing efforts to explore the profound links that exist between Jews and Christians. In particular, I commend the Center for Jewish and Christian Learning to promote Christian-Jewish dialogue. You have clearly helped to make the Twin Cities area one of the principal regions in the U.S. for the promotion of Christian-Jewish dialogue. This was quite evident to all when St. Paul-Minneapolis hosted the last National Workshop on Christian-Jewish Relations. I am happy to say that Chicago will have the pleasure of welcoming the 1990 National Workshop. We will commemorate the twenty-fifth anniversary of the historic Vatican II statement on the Catholic Church's relationship with the Jewish people, the ecclesial document that gave birth to many significant interfaith endeavors.

The very allusion to *Nostra Aetate,* which describes Catholicism's enduring bonds with the people Israel, makes us aware of how far we have come since that monumental day in 1965 when, pursuing the vision of Pope John XXIII, the Second Vatican Council, after careful deliberation, gave final approval to that document.

As you know, the experience of U.S. Catholicism, as well as the leadership of the U.S. bishops, played an important role in its eventual passage. We can truly say that *Nostra Aetate* represents one of the most important contributions of the church in the United States to the Ecumenical Council. That is why we Americans have a particular responsibility to protect and develop its basic understanding and intent. And that, in turn, points to the importance of the work of the College of Saint Thomas on Christian-Jewish relations. My hope is that many more Catholic institutions will follow your leadership.

This evening I would like to share with you my own vision of developments during the last quarter century and to raise some issues that call for additional reflection. I will focus my reflections on four areas: (1) the role of the Hebrew Scriptures, or Old Testament, in the Catholic Church; (2) the growing appreciation of Jesus' profound ties to the Jewish tradition; (3) the sense of a special, deep bonding between the church and the Jewish people; and (4) the significance of the Shoah, or Holocaust, about which some tension remains in our relationship.

THE HEBREW SCRIPTURES AND THE CATHOLIC CHURCH

Even before the Second Vatican Council, Catholic attitudes toward the Old Testament — or the "Prior Testament" as the Pontifical Biblical Commission has called it more recently — had begun to change. A growing number of Catholic exegetes had come to a better understanding of the richness of the first part of the Bible and a deeper appreciation of how these writings had positively influenced the teachings of Jesus and early Christianity.

That process has greatly accelerated since the appearance of *Nostra Aetate*. There has been a gradual, but persistent, shift in emphasis away from the viewpoint that regarded the Hebrew Scriptures simply as background material for understanding the New Testament. In its place has come an emerging sense that the books of the Hebrew Bible are worth studying in their own right, apart from whatever legitimate insights they may offer us into the meaning of Jesus' life and mission. These documents are no longer seen as mere "prelude" or "foil" for the teachings of Jesus in the New Testament. Rather, we are recognizing, however slowly, that, without deep immersion into the spirit and texts of the Hebrew Scriptures, Christians experience an emaciated version of Christian spirituality and know but a very truncated version of Jesus' full religious vision.

While we have made great strides in this regard, we still have a considerable way to travel in order to accord the Hebrew Bible its rightful place in Christian life and spirituality. These inspired books in their entirety — and not only the prophetic and wisdom sections — must be accorded their rightful status as essential, not merely peripheral, resources for Christian retreats, preaching, religious education, liturgy and theology.

This is being done throughout the Catholic Church. When the U.S. bishops wrote their pastoral letter on war and peace, for example, they began with an examination of the relationship between peace and fidelity to God's covenant with Israel. Likewise, in their pastoral letter on the U.S. economy, they drew significantly on the Book of Genesis for insights in regard to human co-creatorship with God in economic decision-making today. Both pastoral letters implicitly acknowledge the importance for Christians to complement the insights of the New Testament with those of the Hebrew Scriptures for a comprehensive biblical spirituality. This same approach is clearly present in Pope John Paul II's first social encyclical, *Laborem Exercens.*

Legitimate questions certainly remain for Jewish and Christian scholars to pursue in regard to the interpretation of the texts of the first part of the Bible. But, as such reflection and study continue, we Christians may draw far more deeply than we have in the past from this spiritual well.

JESUS AND JEWISH TRADITION

Since the Second Vatican Council, the Christian dialogue with Jews and Judaism has begun to demonstrate even greater impact on our understanding of the New Testament, especially in terms of Jesus' links to the Judaism of his day. We are witnessing a genuine revolution in New Testament scholarship, made possible by a much greater understanding of Hebrew and Aramaic, and an enhanced reliance on and availability of Jewish materials from the Second Temple or so-called "intertestamental" period. We are seeing, for example, a rapid end to the dominant hold of that form of biblical interpretation that stressed the almost exclusively Hellenistic background of Pauline Christianity. Such exegesis of the New Testament seriously eroded Jesus' concrete ties with Second Temple Judaism. This, in turn, tended to produce an excessively "universalistic" interpretation of Jesus' message, which contained fertile ground for theological anti-Judaism.

In the last two decades, a dramatic shift in New Testament scholarship has begun to restore Jesus and his message to its original Jewish milieu. This is not to say that complete agreement now exists among scholars regarding the exact form of Judaism that most directly impacted Jesus' teaching. Far from it. In 1985, the Holy See's Pontifical Commission for Religious Relations with the Jews issued its *Notes on the Correct Way to Present Jews and Judaism in the Preaching and Catechesis of the Roman Catholic Church*. These *Notes* regard Jesus as closer in perspective to Pharisaism than to any other Jewish movement of the period but leave the question open for further research and discussion.

Despite the remaining ambiguity, which is likely to continue for some time, there is a growing overall consensus that makes the state of New Testament scholarship today far different with respect to the fundamental vision of Jesus' relationship with Judaism than was the case even a decade ago. That consensus involves a number of central conclusions:

1) The movement begun by Jesus — which grew into the Christian Church — can best be described as a reform movement within Judaism during his

own lifetime. There is little evidence during this formative period that Jesus and his disciples wished to break away from their Jewish context.

2) The missionary movement launched by Paul, as Paul himself understood it, was essentially a Jewish mission that intended to include the Gentiles as an integral part of the divine summons to the people Israel.

3) At the same time, there were conflicts between Jesus and certain Jews. Moreover, the majority of the Jewish people and their leaders did not believe in Jesus, and this strained their relationship with his disciples.

4) Nevertheless, church and synagogue began gradually to walk their separate ways only after the conclusion of the first Jewish war with the Romans (70 CE). Prior to that, Jesus' disciples did not demonstrate a self-understanding of themselves as members of a religious community standing over and against Judaism. And on closer examination, even the later writings of the New Testament, although they manifest signs of the movement toward separation, continue to demonstrate some form of dialogue with the church's original Jewish matrix. Moreover, the inevitable rupture between Judaism and the early church did not and does not eradicate the spiritual "bond" to which *Nostra Aetate* refers.

This recent transformation in New Testament scholarship regarding Jesus' ties with Judaism carries far-reaching implications not only for biblical interpretation but also for contemporary theology, religious education, spirituality and worship. In the past, for example, when we listened to the narrative of the so-called Council of Jerusalem in the book of the Acts of the Apostles, our tendency was to identify fully with the apostle Paul in his dispute with Peter, James and the Jewish-spirited Jerusalem church. But the enhanced appreciation of Jesus' positive Jewish ties now prompts us to take a second look at the passage and its historical context.

From the new perspective, it now appears that Peter and James were trying to hold on to something very important, however inadequately they made their case. Insofar as the fundamental decision recorded in this story played a role in the subsequent severing of all constructive links with Judaism, it also had the effect of deadening an important dimension of the church's soul. It is this buried heritage that Pope John Paul has brought to our attention on numerous occasions during his pontificate.

Nevertheless, this profound shift in Christian exegesis of the New Testament will not have its full impact until it begins to influence all other aspects of church life. We have much work to do in the church to incorporate this new perspective on Jesus and Judaism into our theological statements: our education of clergy, seminarians and lay people; our preaching and our worship. Again, this is being addressed in the church. For example, to provide additional help and guidelines to Catholic preachers in regard to the presentation of Jews and Judaism, the Bishops' Committee on the Liturgy of the National Conference of Catholic Bishops issued an important statement earlier this month. It includes such topics as the Jewish roots of the Christian liturgy, the relationship between the readings taken from the Hebrew Scriptures and the New Testament during Advent and Lent, and suggestions for pastoral activities during Holy Week and Easter. While the episcopal conference will undoubtedly continue to address such matters, the church will also need the assistance of centers, such as yours here at the College of Saint Thomas, for these efforts to be fully effective.

We humbly acknowledge that, regrettably, there has been widespread theological anti-Judaism in the history of Christianity, and it has infected every dimension of ecclesial life. Vatican II gave us a historic mandate to change that tragic legacy. Recent exegesis has, in turn, provided us with the scriptural resources for carrying out this mandate. We must maintain our commitment to this endeavor in the years ahead, for it involves our very faith identity as Christians. If anything, we need to accelerate the work undertaken thus far and give this mandate a renewed priority in the church's life.

THE CHURCH AND JUDAISM

Our renewed appreciation of the thoroughly Jewish context of Jesus' preaching and ministry has inevitably led the church to a reconsideration of how it expresses theologically its relationship with Judaism. It is no secret that many of our past formulations have seriously distorted the role of the Jewish people in human salvation. These distortions undoubtedly played a role in the persecutions borne by Jewish communities in so many parts of the world and tragically helped provide a seedbed for Christian collaboration with the fundamentally antireligious philosophy of Nazism.

Now all that is beginning to change as individual Christian theologians, church leaders and official ecclesial documents increasingly challenge this long-standing theology of total Jewish displacement from the process of salvation after the coming of Jesus. The prevalent "supercessionist" approach to Judaism on the part of much of classical Christian theology is being replaced by a theology of covenantal partnership.

No one has given greater impetus to this new theological understanding of the Jewish-Christian relationship than Pope John Paul II. In recognition of his contribution, the United States Catholic Conference, in collaboration with the Anti-Defamation League of B'nai B'rith, published a collection of his addresses on the topic between 1979 and 1986 (cf. *Pope John Paul II on Jews and Judaism, 1979–1986*, edited with introduction and commentary by Eugene J. Fisher and Leon Klenicki). Several themes emerge in the book as cornerstones of the developing theology of covenantal partnership.

The first theme is that of a "spiritual bond" that links the church to the people Israel. This was a notion central to *Nostra Aetate*. Pope John Paul made it a prominent part of his very first statement on the subject as pontiff in March 1979, when he spoke to an international group of Jewish leaders in Rome. On that occasion he interpreted the conciliar phrase "spiritual bond" to mean "that our two religious communities are connected and closely related at the very level of their respective identities" and affirmed the need for "fraternal dialogue" between them.

Such language makes it clear that the pope wishes to underscore the fact that the Jewish-Christian relationship could not be interpreted as merely marginal for the church's identity. The Holy See's *Notes* of 1985, which build on the pope's own statements, insist that this relationship reaches to the very essence of the Christian faith. Hence to cover over or deny its reality is, in effect, to sacrifice something at the very core of Christian existence, something integral to the church's authentic proclamation of its faith (cf. *Notes,* 1.2).

Earlier that same year, in an address at a twentieth anniversary commemoration of *Nostra Aetate* in Rome, the holy father insisted that the spiritual bond between Christians and Jews must be viewed as a "sacred one, stemming as it does from the mysterious will of God." And during his historic visit to Rome's synagogue in 1986, he further intensified this theme of "spiritual bonding" with the following words:

> The church of Christ discovers her "bond" with Judaism by "searching into her own mystery" (*Nostra Aetate,* 4). The Jewish religion is not "extrinsic" to us but in a certain way is "intrinsic" to our religion. With Judaism, therefore, we have a relationship which we do not have with any other religion. You are dearly beloved brothers and, in a certain way, it could be said that you are our elder brothers.

The second major theme of Pope John Paul's newly emerging theology of the Christian-Jewish relationship focuses on the "living heritage" of Judaism in which Christians share by reason of their inherent bond with the Jewish people. The holy father treads very cautiously here, as well he must, for there is a deep-seated tradition in Christianity that would argue that, by rejecting Jesus as the Messiah, Jews forfeited their patrimony, which then became the sole possession of the church.

Pope John Paul, following in the footsteps of Saint Paul in his Letter to the Romans, will have no part of any "theology of abrogation." During his pastoral visit to the Federal Republic of Germany in 1980, he strongly emphasized that this was a living heritage in which Christians shared. At the Rome synagogue he called on Jews and Christians to witness together in an assertive way to this common patrimony.

In proclaiming the Jewish heritage a "living patrimony" for Christians, the pope is reminding us of an important reality also stressed in the 1985 *Notes* of the Holy See, namely, that this heritage includes far more than the Hebrew Scriptures. The Jewish people have continued to reinterpret their covenantal relationship with God throughout the centuries after the close of the biblical canon. These reinterpretations are to be found in the Talmud and in the writings of Jewish mystics and philosophers, past and present. This literature, too, has great religious value. As Pope John Paul has pointed out, it is important for Christians to know "the faith and religious life of the Jewish people as they are professed and practiced still today" (March 6, 1982). He adds that this body of Jewish literature "can greatly help us to understand better certain aspects of the church."

There is an additional implication to these first two central themes of Pope John Paul's emerging theology of the Jewish-Christian relationship. If we are prepared to integrate the themes of "bonding" and "shared patrimony" into our spirituality as Christians, as the holy father urges upon us, then we must recognize the impossibility of discussing critical contemporary questions in theology and ethics without explicit reference to the ways various Jewish scholars have interpreted covenantal responsibility throughout the ages, including the present day. Hence contemporary Jewish reflections on the meaning of such basic religious issues as the significance of the God of the covenant today, or Jewish deliberations on such pressing ethical issues as peace, power and economic equality assume a very important status.

Let me be clear on this point. There is no question here of incorporating such reflections simply out of interreligious sensitivity, or because of a general commitment to pluralism, as important as such sensitivity and commitment might be. Rather, in light of the renewed theology of the Christian-Jewish relationship rooted in a sense of spiritual bonding and a shared patrimony with

Jews, such reflections now are seen to be integral to the Christian community, not merely as extra resources from a parallel community to be used in a peripheral way.

The third critical theme in the developing Catholic theology of the Jewish-Christian relationship, as articulated by Pope John Paul II, is one to which I have previously alluded: his constant insistence on the permanent validity of the original divine covenant with Israel. On numerous occasions, he has made explicit what was already present, though still in somewhat embryonic form, in the documents of Vatican II, particularly in *Nostra Aetate* and the Dogmatic Constitution on the Church, *Lumen Gentium.*

On a 1980 pastoral visit to Mainz, in the Federal Republic of Germany, the pope, citing Romans 11:29, told a group of Jewish leaders that the original Jewish covenant has never been revoked by God. And, in 1982, meeting with representatives of episcopal conferences and ecumenical leaders in Rome, he underscored the present tense of Romans 9:4 – 5 concerning the Jews, calling them a people "who have the adoption as sons, and the glory and the covenants and the legislation and the worship and the promises." This theme reached a remarkable climax while Pope John Paul was visiting Australia in 1986 when he said that

> The Catholic faith is rooted in the eternal truths of the Hebrew
> Scriptures and in the irrevocable covenant made with Abra-
> ham. We, too, gratefully hold these same truths of our Jewish
> heritage and look upon you as our brothers and sisters in
> the Lord.

Taken together, the three themes that I have just outlined offer us a framework for understanding the Christian-Jewish relationship in a theological context quite unlike what we have known for centuries in the church. On further reflection, this framework, as the holy father has pointed out, is at its heart deeply based in the scriptures. The challenge for all of us in the church today — and I lay that challenge in a special way on all theologians, religious educators and pastors in the audience this evening — is to begin to incorporate this new theology into every aspect of our life as Christian communities. Our theological writings, our liturgical and catechetical volumes, and our preaching must begin to reflect these themes in a consistent and thorough way.

Theologians will continue to pursue better ways of expressing this developing understanding of the Christian-Jewish link. Certainly the pope himself would be the first to acknowledge that not all issues have been fully clarified. But the ongoing discussions should never serve to cloud over the emerging consensus around the three basic themes articulated by Pope John Paul throughout his pontificate.

THE HOLOCAUST

During the last decade, we have witnessed important developments within Christianity in understanding the centrality of the Holocaust for the ongoing life of the Jewish people, in coming to grips with the role that theological and popular anti-Semitism played in undergirding what was at root a militantly anti-religious philosophy, and in beginning to incorporate the Holocaust as a significant experience for Christian theological interpretation in our day. All three dimensions of the Holocaust are crucial for continued Christian existence. Reflection on them should continue in earnest and, as far as possible, in tandem with one another.

The primary goal that led to the Holocaust was an attempt to shape a totally "new person," a "super being," in a social milieu in which growing technological competence combined with bureaucratic proficiency and the gradual erosion of traditional moral restraints to swing open the gates to the virtually unlimited use of human power. The Nazis were convinced that it was now possible to reshape human society, perhaps humanity itself, to a degree never deemed imaginable in the past.

To accomplish this, they were determined to exterminate or subjugate those whom they regarded as inherently inferior. Their calculated plan for "renewing" humankind included gypsies, homosexuals, the mentally and/or physically incapacitated, and the Slavs, especially the Polish nation. First and foremost, they targeted the Jewish people, whom they classified as "vermin," although it has become evident recently that their attack against gypsies had similar features.

Scholars have now demonstrated that, in a significant way, the centuries of Christian degradation of the Jewish image contributed to this Nazi classification of the Jews. Pope John Paul II has summoned Christians to a forthright confrontation with this anti-Semitic tradition. I applaud those scholars who have taken up the challenge in a responsible and thorough manner. Christian theological and institutional collaboration with Nazism must be pursued in depth for the church's moral integrity. In his address in Miami during last year's papal visit to the United States, the holy father announced the establishment of an international project in which Catholic and Jewish experts would probe the significance of the Holocaust in preparation for an eventual statement by the Holy See.

The Holocaust challenges the church today on many theological fronts as well. Most importantly, it raises serious questions about how we might understand God's relationship to creation in our time. In this regard, our new awareness of the deep bonding between Christianity and Judaism assumes great importance. In dialogue with Jewish thinkers, we must pursue the question of God's relationship to the world after the Holocaust. We must also be prepared to turn to the Jewish tradition to discover possible pathways to answer the question.

The Holocaust has also raised profound ethical questions, for its aim was nothing less than the total transformation of human values. How do we anchor moral responsibility in public society in a technological and bureaucratic age in which the basic sensitivity to human life seems to be rapidly eroding at all levels? How do we harness the newly available forms of power for the promotion of good rather than massive destruction? How do we recover an adequate sense of the importance of history as a locus of salvation? How do we make theology more "subject-centered"? Again, Christians need to confront these issues in dialogue with Jews. Above all, we must come to recognize that the face of the Holocaust affects Christian theology as a whole, and not merely the more limited area of Christian-Jewish relations.

This evening, I would like to raise two final issues regarding the Holocaust. The first is the feeling among some within the Jewish community that the Catholic Church — and Pope John Paul, in particular — is "universalizing" the Holocaust or trying to take away its Jewish specificity. This concern has been raised by several prominent Jewish leaders long committed to dialogue, and by Nobel Prize recipient, Elie Wiesel. So they deserve a response — not a superficial apologetic on behalf of the pope but simply a review of his actual record.

In his 1979 visit to Auschwitz, the pope singled out the Hebrew inscription honoring the Jewish victims in that camp. He recalled this event during his address at the Rome synagogue in 1986. His 1987 presentation to the Jews of Warsaw acknowledged both the priority and the uniqueness of Jewish suffering in the Shoah. And in a well-publicized letter to Archbishop John May of St. Louis, president of the National Conference of Catholic Bishops, the holy father emphasized that any "authentic" approach to the Holocaust must first grapple with the specific Jewish reality of the event. And only then may other considerations be added.

Those who express concern about the holy father's direction should be relieved by examining the full range of papal statements these last several years. Taken together, they provide the church with a powerful mandate to countenance no compromise on the question of acknowledging the Jews as the Holocaust's primary victims.

The second issue is the concern of some within the Jewish community that the Catholic Church is trying to "appropriate" the Holocaust, to turn it into a monument to Catholic martyrdom. Their concern is based on the facts that the church, in recent years, has highlighted certain non-Jewish victims of the Holocaust, pointed out the fundamental anti-Christian nature of Nazism and beatified Edith Stein.

These actions might be interpreted as attempts to place Christians exclusively within the victim category, glossing over collaboration by church members and officials. I assure you that I stand ready to repudiate any such effort, were it to arise within the church. But I am convinced that it has not.

Rather, with all due respect for its Jewish uniqueness, the church is trying to grapple with the Holocaust in its own unique way. And we must do this because, unlike the Jewish community, baptized Catholics were not only among its victims but also prominent among its perpetrators. The church unquestionably has the responsibility to bring these other issues to the forefront of its consciousness — and before the world — because they bear a special relevance for contemporary ecclesial and civic life. At the same time, in reflecting on the Holocaust, the church must preserve the primacy of Jewish victimhood. And it has done so.

My sisters and brothers, as I compliment you on your past achievements, permit me also to challenge you to pursue with intensified seriousness some of the critical issues I have just laid before you. In so doing, you truly will bring *tikkun,* "healing," to our world.

Dialogue and collaboration are not options for us. They are a necessity. Never again can Jews and Christians permit themselves to be alienated from one another. Never again can we let our minds and hearts be misshaped by the prejudices and hatreds of the past. Never again can we allow a climate that could produce another Holocaust.

We have so much in common. But ultimately, it is our faith in God, who created us in his image and likeness, that unites us. We need to celebrate that unity always, even while we respect our different traditions.

I trust that my presence among you this evening is a sign of my deep respect and affection for you. This evening I pledge to you my love, my support and my determination to work with you and others on all the matters that concern us as Jews and Christians, as citizens, but most of all, as caring friends.

Cardinal Bernardin in a reflective moment in the courtyard of the Church of the Annunciation in Nazareth. *Photo by Joel Fishman.*

Joseph Cardinal Bernardin speaks to the Catholic-Jewish delegation in the main nave of the Church of the Nativity in Bethlehem on the West Bank. *Photo by Joel Fishman.*

⚜

Jonathan Levine, Michael Kotzin, Shlomo Bourla, Cardinal Bernardin, Father Thomas A. Baima and Carol Marin leaving the press conference at the Western Wall in Jerusalem where the Catholic-Jewish delegation greeted the Sabbath. *Photo by Joel Fishman.*

Rabbi Peter Knobel, the Rev. Dr. John Pawlikowski, Cardinal Joseph Bernardin,
Rabbi Dr. Byron Sherwin and Sister Diane Bergant during the celebration of Havdallah, which bids
farewell to the Sabbath, at the King David Hotel, Jerusalem. *Photo by Karen Benzian.*

Cardinal Bernardin and members of the Catholic-Jewish delegation visit a meeting
of the Focolare Movement at the Ratisbone Center in Jerusalem. *Photo by Joel Fishman.*

The winners of the first Interfaith Awards of the Archdiocese of Chicago.
Rabbi Herman Schaalman, Cardinal Bernardin, Rabbi H. Goren Perelmuter,
Father John Pawlikowski, Marguerite Martini, Cheryl Brown, Father John Harvey,
Monsignor George Higgins. *Photo by Scott Dixey.*

Rabbi Herman Schaalman embraces the Cardinal after receiving the Laureate in Ecumenical
and Interreligious Affairs at the 1995 Interfaith Awards Dinner. *Photo by Scott Dixey.*
Professor Emil Fackenheim and Cardinal Bernardin at the 1996 Jerusalem Lecture in Chicago.
Photo courtesy of Archdiocese of Chicago, Office of Ecumenical/Interreligious Affairs.

✠

Cardinal Bernardin delivers his lecture on "Anti-Semitism: The Historical Legacy
and Continuing Challenge for Christians" in Senate Hall at the Hebrew University of Jerusalem.
Photo by Joel Fishman.

❖

Cardinal Bernardin and the delegation visit an absorption center and meet
the children of new immigrants. *Photo by Joel Fishman.*

❖ Rachael Arons and Raphaela Newman are surrounded by new friends at Saint Joseph School,
(Cabrini-Green neighborhood), Chicago, during one of the programs of the Institute for
Catholic-Jewish Education. *Photo courtesy of Archdiocese of Chicago, Office of Ecumenical/
Interreligious Affairs.*

❖ Mrs. Marge Finch, a second grade teacher at Our Lady of the Wayside School, Arlington Heights,
blows the Shofar during one of the programs of the Institute for Catholic-Jewish Education.
Photo courtesy of Archdiocese of Chicago, Office of Ecumenical/Interreligious Affairs.

❧

Rabbi Herbert Bronstein of the North Shore Israel Congregation in Glencoe talks
with students from Loyola Academy High School in Wilmette about the Torah and Jewish beliefs
as part of a program to increase the Catholic students' understanding of Judaism.
Chicago Tribune photo by José Moré.

FIFTIETH ANNIVERSARY OF KRISTALLNACHT

My dear brothers and sisters, 50 years ago, on November 10, 1938, Bernard Lichtenberg, the dean of the Berlin cathedral, spoke out as follows:

> We know what was yesterday. We do not know what will be tomorrow; but we experienced what happened today. Outside, the synagogue is burning. It, too, is a house of God.

Would that these words of protest had been echoed across Germany that night! Instead, they stand as nearly a solitary witness to a religious rejection of the terrible violence unleashed by the Nazis against Jewish citizens.

This evening I would like to reflect briefly on (1) the experience of *Kristallnacht* itself, (2) why, as Christians and Jews, we must come to terms with its significance for us today, and (3) certain theological considerations that may enable us to reach a deeper level in interfaith dialogue.

KRISTALLNACHT

Auschwitz is perhaps the most widely known symbol of the Shoah. There are no adequate words to describe a visit there. Actually it is impossible merely to visit it. There are so many lessons to learn there about what humans are capable of perpetrating. One cannot visit Auschwitz without taking a firm stand opposing irrational prejudice directed against people who are of a different race, religion or political persuasion. The memory of Auschwitz and the other camps can never be obliterated.

Kristallnacht is especially difficult to come to terms with, because what happened on November 9 and 10 in 1938 was *public, open.* It was impossible for someone *not* to notice the pillars of fire that flared over Germany's synagogue that night. It was not possible to shut one's eyes to the looting and destruction of Jewish shops and homes along the street of one's neighborhood. Someone must have witnessed the arrest of over 30,000 Jewish citizens, the abuse of countless others and the murder of so many of them.

So, the events were observed, but few people spoke out against them. Why were there not more signs of indignation, compassion or willingness to help? The reasons for this tragic silence are complex and still disputed. But a certain moral blindness was undoubtedly to blame. And the church's persistent understanding of its relationship to Judaism also contributed to this blindness.

Because the painful memories of that night still haunt us, and because its full significance continues to impact our current interfaith dialogue and endeavors, we must face honestly this still open wound that affects both Jewish and Christian communities.

A BLEEDING WOUND

We cannot go forward together unless we also remember the past. Moreover, we cannot simply put it behind us, as much as we might like to do so. Christians, and Catholics in particular, must accept their share of responsibility for what happened in the rise of National Socialism to power and domination, as well as for such atrocities as Kristallnacht and the concentration camps.

If it were easy to accomplish this, one might reasonably expect that it would already have been done during the past half century. This past June, the Central Committee of German Catholics published a declaration drawn up jointly by an interfaith discussion group of Jews and Christians. Its title is "After 50 years — how can we talk about guilt, suffering and reconciliation?" The statement notes that

Still today, half a century later, we Jews and Christians are speechless before the incomprehensible horror of what happened during the Nazi regime. It is still difficult for Jews and Christians to overcome the inability to speak.

The statement documents the painful fact that "time alone does not heal wounds . . . Most wounds scar over, but they continue to be painful; however, 'the Shoah is a deep wound that is still bleeding.'"

Despite good will on both sides, despite theological breakthroughs in the Catholic understanding of Judaism, many barriers remain, and will continue to do so, until Christians and Jews can be reconciled in regard to the events of the past.

The German document to which I have referred acknowledges that

> reconciliation does not mean treason toward the dead. However, we Christians have also to learn that we can only ask for reconciliation, not forgiveness, and that we can only ask for it and not demand it. If a Jew does not, or does not yet feel able to, fulfill our request, there are no grounds on which to press him, not even through well-meant "simple expectations." We must bear this lack of simultaneousness.

Those are very powerful words. They are honest and challenging. They give us a sense of direction and hope for the future — the long, difficult road that lies before us.

At the same time, there are other encouraging developments that may ease the journey to some extent. I would now like to outline some of the more significant developments in regard to the Catholic theological understanding of Judaism.

THEOLOGICAL BREAKTHROUGHS

We can trace tensions and alienation between synagogue and church, which resulted in anti-Semitism, back to the patristic period. Perhaps its most important expression is to be found in the theory of supercessionism — the rejection and displacement of the covenantal people Israel from God's plan of salvation and their replacement by the Christian church of the New Covenant. During this same period some popular — and outrageous — notions about the Jewish people became part of the thinking of many Catholics: that the Jews were guilty of deicide, that they engaged in ritual murders and profaned the sacred hosts of the eucharist.

Such ideas persisted in the church through subsequent centuries and were maintained with other economic, political, ideological and social prejudices against Jewish people.

Although some prominent Catholic leaders in prewar Germany unequivocally rejected racial anti-Semitism, many Catholics did not. As you know, this varied from region to region and from person to person. Moreover, after Kristallnacht, as the church itself came under increasing pressure from the Nazis, fewer Catholics spoke out against the social policies of National Socialism.

When faced with the horrible events of the Shoah, however, Catholics began to realize that our traditional theological understanding of the church's relationship with Judaism was inadequate. More than 25 years later, the Second Vatican Council issued its well-known *Declaration on the Relation of the Church to Non-Christian Religions (Nostra Aetate)*. This revolutionary document undermined the theory of supercessionism and described, instead, Catholicism's enduring bonds with the people of Israel.

Our renewed Catholic appreciation of the thoroughly Jewish context of Jesus' preaching and ministry has inevitably led the church to a reconsideration of how it expresses theologically its relationship with Judaism. It is no secret that many of our past formulations have seriously distorted the role of the Jewish people in human salvation. These distortions undoubtedly played a role in the persecution borne by Jewish communities in so many parts of the world and tragically helped provide a seedbed for Christian collaboration with the fundamentally anti-religious philosophy of Nazism.

Now all of that is beginning to change as individual Christian theologians, church leaders and official church documents increasingly challenge this long-standing theology of total Jewish displacement from the process of salvation after the coming of Jesus. The prevalent "supercessionist" approach to Judaism on the part of much of classical Christian theology is being replaced by a theology of *covenantal partnership.*

No one has given greater impetus to this new theological understanding of the Jewish-Christian relationship than Pope John Paul II. In recognition of his contribution, the United States Catholic Conference, in collaboration with the Anti-Defamation League of B'nai B'rith, published a collection of his addresses on the topic between 1979 and 1986 *(Pope John Paul II on Jews and Judaism, 1979–1986).* I respectfully point this out because, while in recent times there have been some misunderstandings and tensions, he is a true friend of the Jewish people.

My brothers and sisters, we must continue to study the past, the events of Kristallnacht, Shoah and their roots in the more distant past. Unless we do so, it will be impossible to bring about a deeper reconciliation between Jews and Christians. We must also face these historical issues squarely and honestly, committing ourselves to ensure that they will never happen again.

At the same time, we must continue the interfaith dialogue and collaboration that has borne such great fruit already, especially in metropolitan Chicago. We must work together to put an end to anti-Semitism and all kinds of racist attitudes and practices.

Finally, we must continue to learn more about one another so that we might arrive at a deeper understanding of one another. As I have noted, Catholics have a new theological base on which to build our contribution to the dialogue.

We are children of the same God. God's design for us has not been violence, racism and alienation but rather mutual respect, harmony and reconciliation. With you I pray with all my heart — never again Shoah, always *Shalom!*

"A SEPTEMBER PRAYER"

"THE NEW WORLD" IS THE OFFICIAL NEWSPAPER OF THE ARCHDIOCESE OF CHICAGO. WHEN HE BECAME ARCHBISHOP, CARDINAL BERNARDIN BEGAN A WEEKLY COLUMN TITLED "THE TRUTH IN CHRIST." HE USES THIS COLUMN AS ONE OF HIS PRIMARY TEACHING VEHICLES TO HIS OWN CHURCH MEMBERS. THIS ARTICLE ADDRESSES A CURRENT ISSUE IN THE NEWS, THE CONTROVERSY REGARDING A CARMELITE CONVENT NEAR AUSCHWITZ.

POETS tell us April is the cruelest month. Winter dies hard, and spring is born painfully. This year, September has presented us with its own season of sadness, especially in the Polish, Catholic and Jewish communities in Chicago.

It has offered us cruel memories of a war that began 50 years ago. Rather than hosting my brother bishop, Cardinal Jozef Glemp, and celebrating with the Polish community of Chicago the encouraging, hard-won freedoms emerging in the governance of Poland, I ponder the power of evil and write a word of reconciliation.

On September 1, 1939, Poland was invaded by Nazi Germany. The subsequent suffering of the people of Poland, Catholics and Jews, in such death camps as Auschwitz-Birkenau remains an incomprehensible tragedy. I vividly remember my own visits to Auschwitz in 1976 and 1985. It is a haunting memory of human depravity. It is a constant invitation to find solidarity in human suffering. Our human family can never forget the consequences of ignoring the most basic teaching of Judeo-Christian morality: "Thou shalt not kill."

Unfortunately, recent events surrounding the Carmelite convent near Auschwitz have tended to obliterate the remembrance of common suffering and the solidarity of Jews and Catholics during that reign of horror. Therefore we ask: Which symbols adequately reflect a religious response to such tragedy?

Responsible leaders from the Jewish and Christian communities were aware of Catholic response to such suffering, a convent for prayer and reparation, was, from a Jewish understanding of death and suffering, an inappropriate symbol in a place where evil had been so tangible. In a spirit of reconciliation it was agreed the convent would be relocated a short distance from the death camp.

Building delays, governmental restriction, incendiary demonstration and insensitive responses further exacerbated the anti-Catholic, and anti-Polish and anti-Semitic sentiments that had developed through centuries of mutual hostility and reappeared and replaced the conciliatory attitudes and commitment to interfaith dialogue of our own times.

Especially since the Second Vatican Council, the Catholic Church has strongly and consistently condemned all forms of prejudices and bigotry toward any group of people. The church has plainly stated anti-Semitism is sinful. I reiterated this fact when I spoke at Quigley Seminary South in 1988. Recent events, however, highlight the fact we have not yet completed the task of replacing all vestiges of racism and anti-Semitism with the love of others mandated by faith. Even at this late date, continual vigilance in this regard is needed.

To promote these ideals, the church — through its leadership in Poland, Rome and the United States — sought to find solutions to the Auschwitz convent controversy that would give clear witness to our commitment to be a sign of reconciliation to the world. The efforts have proved successful.

The Holy See, in a statement issued by Cardinal Johannes Willebrands, said:

> The expressed intention (of the Polish episcopal commission
> for dialogue with Judaism) to proceed with the establishment
> of a center of information, of meeting, of dialogue and of
> prayer, as called for in the Geneva Declaration of February

1987, is received positively, because the Holy See is convinced such a center would contribute in a significant way to the development of good relations between Christians and Jews. . . . The prayer and the life of devotion of the Carmelites, whose monastery will be in some way at the heart of the center, will contribute decisively to its success.

More recently, both Cardinal Marcharski (in whose archdiocese the convent is located) and Cardinal Glemp, as well as the Carmelite authorities, have confirmed they favor moving the convent and reaffirmed the validity of the 1987 statement.

Now I ask that we, the Catholics of the archdiocese of Chicago, who believe in the transforming power of Jesus the Christ, be a reconciling witness to our city in the days ahead.

I ask you to be reconciling witnesses in the spirit that Cardinal Glemp exemplifies in his recent letter to me. We could not host the cardinal this past week with the services and receptions we had planned. But we can honor him by reflecting on his words and joining him in effecting a truthful and just solution to the current controversy.

This is what he wrote to me:

> Your Eminence:
>
> I thank you very much for your words of concern and love. At the same time I apologize for having disappointed you and your collaborators who worked hard to prepare my visit to Chicago.
>
> The moment I realized the pastoral benefit of my visit was at risk, I had no doubts to postpone the visit and to try to settle the controversy at home first. As a matter of fact, it is taking now a peaceful turn. We all pray God may assist us in finding a truthful and just solution. May the blessings of God continue to be with you.

He signed it: "Fraternally yours in Christ . . . Jozef Cardinal Glemp, Primate of Poland."

I pray this September will be more than a season of sadness and disappointment. Rather, may it be a season of hope, a time of understanding and reconciliation.

"TOGETHER WE CAN MOVE MOUNTAINS: REFLECTIONS ON CATHOLIC-JEWISH RELATIONS TODAY"

CHICAGO BOARD OF RABBIS

THE AUSCHWITZ CONTROVERSY CONTINUED TO DOMINATE CATHOLIC-JEWISH RELATIONS INTO 1990. IN THIS TALK, THE CARDINAL REFERS TO MATTERS OF CATHOLIC PUBLIC POLICY, ESPECIALLY ON RIGHT TO LIFE ISSUES SUCH AS ABORTION, CAPITAL PUNISHMENT AND EUTHANASIA. THIS TALK OCCURED ONE MONTH AFTER HE DELIVERED A MAJOR ADDRESS TO THE WOODSTOCK THEOLOGICAL CENTER OF GEORGETOWN UNIVERSITY: "THE CONSISTENT ETHIC OF LIFE AFTER WEBSTER." WEBSTER V. REPRODUCTIVE HEALTH SYSTEM IS THE MOST IMPORTANT ABORTION DECISION OF THE SUPREME COURT SINCE ROE V. WADE AND DOE V. BOLTON CREATED A RIGHT TO ABORTION IN THE UNITED STATES.

❖

DEAR friends, *Haverim,* it is indeed a pleasure to be with you again. Since my arrival in Chicago, I have come to value greatly our ongoing collaboration in various contexts — through the Council of Religious Leaders of Metropolitan Chicago, personal meetings with your leaders and entire membership, and cooperation on various mutual projects, such as the twentieth anniversary celebration of *Nostra Aetate,* the Twelfth National Workshop on Christian-Jewish Relations to take place in Chicago this November, and the many local parish-synagogue dialogues. I admire your dedication to the religious and social well-being of *'am Yisra'el* in the Chicago area as well as the community-at-large. You have been a source of strength to me in my public ministry.

As we meet this morning, I cannot help but recall a very special encounter I had with some of your leaders last summer during the height of the controversy over the location of the convent at Auschwitz. At that time, as you know, we were in the midst of the most serious challenge to the new bond between Catholics and Jews that had emerged as one of the most important contributions of the Second Vatican Council. When I was approached about that meeting, I immediately recognized its potential importance and scheduled it at the earliest possible date.

The memory of that meeting remains very much alive with me because the honest sharing of views in an atmosphere of mutual respect and trust left me convinced more than ever of the value of interfaith dialogue. It truly enables us to move mountains. On that particular occasion, it provided me with a comprehensive assessment of the feelings of the Jewish community about the controversy. I also had the opportunity to support publicly the joint statement released by the group of Catholic and Jewish scholars that the archdiocese and your board co-convened. I have little doubt that this statement — which attracted national coverage — and the support it received from our summer meeting contributed to the ultimate resolution of the conflict.

Heartened by this constructive experience of the sharing of mutual concerns, I would like to discuss some issues that remain sources of possible misunderstanding between our two faith communities. Specifically, I will address the continuing implications of the Auschwitz convent controversy, questions in the Jewish community about aspects of the 1989 U.S. Catholic Bishops' statement on peace in the Middle East, and issues surrounding the involvement of American Catholicism in the political sphere.

I raise these difficult questions not simply to defend Catholic positions. Rather, it is my hope that the end result will be a productive sharing of viewpoints leading to some shared public perspectives. I will conclude my presentation with some observations about the recent closings of certain Catholic parishes and schools. Since the decisions we made affect the entire metropolitan region, I thought you might want to hear from me personally about the matter.

THE AUSCHWITZ CONTROVERSY

Let me begin with some of the issues that remain with us despite the joint decisions of the Holy See, the Polish bishops and the Polish government to relocate the Carmelite convent at Auschwitz outside the camp boundaries. As you know, the official groundbreaking ceremony several weeks ago inaugurated the gradual implementation of the decision.

As a result of the convent controversy, I remain convinced that considerable education is required in both our communities regarding the history of that site of human incarceration and extermination. It has come to symbolize the entire Holocaust because of its central role in the tragic event. Catholic educational institutions at all levels must make a renewed effort to incorporate the story of the Holocaust in their programs. To that end, I have voluntarily committed the archdiocesan school system to full compliance with the recently passed Illinois law mandating Holocaust education in all public schools in the state. And I have agreed to serve as an honorary cochair of the Chicago development committee for the U.S. Holocaust Memorial Museum, now under construction in Washington, D.C., because it will provide national leadership in all phases of Holocaust education.

But I must be candid in saying that, in light of the recent convent controversy, the Jewish community also bears some new responsibilities in terms of Holocaust education. I speak here of an improved understanding of the Nazi attack on peoples other than the Jews, particularly the Polish nation. Some of the comments made by Jewish leaders during the period of tension last summer indicated an inadequate understanding of the history of the Auschwitz camp. After its opening as a camp for German political prisoners, it quickly became the brutal centerpiece for attempts to liquidate the Polish leadership elite, including the Polish clergy, with the ultimate goal of reducing the Polish people to a nation of indentured servants.

I agree that we must always remember that, eventually, Auschwitz became the major point of Jewish extermination and that, in the end, the overwhelming number of its victims were Jews. We should never blur this distinction any more than we should lessen the distinction between the Jewish and the non-Jewish victims overall. However, until Jews better appreciate how Auschwitz has also acquired a central role in postwar Polish identity, we will never achieve the mutual understanding necessary to defuse permanently the possibility of conflict over the campsite.

Improved understanding of Polish victimization at Auschwitz is a need everywhere, especially here in metropolitan Chicago, which is the home to so many Polish Catholics. That is why I urge you to take a special leadership role on this matter within your community. I welcome and firmly support the recently announced plans for a Polish-Jewish dialogue for a variety of community-based programs on this matter. My sincere hope is that you also will give this effort your full support and cooperation.

Dr. Stanislaw Karjewski, a young Polish Jew at the Institute of Mathematics in Warsaw, has summed up well the situation that confronts us as religious leaders. He admits that "most Poles do not recognize the exceptional character of the project to wipe out the Jewish people and either poorly understand or altogether ignore the Jewish significance of Auschwitz." But he likewise insists that people in the West, including Jews, simply do not appreciate the depth of the Polish suffering at Auschwitz:

> The historical fact is that the Nazis tried to crush the Polish nation; they not only introduced bloody terror but began to murder Polish elites and destroy Polish culture. The Auschwitz camp was used also for this purpose, and during its first two years of existence, *this* was its main function. (SIDIC 22:3 [1989], 16)

The question of Polish anti-Semitism, past and present, must be a part of any reconciliation effort in regard to the convent controversy. We may never achieve a total meeting of the minds on this question between the two communities. But each must be prepared to probe the issue far more extensively than has been the case until now if the syndrome of wholesale indictment and stubborn denial, which has unfortunately characterized Polish-Jewish relations until now, is to be overcome.

As I have intimated, Poland, like other nations, will have to come to grips with its legacy of anti-Semitism. The church in Poland and certain Polish academic centers, such as the Jagiellonian University, have begun this process. As you know, one important event in this regard took place here in Chicago last summer when 22 professors — 21 Catholic and 1 Orthodox — from theological faculties throughout Poland came to the Spertus College of Judaica for eight weeks of intensive study of Judaism, Jewish-Christian relations and American pluralism. The program — sponsored by the archdiocese, the Polish episcopal conference and Spertus College — also involved intensive exposure to the diversity of life within the Jewish community in metropolitan Chicago.

As one of the principal cosponsors of the institute, I take this occasion to thank the Chicago rabbinic community for the participation of many of its members and synagogues in this program. From the evaluations of the program, we know that it proved to be an enlightening experience for the participants and will surely have a positive impact on Polish society in the days ahead. Its value has already been demonstrated by the fact that several of the participants wrote articles, based on their Chicago experience, in leading Polish journals, urging reconciliation between Jews and Catholics based on the church's faithfulness to the 1987 Geneva accord in regard to the Carmelite convent at Auschwitz.

It also will be necessary for the Jewish community to confront the frequent stereotyping of Poles still current in world Jewry. Some of this is due simply to lack of knowledge, both of the complex history of Jewish life in Poland as well as Polish sufferings during the Nazi onslaught. This is not to say that many Jews today do not vividly remember anti-Semitic attacks against them or their immediate families in Poland. But these memories are often generalized, in particular, not placed in the total socio-political framework of the interwar years.

There is need in the Jewish community for a heightened understanding of the constructive periods in Polish-Jewish history in Poland where Jews often immigrated at times when many other European nations excluded them. A more sophisticated analysis of the multifaceted role of the large Jewish community in pre–World War ɪɪ Poland is also necessary. For Jews played significant roles in the fields of commerce, industry, law and medicine, even though they may have been somewhat more restricted in other social freedoms in comparison with the West.

THE U.S. BISHOPS' STATEMENT ON PEACE IN THE MIDDLE EAST

Turning now to my second topic, the 1989 U.S. bishops' statement on peace in the Middle East, I know there are continuing questions among you and your people regarding certain of its perspectives. Some of these are primarily due to misinterpretations or the failure to place this document within the larger body of recent reflections by the pope and the Holy See on the issue.

I welcome dialogue on this issue because it will help us find a way to forge a new interreligious coalition to pursue the path of peace in the Middle East. It is vital that we end the violence that wreaks so much havoc on both Israelis and Palestinians, especially the younger generations. Next month I will participate in an interfaith service for peace in the Middle East at Saint James Episcopal Cathedral. It is being held in connection with a two-day conference sponsored by the U.S. Interreligious Committee for Peace in the Middle East. My fervent prayer is that it may spark a new commitment to a just resolution of the devastating conflict in that part of the world.

The search for a political accord between Palestinians and Israelis is premised in my own mind and that of my brother bishops in the U.S. on certain critical *givens*.

First, with Pope John Paul ɪɪ, we recognize that Israel has legitimate *national* claims in the Middle East, not merely claims rooted in biblical tradition, history and Shoah. As the holy father stated unequivocally in 1984 regarding the Jewish people, "They have a right to a homeland, as does any civil nation, according to international law." (*Redemptionis Anno,* April 20, 1984)

We also recognize the continuing security threat to Israel. The bishops' statement acknowledges this at the very outset as a serious obstacle to peace in the Middle East. While the statement does not go into the matter in detail, I am well aware that the statements from Palestinian and Arab governmental sources continue to speak of the wholesale elimination of the State of Israel despite the official bilateral state stance of the Palestinian Liberation Organization. It is vital that Israel take constructive first steps toward peace negotiations with the Palestinians. But it is equally imperative that Palestinian leaders and their supporters demonstrate a clear shift in thinking about Israel and the Jewish people by substantially altering the tone and content of their pronouncements. What is needed is not merely an exchange of "land for peace," as the formula has been put, but a permanent commitment to reconciliation and national accommodation on the part of all parties to the conflict.

Finally, I appreciate the deep Jewish attachment to the city of Jerusalem, while recognizing the profound attachment to it in the hearts of Christians and Muslims as well. Pope John Paul II alluded to this in his recent meeting with representatives of the American Jewish Committee by referring to Jerusalem as "the city considered holy by millions of believers: Jews, Christians and Muslims (*L'Osservatore Romano,* March 26, 1990, 11)." The U.S. bishops know that there cannot be genuine and just peace in the Middle East without ample provisions for this deep tie to Jerusalem that has roots in the biblical tradition. In so doing, the bishops are echoing the sentiment of Pope John Paul II, who has spoken of how

> Jews ardently love her [Jerusalem] and in every age venerate her memory, abundant as she is in many remains and monuments from the time of David, who chose her as the capital, and of Solomon, who built the Temple there. Therefore, they turn their minds to her daily, one may say, and point to her as the sign of their nation. *(Redemptionis Anno)*

While speaking of Israel, I wish to bring up a delicate topic that continues to divide our communities. I mention it only as an issue that needs to be discussed lest it continue to create tension between us. I am speaking of reports of human rights violations in Israel, particularly in the occupied territories, especially as these affect our Arab Christian brothers and sisters. Within the Catholic community — especially those who work in Israel or who have studied or visited there — there is a deep conviction that a double standard is at work. The Jewish perception, I know, is quite different. I must admit that my knowledge of the situation is not personal or direct. But I know that this concern exists in the Catholic community. I would like, on some occasion in the future, to discuss the matter with you, both for my own education and to promote greater harmony between our two communities.

POLITICAL INVOLVEMENT BY THE CATHOLIC COMMUNITY

I turn now to the issue of political involvement by the Catholic community in the United States, especially in the national debate about such life issues as abortion, euthanasia and capital punishment. At times, our involvement — as a church or faith community rather than as individual citizens — has itself become a matter of some controversy. This is especially true in regard to abortion, which is being debated with renewed intensity since last year's *Webster* decision that restored to the states some authority to restrict or regulate abortions. The proper role of religious groups in the shaping of public policy is a challenging issue. Our future as a moral voice in the world may well depend on how it is resolved.

This is not a new theme in our history as a nation. From Washington's first inaugural to Lincoln's second inaugural, from the Declaration of Independence to the decisive issues of our time, the themes of religion, morality and politics are woven through the American experience. Intellectually and politically, the key question in every stage of the American civil experiment has not been *whether* these themes should be discussed but how to structure the debate for the welfare of the state and the church in a religiously pluralistic society.

As a society, we are increasingly confronted with a range of issues that have undeniable moral dimensions. It is not possible to define, debate or decide these policy issues without addressing explicitly their moral character. The issues span the whole spectrum of life from conception to natural death, and they bear upon the major segments of our domestic and foreign policy.

When should the civil law incorporate key moral concerns? Quite simply, when the issue at stake poses a threat to the public order of society. But at the very heart of *public order* is the protection of human life and basic human rights. A society that fails to protect either or both is rightfully judged morally defective.

Neither the right to life nor other human rights can be protected in a society without the civil law. To hold the moral position of the Catholic Church — for example, that all directly intended abortion is wrong — and not to relate this moral position to civil law would be a serious abdication of moral responsibility. Precisely in a pluralistic society, where moral views differ, we cannot depend on moral agreement alone; protection of fundamental rights is directly dependent on the content of the civil law.

But does this imply that we are imposing our religious beliefs on society as a whole? I would argue that this is *not* the case for two reasons.

First, in making the case for a legal order that protects the unborn, we present our views in terms of the dignity and equality of human life, the bond between human dignity and human rights, and the conviction that the right to life is the fundamental human right, not in religious or sectarian terms. In the final analysis, our success depends on the persuasiveness of our arguments. And it is the voters who decide that, not ourselves.

Second, our objective, that the civil law recognize a basic obligation to protect human life, especially the lives of those vulnerable to attack or mistreatment, is not new in our society. The credibility of civil law has always been tested by the range of rights it defends and the scope of the community it protects. The civil rights struggle of the 1960s was precisely about extending the protection of the law to those unjustly deprived of protection. The people of the United States did not need a religious consensus to agree on this proposition then; they do not need religious agreement today to understand the argument that a part of the human community — the unborn child — is without fundamental protection of the law.

However, the extent or kind of legal protection that can be achieved for unborn children is partly dependent on the degree of public consensus that can be built to sustain a legal norm. Since civil law does not incorporate the moral law *in toto,* to build such a consensus, a convincing case must be made that abortion *is* a public order issue.

Religious institutions in a democracy stand at the intersection of public opinion and public policy decisions. In a complex democracy like ours, public opinion seldom translates directly into policy decisions. But it does set a framework for policy decisions. It sets limits for policy choices and provides indications of policies desired by the public. The Catholic Church — and other religious communities — influence this intersection of opinion and policy through their access to the conscience of citizens.

The church, I believe, should speak its mind, seek as a community to live its convictions, but leave space for others to speak to us, help us to grow from their perspective, and to collaborate with them. I am confident that, while we may not agree on all such matters, we can learn from one another. That is why I have included this topic in my address this morning.

You have read and heard a great deal in recent months about the financial difficulties facing the archdiocese and the consolidation and closing of a number of parishes and schools. While some of the reporting has been accurate, some has been misleading in that it has not given a true picture of what is occurring.

The archdiocese is not about to fold! It continues to be one of the most active and vital in the country. Rather, it is facing up to certain realities and making some long overdue decisions so as to ensure its ministerial and financial well-being in the future.

One of those realities is the demographic changes of the past 20 to 30 years. Quite simply, many of the people who supported our parishes and schools in the central city often served — especially in the fields of education and social services — many who are not of our faith. We have taken pride, for example, in our inner-city schools, which have provided a quality education to thousands of minority students, over 40 percent of whom are not Catholic.

But today we have too many older, under-used facilities in the inner city. Sometimes they are only a block or two apart. This past year, more than 25 percent (108) had to be subsidized in the amount of $18 million. While we have no intention of leaving the inner city or minimizing our outreach, we must close some of our marginal facilities and consolidate others so that we can deploy our financial resources and personnel more productively. The actions we have taken are the result of careful research and planning so as to ensure our ability to continue providing the needed religious, educational and social services. No one will be deprived of the services that he or she has been receiving as a result of the restructuring that is taking place.

Those who are directly affected by the changes, quite naturally, feel them the most. Some are angry, hurt. And some have been very vocal. I am sensitive to their feelings. We are doing everything we can to assist them in this period of transition. In the end, I am confident that all will turn out well. All indications are that I have the support of the vast majority of the archdiocese.

Even as we are engaged in the process of cost containment through closures and consolidations, we also are embarking on a plan for revenue enhancement, because our people generally give less than other religious communities. We also are making plans for opening new parishes in the suburbs where existing facilities are unable to provide for the religious needs of their growing congregations. I expect to announce the openings of the first of these new parishes in the next month or two.

What I have just presented is but a brief summary of a very large and complex reality. But I hope that these few remarks will put the matter in correct perspective for you.

CHICAGO CONVOCATION FOR PEACE IN THE MIDDLE EAST

IN JUNE 1987, 50 AMERICAN CHRISTIAN, JEWISH AND MUSLIM LEADERS FOUNDED THE
U.S. INTERRELIGIOUS COMMITTEE FOR PEACE IN THE MIDDLE EAST. FROM FALL 1989
THROUGH SPRING 1990, THE COMMITTEE HELPED TO ORGANIZE LOCAL CONVOCATIONS FOR
PEACE IN A DOZEN U.S. CITIES. THIS TALK TOOK PLACE AT THE CHICAGO CONVOCATION.

IN this passage from the New Testament, we heard Jesus' Beatitudes from the Sermon on the Mount. Those who hunger and thirst, not for food but for justice, are the fortunate ones. They are gifted by God because they have undergone a change of heart. The poor in spirit, the meek, those who mourn, the merciful, the pure in heart, and those persecuted for holiness' sake are promised happiness.

The peacemakers — those who put an end to violence, who lay down the sword, who work for harmonious relationships, who break the patterns of hatred, who love even their enemies — will be called "children of God," the ultimate blessing. These "children of God" — be they Jews, Christians and Muslims in the Middle East, or ourselves gathered here — are mandated by our great religious traditions to be peacemakers.

The familiar methods of conflict from the past and the present are painfully reflected in the Middle East today. There has been a tragic, but perduring, reliance on violence, even on aggression, to claim and protect interests, and to demand a security that can never be achieved solely by resorting to armed struggle. Why do people commit themselves to fight to the death over the totality of their claims? Why are they unwilling to talk to each other until every prior wrong is healed? No just solution to the long and tragic conflict between the Israelis and the Palestinians will ever occur through armed conflict or inflammatory rhetoric.

Only strong people can resolve deep conflict. And we know from our religious traditions and current world events that effective solutions to problems today demand a new perspective, a fresh way of looking and thinking. The strength needed to resolve conflict may be found in the gentle, yet powerful, strength of the Beatitudes — a strength that is available to every person who seeks the truth and strives to live justly. Such gentle strength, affirmed in our three religious traditions, acknowledges obstacles to peace, makes efforts toward harmony, and responds courageously to the challenges of violence and injustice.

Surely there are enormous obstacles to peace. Wrongs committed by all of us — Christians, Muslims and Jews — are indelibly written in the history of the Middle East.

At the present time, in our country and in the Middle East, the tolerance of anti-Jewish and anti-Arab prejudice undermines the trust that is the necessary foundation of peace. Anti-Arab prejudice and stereotypes are alarmingly widespread forms of bigotry in the United States and Europe. So, too, we were outraged by the recent desecration of Jewish cemeteries in France. Such actions greatly impede efforts for peace.

Gentle, but strong, efforts now taking place can lead to a mutual understanding and trust on which to build a just and lasting peace between Palestinians and Israelis. Groups of Israelis and Palestinians, and of Jewish Americans and Palestinian Americans, are engaged in serious discussions to pave paths toward peace in the Middle East.

The archdiocese of Chicago continues to promote dialogue and interaction with Muslims and Jews. Our cooperative ventures with members of the Jewish community have a longer and more extensive history, but we are very pleased that our participation with other Christians in dialogues with the Muslim community is moving beyond its initial stages.

In November 1989, the U.S. Catholic bishops issued a statement in regard to peace in the Middle East. It was the result of extensive on-site visits and consultation with the respective parties involved in the disputes of that region. In this statement, *Peace in the Middle East: Perspectives, Principles and Hopes,* the bishops reaffirmed Israel's right to exist within secure borders. They also recognized the right of the Palestinians to self-determination, including their option for an independent homeland. The bishops urged a "more active diplomatic engagement by the United States in the process of seeking and making peace in the Middle East."

In a recent address to the Chicago Board of Rabbis, I stated that it is vital for Israel to take constructive first steps toward peace negotiations with the Palestinians, and for the Palestinians to demonstrate in their pronouncements a clear shift in their thinking about Israel and the Jewish people. I added that, besides the so-called "land for peace" strategy, a permanent commitment to reconciliation and national accommodation on the part of all parties to the conflict is needed. In that address I also committed the archdiocese and myself personally to renew efforts to incorporate in our Catholic educational programs the story of the Holocaust — the savage attempt to destroy the Jewish people and to devastate the Polish nations and other peoples.

Today — tragically — physical, mental and moral suffering are all too much a part of the daily life of many people in the Middle East. Although the incident was not political in nature, even today a number of Palestinians were killed. How much longer can they live without peace and justice? How much longer can we allow this to happen?

This evening I re-commit the archdiocese and myself personally, insofar as we are able, to keep the issue of Middle East peace before us and to work toward it, within the framework of the U.S. bishops' statement, until it is achieved.

To place the issue of peace in the Middle East before us is the purpose of this Chicago Convocation that brings together Jews, Christians and Muslims. I trust we will all give our time, energy and support to walking the difficult road toward a just peace.

The Beatitudes are a wonderful expression of trust in God. They teach us that right will ultimately prevail. Apparent weakness hides an abiding inner strength. Those who seek justice are the first citizens of the reign of God. Gentle strength responds to challenges. Dare we act in the spirit of the Beatitudes?

Will the Christians of our nation invest the time to care about the faraway region of the world where Jesus once walked? Will our religious communities become more involved in peacemaking and concern for the people who live in the land esteemed as holy by Muslims, Jews and Christians? Will we get to know one another well enough to be confident of one another's good will? Are we willing to support joint efforts to build the kind of trust and respect that are necessary for the resolution of conflict?

Are we willing to help persuade the U.S. government, as well as the representatives of Israel and the Palestinian people respectively, to work steadily toward the first stages of mutual trust that will ensure successful peace negotiations? Will we assist the legislators and members of the U.S. government, as well as Palestinians and Israelis, who take personal risks to work for peace in the Middle East? Will U.S. citizens help shape a foreign policy that moves the Middle Eastern nations toward peace?

Will we join with others in a larger quest for peace that cannot be ignored or pushed aside? Will we support Israelis and Palestinians who must, in the end, achieve real peace in the Middle East — active cooperation, not merely the cessation of hostilities?

A great challenge lies before us. It leads us to bow humbly in prayer before the one God we worship in our respective ways, acknowledging that we are powerless without God's help. Let us implore him to give us the gifts of wisdom, strength and perseverance to carry out his will.

"RELIGION AND POWER: THE URGENCY OF A NEW SYNTHESIS"

TWELFTH NATIONAL WORKSHOP ON CHRISTIAN-JEWISH RELATIONS

THE NATIONAL WORKSHOP ON CHRISTIAN-JEWISH RELATIONS IS A MAJOR INTERFAITH CONFERENCE THAT ATTRACTS RELIGIOUS, EDUCATIONAL AND CULTURAL LEADERS AND LAY PEOPLE FROM THE UNITED STATES AND ABROAD. IN 1990 THE WORKSHOP WAS HELD IN CHICAGO.

IN a perceptive comment on our times, the Catholic philosopher, Romano Guardini, spoke directly to the question of power in the late twentieth century. In the years ahead, he insisted, power will surely continue to increase at an even swifter tempo than it has. As a result, coming generations will face the task of curbing its excesses. "The core of the new epoch's intellectual task," according to Guardini, "will be to integrate power into life in such a way that man can employ power without forfeiting his humanity. For he will have only two choices: to match the greatness of his power with the strength of his humanity, or to surrender his humanity to power and perish" (*Power and Responsibility,* Henry Regnery, 1961, xiii).

Guardini's point, and it remains a crucial one, was that it would be just as false to abandon all efforts to employ power as it would be to jettison all restraints on its use. Our modern challenge is far more complex. It involves nothing short of a new synthesis, one that combines the ever-increasing power that modern technology and communication have placed in the hands of the human community with a fundamental sense of respect for personal dignity and the integrity of all creation.

Put another way, the humanization of power involves the creation of a public culture that serves both as a lid on the destructive potential inherent in all accumulation of power and a guide as to how this power should be used for the enhancement of the quality of life at every level. Today we do not have to search very long for a graphic reminder of a period when this balance went awry. It was, of course, during the Holocaust. And so, as we pursue our contemporary reflections on the question of power at this National Workshop on Christian-Jewish Relations, it might be well to pause at the outset to recall what happened just a few decades earlier in this century when, as a prisoner described it in Alexandre Donat's *The Holocaust Kingdom,* Europe seemed to show itself "pagan at heart."

Nazism was generated by the rapid growth of technological capacity combined with an increase in bureaucratic efficiency. This gave the leadership of the Third Reich a sense of power unparalleled in human history. Both the historic religious traditions and the new liberal democratic philosophies found themselves incapable of stemming its tide. The Nazis aimed at the total transformation of human values. Basic religious ideas that had shaped the public culture of Europe for centuries were transformed into purely political and anthropological concepts. In this sense, as the late Israeli historian Uriel Tal insisted, the Holocaust becomes a chapter in the history of civilization as such and not only a chapter in the history of the Jews.

All restraints on the use of human power had now disappeared in the eyes of the Nazis. Once they had totally consolidated control over every aspect of public life through their takeover of education, politics, law and medicine, they were free to become absolute arbiters of who could live and who could die. All those deemed inherently unfit were to be exterminated — Jews first and foremost but also the Polish leadership elite, the mentally and physically impaired, gypsies, gay persons and others.

The Nazis had come to the point of feeling they had total power in their hands. God and religion had been rendered meaningless as effective checks on this power. The late Jewish historian Jacob Talson posed the critical question in the light of such massive consolidation of power when he asked, "Has Auschwitz become an eternal warning, or merely the first station on the road to the extermination of all races and the suicide of humanity?" ("European History — Seedbed of the Holocaust," *Mid-Stream,* May 1973, 24).

Seeing the Holocaust as something far more than another manifestation of traditional Christian anti-Semitism makes it a problem not only for Christian morality but for the whole value structure of Western society generally. The very moral integrity of Western liberal democratic society is threatened by the Holocaust, for the event took place in a society supposedly embodying the best impulses of Western liberalism. It was the creation of people who were in many cases highly educated, who prided themselves on personal integration of the wellspring of Enlightenment morals. In retrospect, the nineteenth-century polemic against religion led by such individuals as Feuerbach and Nietzche appears to be hopelessly simplistic.

One of the deepest and most difficult questions posed by the Holocaust experience is how to begin the reconstruction of public values. Sole reliance on traditional religious values is insufficient as a response by the church because of demonstrated Christian collaboration in some quarters. Nor can we naively trust the rational ideals of democratic liberalism to prevent exaggerated concentrations of power.

The answer involves a new partnership between religion and public reason, one that recognizes the reality brought home to us by the Second Vatican Council in its *Pastoral Constitution on the Church in the Modern World:* namely, the primacy of culture in shaping the moral fabric of any society. At the minimum, this requires an acknowledgment that society needs to foster a sense of transcendence in its cultural life. Its ethos must enhance an appreciation and acceptance of transcendence on the part of its citizenry, rather than subtly or directly encouraging a one-dimensional approach to human living.

Although the historic religions, such as Christianity, must remain fully conscious of their participation in previous acts of human degradation, they must push for a consensus that, unless a spirit of transcendence prevails in public self-awareness, we will continue to experience repetitions of the massive destruction of human life akin to what happened in the Holocaust. While there is little doubt that some anti-transcendence philosophies have produced a betterment of the quality of life on several levels, the abuses we have seen in them, now becoming so openly visible in Eastern Europe, as well as the potential for even greater destructiveness (which has shocked us in the Holocaust), cannot be curbed without firmly maintaining a belief in a transcendent God. Unless people can once again come into contact with a personal power beyond themselves, unless there is a sense of a moral norm greater than themselves that can guide and judge conduct toward fellow human beings and the earth entrusted to our care, and unless such a sense is sustained by the general cultural milieu, there is little hope of avoiding another disastrous social experiment such as Nazism.

Rabbi Irving Greenberg has grappled with this problem in his reflections on the Holocaust's impact on Western society. It is his firm conviction that the lessons of the Holocaust require believing women and men firmly to resist the "absolutization" of the secular realm, a phenomenon that appears to be growing in the Western world. He writes:

> Secular authority unchecked becomes absolute. Relative values thus become the seedbed of absolute claims, and this is idolatry. This vacuum was a major factor in the Nazi ability to concentrate power and carry out the destruction without protest or resistance. ("Cloud of Smoke, Pillar of Fire: Judaism, Christianity and Modernity after the Holocaust," in Eva Fleschner, ed., *Auschwitz: Beginning of a New Era?* KTAV, 1977, 17)

I fundamentally agree with Rabbi Greenberg's assessment. In my perspective, therefore, one of the primary tasks for religion in the public sphere is to serve as a continual counterforce against any efforts to consolidate power in the hands of a few, a phenomenon that has inevitably inflicted massive suffering on human communities and significant destruction on the rest of creation. I might add here that the recent stress in official Catholic social ethics, including the U.S. Catholic bishops' pastoral letter on the U.S. economy, on participation as a central moral value is very much in line with this emphasis on religion's role in the permanent breakup of power. Power that is truly shared by all citizens is far less likely to be abusive.

As a Catholic leader deeply committed to the vision of the Second Vatican Council, I recognize that religion's role in keeping power concentrations at bay must be promoted within certain parameters set by the Council. In its *Decree on Religious Liberty*, so strongly shaped by the American democratic experiment, Vatican II decisively affirmed the secular, democratic state as the new Catholic ideal. There is no going back on these basic affirmations. When I speak of religion's contribution to framing the public culture, I do so with the explicit recognition that no religious group can (or should) impose its will on the body politic. As I have emphasized in a number of my statements on church-state relations in the context of the need for a consistent life ethic, persuasion and dialogue must be our preferred route in the public sector.

Nonetheless I am faced with a dilemma. Since, in keeping with Vatican II, I also affirm the centrality of public culture in shaping morality, I cannot be content with confining the matter exclusively to the sphere of what Professor Manfred Vogel has termed "vertical relations." Rather, I agree with Dr. Vogel that, unless religion can have a direct impact on the sphere of "horizontal relations" as well, we may risk having religion "commit suicide" — in Vogel's words — or "merely smooth and grace its own exit from the state" (cf. Walter J. Burghardt, sj, ed., *Religious Freedom 1965 and 1975: A Symposium on a Historic Document,* Paulist Press, 68). Or as the church historian Clyde Manschreck put it, we may be opening the public sphere to the emergence of "naked state sovereignty" (cf. "Church-State Relations — A Question of Sovereignty," in Clyde L.

Manschreck and Barbara Brown Zikmund, eds., *The American Religious Experiment: Piety and Practicality,* Exploration Press, 121).

The above realization makes it evident, as do a number of past social situations, that while dialogue and persuasion must be religion's first impulse in the public sector, we cannot automatically exclude the possibility that, at certain moments, religious groups may have to move into the power mode in order to preserve certain basic moral values in a society. I feel American Catholicism should have been more active in this regard when the abolition of slavery and basic political rights for women first became national issues. It was significantly involved, somewhat later, in historic coalitions with the Protestant and Jewish communities, in an organized effort to improve the conditions of the American worker during the thirties and forties and, then, again in the sixties to guarantee civil rights for African Americans and other minorities. Both are successful examples of a selected use of the power and influence of religion on an interreligious basis to shape public life in this nation. They also are a reminder that, although dialogue and persuasion ought to remain religion's primary option in the public sphere, there are clearly times when religious institutions must go beyond this approach.

In the coming years, we may be forced to confront similar situations. The escalating power of the communications media, for example, is a growing cause of concern because of its ever-increasing ability to mold the public ethos of the contemporary world, far more perhaps than either the political or legal realms. The new power of the media can, of course, serve a useful purpose, just as much as enhanced technology has. But this power also may be used for the promotion of values that will ultimately degrade and destroy the very moral fabric of this land. I think, for example, of the power of media relative to pornography, an area that has especially concerned me these past several years and on which I have tried to exercise leadership in an interreligious setting. We may see a growing number of troubling situations relative to the media that only a well-organized, broadly based group of religious leaders can confront.

Finally, I would point to the area of the growing depersonalization of language in our society. Control of language is an immensely powerful force in any society. We must honestly ask whether this immensely powerful vehicle is not now becoming increasingly a source of the degradation of human persons, especially in certain areas of the communications arts. Actually, as scholars have shown, there is a direct tie between this phenomenon and the Holocaust with which I began this set of reflections. The efforts by the Nazi theoreticians to neutralize the moral impact of Auschwitz and its sister death camps is intriguing to study. Their goal was to reduce the operations at these camps to the level of mere technical activity by the utilization of totally depersonalized terms to describe the human slaughter taking place. The daily work output of a camp was reported in much the same manner as one might make public the daily production line record of an industrial plant.

Some commentators see this as the dawn of a new phase in making mass destruction thinkable and morally acceptable. It is a process similar to the reporting of deaths during the Vietnam era and continues in use to clothe torture activities by certain governments. The same thing is happening, I submit, in the abortion debate where often the fetus is referred to as mere "tissue." What is taking place in the language of popular culture today may be another step in the process. Clearly it is incumbent on the religious communities to work together to counter such depersonalization of language.

The question of relating religion and power remains very much an open-ended one that must continually respond to new challenges in the public sphere. The primary goal of any efforts in this area, let me repeat, must always be the preservation of the face of God in all of creation, not the triumph of one religious tradition over another. Professor Emil Fackenheim has said that the Nazis' ultimate goal was to wipe out the divine image in history (*The Jewish Return Into History,* Schocken, 246). They did not succeed in the end. And no other group must succeed in the future. That remains our ongoing challenge for the future.

"RECONCILING CHURCH AND SYNAGOGUE"

"THE NEW WORLD" IS THE OFFICIAL NEWSPAPER OF THE ARCHDIOCESE OF CHICAGO.
WHEN HE BECAME ARCHBISHOP, CARDINAL BERNARDIN BEGAN A WEEKLY COLUMN TITLED
"THE TRUTH IN CHRIST." HE USES THIS COLUMN AS ONE OF HIS PRIMARY TEACHING
VEHICLES TO HIS OWN CHURCH MEMBERS. EACH YEAR, HE DEVOTES AT LEAST ONE COLUMN
TO CATHOLIC-JEWISH RELATIONS.

LAST October 28 marked the twenty-fifth anniversary of Vatican II's *Declaration on the Relation of the Church to Non-Christian Religions.* Its Latin title is *Nostra Aetate.* It is quite impossible to overemphasize its importance in the history of Christianity. As Cardinal Willebrands, a leader in ecumenical and interfaith dialogue for 40 years, has pointed out, "For the first time in history a general Council acknowledged the search for the absolute by non-Christian races and peoples, and honored the truth and holiness in other religions as the work of the one living God."

While the document briefly covers relations between the Catholic Church and Hinduism, Buddhism, Islam and other non-Christian religions, it has so far had the greatest impact on relations between the church and the synagogue — the focus of this column.

Despite its origins within the Jewish community, a rift gradually developed between Christianity and Judaism. For their part, Christians began to think that, because many Jews did not recognize Jesus as the expected Messiah, God had rejected them and replaced them with Christians in his plan of salvation. The next step was to accuse all Jews of guilt for Jesus' death. From these theological distortions emerged false charges of Jewish ritual murders and profanation of the eucharist. For many Catholics, anti-Semitism, unfortunately, appeared to have a solid theological basis.

While anti-Semitism reared its ugly head from time to time during the centuries, it was carried out with extreme brutality in this century by the Nazis. The Congregation of the Holy Office explicitly condemned anti-Semitism in 1928, but this did not automatically eradicate prejudice against the Jews among all Catholics. Since the Holocaust, Christians have learned the significance of that horrible experience for Jews throughout the world. But we have yet to recognize its significance for ourselves. We tend to place all the guilt on the godless Nazis and to overlook Christian treatment of the Jews through much of church history and the complicity of some Catholics in the Holocaust itself.

This was not true of all Catholics by any means. One, Angelo Roncalli, the apostolic nuncio in Bulgaria and Turkey during this period of Nazi terrorism, saved thousands of Jews from deportation. Later as Pope John XXIII, he removed the objectionable words "perfidy" and "perfidious Jews" from the Good Friday liturgy. During his pontificate a dramatic shift in the church's attitude and thinking about Jews took deep root. It reached greater maturity under Pope Paul VI and the promulgations of *Nostra Aetate*.

Nostra Aetate represented a definitive, new step in the church's understanding of Judaism. As Cardinal Willebrands has said, "Never before has a systematic, positive, comprehensive, careful and daring presentation of Jews and Judaism been made in the church by any pope or council." The conciliar document acknowledged the Jewish people, affirmed their special position under Christ, fostered mutual understanding and respect between us, and condemned anti-Semitism.

Because it took nearly 2,000 years to arrive at a document like *Nostra Aetate,* we should not expect that all prejudice, stereotype, mistrust and enmity will be promptly dispelled on either side, or that the new ideas will be quickly disseminated or accepted within either community. Dialogue and collaboration are the ways that can lead to our reconciliation as brothers and sisters and a deeper mutual understanding and appreciation of church and synagogue. But this is not an easy process. It demands mutual trust and respect. Given the history of our relationship, it will naturally take time for such trust to develop.

Since the Council, the Holy See has taken additional steps regarding the church's relation with Jews and Judaism. In 1974, it issued *Guidelines on Religious Relations with Jews,* covering such topics as dialogue itself, liturgy, teaching and education, and joint social action. In 1985, it published *Notes on the Correct Way to Present Jews and Judaism in Preaching and Catechesis.* In 1989, the Pontifical Justice and Peace Commission promulgated *The Church and Racism,* which devoted considerable space to a condemnation of anti-Semitism, including anti-Zionism. Moreover, Pope John Paul II himself has made many significant contributions to the church's theological understanding of Jews and Judaism. In particular, he has stressed the underlying permanent bond between the church and the Jewish people, a bond that impacts the church's very identity as a faith community.

As a result of all of this, Catholics have become more aware of the value of the Old Testament, the Jewish context of Jesus' preaching and teaching, the spiritual bond between us and our Jewish brothers and sisters, the permanent validity of the original divine covenant with Israel, and the living heritage that we share with Judaism.

At the same time, Catholics and Jews remain divided in many ways and on many issues. For example, there have been recent controversies regarding the Carmelite convent at Auschwitz and the visits of the holy father with Kurt Waldheim and Yasser Arafat. Moreover, many Reform Jews disagree with the Catholic community's stand in the public policy debate on abortion.

While there are other points of contention, the most serious obstacle toward improving relations between the Catholic Church and the Jewish people centers on the State of Israel. Many Jews want the Holy See to establish formal diplomatic relations with the State of Israel. The Holy See has not done this because serious problems in the Middle East are unresolved. Nonetheless, various popes, including Pope John Paul II, have spoken with great sensitivity about Israel's continued attachment to the land of Israel.

We still have a long way to go in the Jewish-Catholic dialogue, but *Nostra Aetate* has helped make the dialogue possible.

"PRESERVING THE DIGNITY OF ALL CREATION: TOWARD A RENEWED CHRISTIAN-JEWISH RELATIONSHIP"

JEWISH-CATHOLIC INTERNATIONAL LIAISON COMMITTEE

THE INTERNATIONAL LIAISON COMMITTEE COORDINATES THE CATHOLIC-JEWISH DIALOGUE AT THE GLOBAL LEVEL. THIS MEETING IN BALTIMORE MARKS THE FIRST TIME THE COMMITTEE MET OUTSIDE EUROPE.

BROTHERS AND SISTERS,

At the outset I wish to express my gratitude to His Eminence Edward Cardinal Cassidy, Mr. Edgar Bronfman, Archbishop William Keeler, Bishop Pierre Duprey and the members of the International Liaison Committee (ILC) and the International Jewish Committee on Interreligious Consultations (IJCIC) for the invitation to address you in this opening plenary. I also extend a warm welcome to those from foreign lands. We are pleased that the official international dialogue has arrived on this continent, for decades the scene of considerable important creative activity in terms of the Catholic-Jewish relationship. Certainly the continuing experience of Jews and Christians interacting in religious dialogues and community activities in the pluralistic societies of Canada and the United States remains indispensable for the growth of Jewish-Catholic solidarity on a global scale.

The focus of our gathering this evening is on the future. But I would be remiss if I neglected to relate some of the history of our relationship in North

America, a history that had a decided impact on the passage of chapter four of *Nostra Aetate* at Vatican II.

American Jews and Catholics shared a special destiny for a good part of the first two centuries of this country's existence. While our communities enjoyed the protection accorded all citizens by the U.S. Constitution and Bill of Rights, in practice we experienced widespread discrimination in many areas of daily life. Indigenous hate groups such as the Ku Klux Klan targeted us both. Signs proclaiming "neither Catholics nor Jews need apply" (for example, for housing or jobs) were not uncommon in cities such as New York as late as the first part of the twentieth century. Yet, despite such discrimination, we developed a profound sense of appreciation for the freedom and opportunity that America's pluralistic setting provided us, including the opportunity to nurture our faith traditions.

From the Catholic side, this appreciation was poignantly expressed by one of our great ecclesiastical figures, James Cardinal Gibbons of Baltimore. Speaking in Rome in 1887, Cardinal Gibbons affirmed his belief in the positive dimensions of Catholicism's experience of America:

> For myself as a citizen of the United States, without closing my eyes to our defects as a nation, I proclaim, with a deep sense of pride and gratitude, and in the great capitol of Christendom, that I belong to a country where the civil government holds over us the aegis of its protection without interfering in the legitimate exercise of our sublime mission as ministers of the gospel of Jesus Christ.

For the progress that the Catholic Church in the United States had made, Gibbons continued, "Under God and the fostering care of the Holy See, we are indebted in no small degree to the civil liberty we enjoy in our enlightened republic."[1]

The spirit of religious pluralism that characterized this nation made possible the slow but steady growth of trust between Jews and Catholics. We no longer feared and distrusted each other as had so often been the case in many parts of the world. As a result, in time we were able to build coalitions for common action on a social agenda that was unprecedented in previous centuries. Many Protestants joined us in this unique coalition that helped transform the social profile of U.S. society. True, many deep and persistent problems remain. But it was this social coalition that first created a sense of bonding between us that eventually would lead us to examine our specifically religious teachings about one another.

Christian-Jewish cooperation in this country began with a common concern for the conditions of the nation's working class that embraced the majority of Catholics and Jews. As early as 1919 and 1927, we began to speak out in support of striking workers. This was followed by two decades of intensive joint activities coordinated by the National Catholic Welfare Conference and the Central Conference of American Rabbis as we joined the Federal Council of Churches in support of extensive new legislation aimed at eliminating chronic unemployment, protecting children and women from abuse in the workplace, insuring more equitable taxation, and guaranteeing workers basic collective bargaining rights. For the Catholic Church in the U.S., this was our response to the social encyclicals of Popes Leo XIII and Pius XI.

Social researchers of the period took note of this new tri-faith religious coalition in America and its growing social impact. Writing in 1934, Claris Silcox and Galen Fisher explicitly attributed the abolition of the 12-hour work day in the steel industry, for example, "in considerable measure" to these tri-faith efforts. Overall they concluded:

> This close collaboration by these three agencies, speaking for tens of thousands of churches and synagogues, is considered by thoughtful men to have done much toward educating the conscience of the nation and toward demonstrating the courageous concern of all the creeds with justice and the good life.[2]

The efforts of the 1930s and 1940s were directed primarily at the dignity and economic well-being of peoples of European extraction. In the '60s, our faith communities faced yet another challenge: racism. With the civil rights marches led by Dr. Martin Luther King, Jr. bringing this major unresolved issue to the surface, Jews and Christians once more were summoned to partnership. The response was the historic Conference on Religion and Race, convened in Chicago, which generated joint action toward the passage of comprehensive civil rights legislation affecting African Americans and other minorities. This work is far from finished, as recent events in Los Angeles and other cities have shown.

It was also in the late '50s and early '60s that we began to examine our teaching materials for their portrayal of other religious groups in light of the trust and understanding that had come about as a result of our cooperation in the pursuit of social justice. As each religious body began to examine these materials (Catholics at Saint Louis University[3] and Jews at Dropsie College in Philadelphia, with the overall support of the American Jewish Committee), it became obvious that many religious stereotypes of Jews and Judaism were present in the Catholic texts and that Jewish books were generally devoid of much concrete information on Catholics and their beliefs. As a result of these studies, a wholesale reevaluation of the portrayal of Jews and Judaism began among the principal Catholic publishers. The Jewish response has been somewhat slower in coming, but recently new efforts have been launched to improve Jewish understanding of Catholicism.

This was the context that prepared the U.S. Catholic bishops for their participation in the Second Vatican Council's discussions on the proposed conciliar statement regarding the church's relationship to the Jewish people. The positive experience of U.S. Catholicism in working with Jews for several decades on a common social agenda solidified episcopal support for the passage of this historic document. While many prominent Europeans contributed to the formulation of chapter four of *Nostra Aetate*, some from their experience in helping in the efforts to rescue Jews during the Shoah, the strong endorsement given this document by the U.S. hierarchy proved especially crucial in its eventual approval in the Council's fourth and final session in 1965.

And so there is little doubt in my mind that, by turning outward to confront social injustice, Catholics and Jews established a sense of trust and confidence that, in the end, enabled them to deal constructively with the long-standing theological misperceptions that over the centuries had often caused immeasurable suffering for the Jewish community.

After Vatican II the process of implementing *Nostra Aetate* led to a full range of activities on the local and national levels. Some of these efforts focused on removing the last vestiges of anti-Semitic stereotypes from teaching materials and beginning the task of retraining teachers. The 1974 *Guidelines* of the Holy See, those of our own episcopal conference of 1967 and 1975, and the 1975 *Notes* of the Holy See provided the framework for this process.

We also continued the preconciliar efforts to examine together issues of social concern. Several conferences took place at the University of Notre Dame under the joint sponsorship of the Synagogue Council of America and the National Conference of Catholic Bishops. And, more recently, the Synagogue Council of America and our episcopal conference have sponsored important discussions on education and moral values, religious freedom, the Middle East and developments in Eastern Europe.

So, as we gather together this evening in public plenary at the start of these critical international conversations, the spirit of interreligious cooperation that remains a cherished legacy on this continent should serve to rekindle among us a new commitment to the mutual pursuit of justice and reconciliation on a worldwide scale. There is always a danger that our dialogue may become overly insular in its concerns. While many of the issues that relate more directly to our relationship as Catholics and Jews surely need to be pursued, we should never make them the exclusive agenda of our discussions and actions.

Certainly this is the clear direction for our dialogue given in the many statements by the Holy See on Catholic-Jewish relations. In his 1980 address to the people of Mainz, Germany, for example, Pope John Paul II termed this dimension of our dialogue a "sacred duty." Jews and Christians, as children of Abraham, are called to be a blessing for the world by committing themselves to work together for peace and justice among all peoples.[4] And I am pleased that the most recent meeting of some members of the International Liaison Committee and International Jewish Committee on Interreligious Consultations held this past February in Poland reaffirmed the pledge made at the gathering of the two bodies in Prague in September 1990 regarding the need for a unified Catholic-Jewish response against the rise of xenophobia, anti-Semitism, racism and extreme nationalism in many parts of the world, and for joint support of legislation protecting the human, religious and civil rights of minorities. My profound hope is that our meeting here in Baltimore will deepen this pledge. I would like to offer some suggestions regarding areas that call for our attention.

Meeting as we are here in Baltimore, with a special focus on the implications of the Holocaust for our relationship, let me begin consideration of our future joint agenda with some reflections on challenges of that period that Elie Wiesel has called "night." The Holocaust surely presents itself as a complex reality, one that may ultimately defy human explanation. Yet there are some important conclusions we can draw from a study of the Nazi era. For, the more we examine the Holocaust, the more it appears as a significantly new stage in human history.

The combination of greatly enhanced technological capacity, a new level of bureaucratic organization, and the erosion of traditional moral standards paved the way for the mass extermination of human life in a seemingly guiltless fashion. The door was now ajar for an age when dispassionate torture and the murder of millions of innocent people could become not merely the acts of crazed despots, not merely an irrational outbreak of xenophobic fear, not only a desire for national security, but a calculated effort to reshape history supported by intellectual argumentation from the best and the brightest minds in a society. It was an attempt, Professor Emil Fackenheim has written, to wipe out the "divine image" in history. "The murder camp," Fackenheim insists, "was not an accidental by-product of the Nazi empire. It was its essence."[5]

What emerges as a central reality from a reflection on the Holocaust is the Nazi attempt to create a fully liberated humanity to be shared in only by the Aryan race. In Nazi belief this new humanity would be capable of exerting virtually unlimited power in shaping the world and its inhabitants. To their mind God was dead as an effective force in governing the universe. To attain their objective, the Nazis were convinced that the "dregs of humanity" had to be eliminated or at least their influence on culture and human development greatly curtailed. The Jews fell into this category first and foremost. They were classified as "vermin." But the Poles, the gypsies, homosexuals, and the mentally and physically impaired were also looked on as polluters of humanity, as obstacles to the growth of human consciousness to a new level of insight and power. Their extermination under the rubric of humankind's purification assumes a theological significance intimately related to the Jewish question.

The late Israeli historian, Uriel Tal, captured well the basic moral challenge of the Holocaust. The so-called "Final Solution," he says, aimed at a total transformation of human values. Its stated goal was the complete liberation of humanity from previous moral ideals and codes. When the Nazi program had reached its completion, people would no longer feel bound by any sense of moral responsibility rooted in an understanding of a Creator God.

Professor Tal argued that the Holocaust, while related to classical forms of anti-Semitism (including those found in popular Christian belief), was in many ways the direct result of central forces in modern Western society. And so it presents a profound challenge to all of us whose countries are heirs of the liberal political tradition. The basic issue that now confronts all of us — Jew, Christian, Muslim, Hindu — is whether it is any longer possible to maintain a society whose public value system clearly depends on the acknowledgment of God who is the ultimate source of life. This is a premise that increasingly we cannot take for granted in the Western world. The forces that generated the Holocaust did not completely disappear from the scene with the demise of the Third Reich. That is why the discussion on moral values recently inaugurated between the Synagogue Council of America and our episcopal conference, to which I referred earlier, assumes such importance.

The response to the growing challenge of total secularism in so much of our public life will not be met simply by nostalgic calls for a return to previous forms of Christian-dominated societies. Nor is the kind of fundamentalism in religion preached by many today what we need. The societies of the Western world, and to a degree the Orient as well, are becoming increasingly pluralistic. For this reason, the dialogue that we continue here this week in Baltimore needs at some point to touch base with the entire religious family. For Catholics, Pope John Paul II has clearly shown us the way with his leadership in convening the meeting of world religious representatives around the theme of peace in Assisi several years ago.

My friends, I truly believe that the religious traditions of the world, including Judaism and Catholicism, stand at a crossroads in terms of the world's future. Either we will begin to work constructively for what Professor Fackenheim has called "the restoration of God's image" in history after the Shoah, or we will more and more find ourselves surrounded by a new secular absolutism. Rabbi Irving Greenberg has spoken to this in the light of the Holocaust. "Secular authority unchecked," he says, "becomes absolute. Relative values thus become the seedbed of absolute claims, and this is idolatry. This vacuum was a major factor in the Nazi ability to concentrate power and carry out the destruction without protest or resistance."[6]

The effort to restore Christians and Jews to the forefront of moral leadership in addressing the problems of global justice will not prove easy. It is no secret that key people in the scientific and technical communities regard us as insignificant, if not an actual obstacle, to the cause of the earth's survival. These are not easy words for us in the religious community to hear. We will only convince the skeptics with concrete actions, not mere protestations, as we did through the highly effective interreligious coalitions mounted in the '30s, '40s and '60s in this country.

Two additional points need to be made at this juncture. The first relates to the reestablishment of full Christian moral integrity after the Shoah. As the church enters into a new coalition with Jews and others in support of an agenda of global justice, this commitment must be accompanied by a concomitant effort to purge any remaining stereotypes of Jews and distortions of the Jewish tradition that remain in Catholic theology, catechetics and liturgy, and to submit its World War II record to a thorough scrutiny by respected scholars. In terms of the latter, the recent 400-page report by a panel of historians commissioned and supported by the cardinal archbishop of Lyons in France serves as an excellent model for the direction in which we need to move. It is only through such candor and willingness to acknowledge mistakes where documentary evidence clearly warrants it that Catholicism can join in the pursuit of contemporary global justice with full moral integrity.

Secondly, there is need to recognize from the very outset that, on some important issues of public policy, major differences have surfaced between Catholics and Jews, and will continue to do so. We should try as far as possible to continue to dialogue on these issues as we have, for example, on the Middle East and abortion on both the national level and local levels here in the United States. Even with such dialogue, we may, at times, find ourselves on opposite sides of proposed legislation. One such example is our difference of opinion regarding the Religious Freedom Restoration Act. But we must always be guided by the recognition of the right of conscience and the inherent dignity of each human person that are so central both to the Second Vatican Council's document on religious liberty and Pope John Paul II's first encyclical on human redemption.

Having sketched the overriding challenge confronting Jews and Catholics today, let me now address briefly several more specific areas, all of which ultimately are in one way or another affected by the post-Holocaust condition of humanity.

The first is the unprecedented crisis facing the entire human family because of the rapid deterioration of the environment that we share together, no matter what our faith. Never before in the history of civilization have men and women needed to be so concerned about the survival of the natural world on which we are increasingly recognizing our dependence. Nature has had the inherent recuperative powers to overcome any ecologically destructive act the human community might perform. But respected scientists now warn us that this situation is rapidly coming to an end. We may now be pushing the natural world to its recuperative limits, and even beyond, through pollution and other forms of environmental destruction.

The religious community, sad to say, has been somewhat slow in responding to this rapidly escalating crisis. Many still do not give ecological preservation a high place on the global justice agenda. Hopefully, the coming world summit on the environment in Rio de Janeiro this summer will awaken the conscience of us all.

Pope John Paul II, in his 1990 World Day of Peace message, strongly urged Catholics, and all peoples of good will, to take up the ecological challenge. He wrote,

> Today the ecological crisis has assumed such proportions as to be the responsibility of everyone. . . . Its various aspects demonstrate the need for concerted efforts aimed at establishing duties and obligations that belong to individuals, peoples, states and the international community.[7]

He repeated this challenge in his recent encyclical, *Centesimus Annus,* issued in 1991 in commemoration of the 100th anniversary of the first papal encyclical on social justice, *Rerum Novarum.*

And this past November, I joined my brother bishops in the United States in approving a statement on environmental concerns, entitled "Renewing the Earth."[8] This statement emphasized that safeguarding creation will require the peoples of the globe to live responsibly within it rather than trying to direct the planet's course merely as outsiders. We have lost a fundamental awareness of the basic linkage between humanity and the natural world. Recovery of this awareness, which involves development of a new sense of dependence on the world of nature, is critical for human survival as well as the well-being of the entire planet.

Ecological concern, however, is not a matter of scientific expertise alone. If we are to see its growth in our day, there must be an emergence of a spirituality that takes very seriously the enhanced role of the human community as "co-creators." This term has gradually taken on a new prominence in Catholic social thought. Pope John Paul II made it a centerpiece of his encyclical on human work, *Laborem Exercens.* And the U.S. and Canadian bishops have both drawn on this biblical notion, the former in the documents on energy (1981) and the national economy (1986), and the latter in their statement on economic justice (1983).

But if this notion of co-creatorship is not to lead to disastrous misinterpretations of human power, it must be accompanied by serious reflection on the biblical sense of human dependence on the Creator God who alone remains the Lord of the earth. The Christian-Jewish dialogue can provide an important setting for an in-depth study of the religious roots of authentic ecological responsibility, of how the human family can fulfill its newly demanding co-creatorship role in a genuine partnership with God, the source of all life.

As a Christian, I recognize that the church stands to gain much insight from its Jewish partners in the conversation on this topic. This is already acknowledged in the papal and episcopal documents mentioned above that rely in an important way on the tradition of the Hebrew Scriptures in setting forth their vision of co-creatorship. This is but one illustration of the changing attitude within Catholicism that increasingly is coming to recognize the First Testament as an integral part of Christian faith in its own right and not merely a prelude to the teachings of the New Testament.

But the Hebrew Scriptures are not the only part of the Jewish religious tradition that will serve us well in a dialogue about our growing co-creational responsibility. We also stand to gain much from mutual reflections on the Jewish mystical tradition and on the writings of such contemporary figures as

Rabbi Joseph Soloveitchik and Dr. David Hartman,[9] where the notion of the human person's role as co-creator is particularly prominent. Such reflections will only underscore the point emphasized in the 1985 Holy See's *Notes on the Correct Way to Present the Jews and Judaism in Preaching and Catechesis in the Roman Catholic Church*,[10] namely, that in approaching the Jewish tradition Christians should not restrict themselves to the biblical era.

A second issue of global significance that ought to be part of the global outreach of our dialogue is that of peace and war. Recent experiences have left us with complex feelings in this area. On the one hand, we are living through the final stages of the "Cold War" with its continual threat of nuclear annihilation. On the other hand, last year we witnessed the destruction and the fear that even a limited "technological" war can engender. Some of you here this evening may have personally lived through those threatening days and nights or had family or friends who did.

As chairman of the U.S. Bishops' committee that prepared the 1983 pastoral letter entitled *The Challenge of Peace: God's Promise and Our Response,* I came to understand the profound difficulty involved in making concrete moral judgments in this area. But I also was convinced of the urgent need to try to move to such judgments. I also became convinced that, ultimately, these judgments would bear little practical effect unless they were accompanied by a true change of heart rooted in a deep spirituality of peace. Many Christians have mistakenly seen the Hebrew Scriptures and the Jewish tradition as advocating war far more than peace. This is a very simplistic understanding of the Jewish perspective, past or present. At the same time, the long tradition of Christian reflection on war and peace may help the Jewish community to sort out its contemporary responsibilities, particularly with respect to the policies of the State of Israel.

Our dialogue about war and peace, which must focus primarily on the religious resources of both our traditions, needs to include both the global dimensions as well as the more limited issues involved with the Israeli/Arab/Palestinian conflict. Catholics cannot ignore the serious reservations about the recent Gulf

War raised by Pope John Paul II as well as by a number of U.S. bishops. But they also need to hear firsthand Jewish perceptions of the conflict. The conversations may not always be easy in this regard, but, in the end they will, I am convinced, prove mutually beneficial. The dialogue must also continue to focus on the more limited crisis in the Middle East. The exchanges that have taken place in the last several meetings between the Bishops' Secretariat for Ecumenical and Interreligious Affairs and the Synagogue Council of America need to continue and even expand.

One particular concern of mine in recent years has not received much, if any, attention in the recent dialogue. I speak of the growing exploitation and deprivation of children. In this country, one out of every five children is undernourished. And here and in many other countries of the world there is an increased trafficking in child pornography. As a leader of a U.S. interreligious alliance established to combat this insidious problem, I see it eating away at the moral fiber of the nation. And the exploitation of children for economic gain, something that Jews and Catholics together opposed in the '30s and '40s, is surfacing anew in many Third World countries.

The recent U.S. Catholic bishops' document on children, *Putting Children and Families First,* may serve as an important starting point for a full-fledged discussion of this pressing issue between our two faith communities. We can no longer ignore it. How we treat children is very much a barometer of our general respect for human life and dignity.

Finally, in addition to addressing the specific issue of protecting and enhancing the well-being of children, we need to engage in discussion and common action against all forms of social discrimination and lack of human rights. In a special way, I believe we must be sensitive to continuing attacks against those who were directly victimized by the Nazis — Jews, East European ethnics, homosexuals, the Romani people (gypsies) and the handicapped. Jews and Catholics played an important role in combating recent manifestations of anti-Semitism and attacks on African Americans during political campaigns in this country. In Europe, where anti-Semitism and other forms of social

136

discrimination appear on the rise against Jews and gypsies in some areas, Jewish-Christian coalitions have likewise emerged. But these joint efforts must grow and stay their course. The social dislocation affecting many parts of the European continent as a result of the collapse of the Communist empire, and the increasing economic difficulties surfacing practically everywhere, make it likely that the specter of prejudice and discrimination will be part of global reality for the foreseeable future. If we have learned one lesson from the period of the Holocaust, it is that no one group can successfully preserve its own well-being while ignoring blatant assaults against the dignity of others. Sooner or later, the bystanders become the victims as well.

Catholics and Jews need to converse about ways in which our two communities can actively promote the preservation of human dignity in various spheres. Human rights legislation on a national and global scale, greater economic opportunities for women who suffer greatly in many parts of the world in this regard, new legislation to protect children — these are but some of the areas that call for our attention.

The list of our joint responsibilities in the social sphere could easily be extended. But if we were to address seriously the ones I have highlighted, we would truly be taking the first step toward *tikkun olam,* the "healing of the world."

In short, my brothers and sisters, the present global realities are calling us to a kind of moral madness, as Elie Wiesel has termed it. As Rabbi Byron Sherwin of the Spertus College of Judaica in Chicago, who has been central in the work of the Bernardin Center at that institution, has said of Wiesel's approach, " . . . madness means: not to be seduced by appearance and social convention; to love where there is only indifference and hate; to try to live humanely in an inhumane world; to believe in humankind in spite of what we have done."[11] Such moral madness, if jointly shared, will help both our communities resist the apathy and hatred all too common in our societies. For, as a Brazilian proverb puts it, when we dream alone, it is only a dream, but when we dream together, it is the beginning of reality.

[1] As quoted in George G. Higgins' introduction to Walter J. Burghardt, SJ, ed., *Religious Freedom: 1965 & 1975: A Symposium on a Historic Document.* Woodstock Studies 1. New York: Paulist Press, 1977, 68.

[2] Cf. Claris Silcox and Galen Fisher, *Catholics, Jews and Protestants: A Study of Relationships in the United States and Canada.* Boston: Institute of Social and Religious Research, 1934, 301 – 31.

[3] Cf. John T. Pawlikowski, OSM, *Catechetics & Prejudice: How Catholic Teaching Materials View Jews, Protestants and Racial Minorities.* New York/Paramus/Toronto: Paulist Press, 1973; for subsequent developments cf. Eugene Fisher, *Faith Without Prejudice: Rebuilding Christian Attitudes Towards Judaism.* New York/Paramus/Toronto: Paulist Press, 1977, and Philip A. Cunningham, *A Content Analysis of the Presentation of Jews and Judaism in Current Roman Catholic Religion Textbooks* (PH.D. dissertation, Boston College, 1992).

[4] Cf. Eugene J. Fisher and Leon Klenicki, eds., *Pope John Paul on Jews and Judaism, 1979 – 1986.* Washington: NCCB Committee for Ecumenical and Interreligious Affairs, and New York: Anti-Defamation League of B'nai B'rith, 1987, 35 – 36.

[5] Emil Fackenheim, *The Jewish Return Into History.* New York: Schocken, 1978, 246.

[6] Irving Greenburg, "Cloud of Smoke, Pillar of Fire: Judaism, Christianity and Modernity after the Holocaust," in Eva Fleischner, ed., *Auschwitz: Beginning of a New Era?* New York: KTAV, The Cathedral of Saint John the Divine, and the Anti-Defamation League of B'nai B'rith, 1974, 29.

[7] As quoted in National Conference of Catholic Bishops, "Renewing the Earth: An Invitation to Reflection and Action on the Environment in Light of Catholic Social Teaching," *Origins,* 21:27 (December 12, 1991), 429.

[8] Ibid., 425 – 32.

[9] David Hartman, *A Living Covenant: The Innovative Spirit in Traditional Judaism.* New York: The Free Press, 1985.

[10] Cf. Helga Croner, ed., *More Stepping Stones to Jewish-Christian Relations: An Unabridged Collection of Christian Documents 1975 – 1983.* New York/Mahwah: Paulist Press (A Stimulus Book), 1985, 22 – 232.

[11] Byron Sherwin, "Elie Wiesel on Madness," *CCAR Journal,* 19:3 (June 1972), 32.

INTERFAITH CLERGY INSTITUTE

❈

ALLOW me to begin by expressing my appreciation for the opportunity to participate in this Interfaith Clergy Institute. I am convinced that one of the strengths of the Chicago metropolitan area is the level of interreligious dialogue and cooperation. In particular, the ever-deepening Jewish-Christian relationships ought to be cherished and nourished. Opportunities such as this Institute are invaluable. I truly regret that my schedule does not allow me to participate in today's full program. I am confident, however, that it will be a worthwhile experience for all who are able to do so.

In his invitation to serve as today's keynote speaker, Rabbi Schaalman asked that I address the topic "authority and autonomy." As I reflected on the topic and the complexities of perspective and experience present within this room, I found it difficult to identify a helpful starting point. As I thought more about the topic, I realized that in one sense the current context or motivation for this issue is as much cultural as it is religious. Let me explain.

One of the great intellectual lights of the Roman Catholic Vatican II era was Father Bernard Lonergan, SJ. His theological synthesis has influenced a great deal of contemporary Catholic thinking. In one of his seminal articles, he discussed what he described as the post-Enlightenment shift in cultural consciousness or awareness. He described this shift as a movement from a classicist to a historicist awareness.

According to Lonergan, the classicist worldview assumed that the source of reality was to be found in the eternally immutable Godhead. The purpose of life in this context was to discover the divine truth that is the origin and destiny of life. The methodology of this search was *deductive* in nature: look to God and apply what one finds to daily living. The Cartesian "turn to the subject" altered this worldview in the most significant manner. Rather than God, it was the individual experience that became the primary referent for the "really real." The search now was not so much for truth as for meaning — meaning that began with the concrete and moved forward in a more *inductive* fashion.

Such a shift obviously has great bearing on today's topic. In a classicist world, human authority was an external reality that mediated divine authority. The individual was expected to bow before and conform to the demands of such authority. In a sense, freedom was an attribute whose purpose was to give an individual the opportunity to find external truth, goodness and beauty, and apply those realities to the concrete and mutable circumstances of life. One could say that autonomy was a concept foreign to this world because the individual had no real purpose apart from the community in which authority was situated.

In a historicist world, the process is reversed. Autonomy now is center stage. The individual is primary. Meaning is that which fulfills the individual quest. In this view, universals give way to particulars. Authority is granted only as much prerogative as it earns, and as is needed to provide the social space necessary for the individual search for well-being.

It could be said, then, that the world authority is expressive of a classicist worldview while autonomy celebrates a historicist perspective. As such they are concepts that many might consider to be in opposition to each other or, at the very least, are not easily reconcilable.

But how does this cultural analysis relate to our religious heritage? Many philosophers of religion would suggest that it is impossible for a religious heritage not to be impacted by the culture in which it is situated. On a continuum that goes from a religious sect's posture of withdrawal or avoidance to an openness to assimilation that eliminates any distinctive religious identity, every religious tradition engages culture in one way or another. In this context, some would suggest that within the religious tradition the Protestant Reformation was a Christian response to shifting cultural context just as Reform Judaism was a Jewish response. Others would propose that one of the sources of current tensions in the Roman Catholic tradition is the discomfort some experience with the Second Vatican Council's recognition of modernity, especially as it is found in the *Pastoral Constitution on the Church in the Modern World* and in the *Decree on Religious Liberty*. One commentator, in fact, has suggested that all our religious denominations are experiencing what he describes as "culture wars." Battles between religious conservatives and liberals over issues that many thought had been resolved by the Scopes trial and other events, such as the Second Vatican Council, are being waged with various levels of intensity.

I will leave it to you to discuss the adequacy of this analysis. Aware of it, however, I would like to move the conversation forward by making two assertions. First, that the current cultural antinomy between authority and autonomy is not healthy. Second, that just as religion is affected by culture, so, too, religion can and should affect culture. Unfortunately, in the United States this is not happening as it should.

Regarding the first point, developmental psychologists and certain schools of sociological analysis argue persuasively that the human person is essentially interpersonal in nature and needs to be part of some type of community. This perspective would suggest that human autonomy is not absolute because human beings do not live in a vacuum; they necessarily exist in relationship with others. Similarly, authority is not an end in itself. It is exercised — or should be — in the service of the commonwealth that sustains individuality, interpersonal relationships and the common life and concerns of the community. Authority and autonomy are seen as existing in tension. But that tension must be creative. Otherwise, the distrust and pessimism that now permeate large parts of our society will likely worsen.

As for the second point, allow me to quote from Robert Bellah.

> For a long time our society has held together, even in times
> of rapid change, by a religious center that sought to reconcile

the claim of community and individuality. Rejecting both chaotic openness and authoritarian closure, representatives of this cultural center defended tradition . . . but not traditionalism. They sought to reappropriate the past in light of the present, mindful of the distortions that mar the past of every tradition.

I am inclined to agree with Bellah on this point. I also agree with his assertion that the voice of religion in the United States "seems less evident in our public life and less articulate about where we should be heading than was the case in the past." One reason for this silence is the religious cultural wars I just mentioned. I wonder, though, whether there is not another, more profound reason. Could it be that as religious professionals we have been co-opted by the cultural malaise that surrounds us and have begun to doubt whether our religious traditions have anything of real significance to offer the contemporary world? Have we been so assimilated that we have forgotten the distinctive transforming elements of our Judeo-Christian heritage? Or have we simply grown tired of the never-ending dialogue within our religious communities and with society at large?

Whatever the reason, I believe that it is time for us, as religious leaders, to consider how we can become more active participants as our society struggles with the issues of autonomy and authority. Let us both research our common heritage and our distinctive traditions and listen attentively to the signs of the times that speak to us of God's grace. Let us talk, pray, celebrate and work with each other for the betterment of all.

VISIT TO YAD VASHEM

ON MARCH 20, 1995, CARDINAL BERNARDIN LED A DELEGATION OF CATHOLICS AND JEWS ON A VISIT TO THE MIDDLE EAST. THE DIALOGUE VISIT WAS THE FIRST TIME A CARDINAL OF THE CATHOLIC CHURCH EVER TRAVELED TO THE HOLY LAND AS PART OF AN INTERFAITH DELEGATION. THE DELEGATION VISITED THE STATE OF ISRAEL, THE WEST BANK AND GAZA. THEY MET WITH RELIGIOUS, COMMUNAL AND POLITICAL LEADERS IN THE ISRAELI AND PALESTINIAN COMMUNITIES.

As we Christians and Jews gather here this morning at this place of memory, the words of Pope John Paul II, spoken on the occasion of the fiftieth anniversary of the liberation of Auschwitz-Birkenau, challenge each of us. The holy father described the Holocaust as a time marked by "a darkening of reason, conscience and the heart." Truly it was a period in history when humankind lost all sense of the value of human life. How else are we to explain, in particular, the loss of over one million children who are now so movingly remembered at this memorial site? Each of us stands in the presence of the ashes of camp victims in humble reverence, with a sense of pain for some and a sense of remorse and responsibility for others.

We cannot be satisfied, however, with only remembering, as sacred a duty as that remains. We need to hear Pope John Paul II's plea for the development of fraternal solidarity between Christians and, as he said in his remarks for the Auschwitz-Birkenau commemoration, "those who bear the indelible mark of these tragedies." This new sense of solidarity must enable us to stand together against all continuing manifestations of anti-Semitism, ethnic hatred and genocide. As Elie Wiesel has insisted, ultimately we continue to remember the victims by our protest against all contemporary forms of death from violence, social hatred and injustice. May the names of the victims of the Shoah, as well as those of the righteous, remain forever blessed. Amen.

"ANTI-SEMITISM: THE HISTORICAL LEGACY AND CONTINUING CHALLENGE FOR CHRISTIANS"

HEBREW UNIVERSITY

THE ESSENCE OF THE DIALOGUE VISIT IS FOUND IN THIS ADDRESS AT HEBREW UNIVERSITY. CARDINAL BERNARDIN RECEIVED THE HONORARY FELLOWSHIP OF THE UNIVERSITY AND DELIVERED THIS ADDRESS IN THE SENATE HALL ON MOUNT SCOPUS.

LADIES and gentlemen, I am greatly honored by your conferral on me of the Honorary Fellowship of the Hebrew University of Jerusalem. It is a humbling experience, indeed, to receive such an honor from this distinguished scholarly community. I am also very grateful for this opportunity to address you on the subject of anti-Semitism from a Catholic point of view.

In recent years the Catholic Church has undertaken important efforts to acknowledge guilt for the legacy of anti-Semitism and to repudiate as sinful any remaining vestiges of that legacy in its contemporary teaching and practice. In 1989, the Pontifical Commission for Peace and Justice issued a strong declaration on racism, which had an international impact. The document, entitled *The Church and Racism: Towards a More Fraternal Society,* insisted that "harboring racist thoughts and entertaining racist attitudes is a sin" (24).[1] And it clearly included anti-Semitism on its list of continuing manifestations of racist ideologies that are to be regarded as sinful. In point of fact, *The Church and Racism* calls anti-Semitism "the most tragic form that racist ideology has assumed in our century" and warns that certain forms of anti-Zionism, while not of the same order, often serve as a screen for anti-Semitism, feeding on it and leading to it (15).[2]

Pope John Paul II has taken up the challenge to anti-Semitism put forth by the Pontifical Commission on several occasions in recent years. During a visit to Hungary in 1991, conscious of the post-Communist era resurgence of anti-Semitism in certain parts of Central and Eastern Europe, the pope spoke of the urgent task of repentance and reconciliation:

> In face of a risk of a resurgence and spread of anti-Semitic feelings, attitudes and initiatives, of which certain disquieting signs are to be seen today and of which we have experienced the most frightful results in the past, we must teach consciences to consider anti-Semitism, and all forms of racism, as sins against God and humanity.[3]

And in his current book, *Crossing the Threshold of Hope,* the holy father repeats this theme as he calls anti-Semitism "a great sin against humanity."[4]

In my address this afternoon I will reflect on how we can work to eradicate the evil of anti-Semitism from our midst. This is not an easy task; it is one to which I have been dedicated for many years. My reflections will have four parts: (1) the roots of anti-Semitism in Christian history, (2) contemporary developments in Catholic theology, (3) thoughts on the relationship between anti-Semitism and Nazism, and (4) actions that can be taken to ensure that anti-Semitism is not part of the future.

ORIGINS OF ANTI-SEMITISM

Allow me to explore briefly some of the reasons why anti-Semitism has been part of Christian life. It is important that we do this because anti-Semitism has deep roots in Christian history, which go back to the earliest days of the church. In fact, as Father Edward Flannery has shown in his classic work on anti-Semitism, *The Anguish of the Jews,*[5] the early Christian community inherited a cultural tradition from the Graeco-Roman civilization that included a prejudicial outlook toward Jews. Jews were disliked in pre-Christian Greece and Rome for their general unwillingness to conform to prevailing social mores. It is regrettable that this long history of anti-Semitism in a Christian context has been virtually eliminated from our history texts and other educational materials. Inclusion of this history, as painful as it is for us to hear today, is a necessary requirement for authentic reconciliation between Christians and Jews in our time.

In addition, there were many other factors that likely contributed to the growth of anti-Jewish feelings among Christians in the first centuries of the church's existence. For one, the overwhelming number of early Christians came from Graeco-Roman communities with little personal acquaintance with Jews and Judaism. We now know from scholars dealing with early Christianity, such as Robert Wilken[6] and Anthony Saldarini,[7] that the final break between Judaism and Christianity was a far more gradual process than we once imagined, extending into the third and fourth centuries in some areas of the East. Nevertheless, the formative influence of Jewish Christianity on the church as a whole declined rapidly after the pivotal decision reached by Paul and the representatives of the Jerusalem church at what is often called the Council of Jerusalem. This resulted in the loss of any countervailing positive identification with Jews and their religious heritage that could overcome the new converts' inbred cultural prejudices. This tendency toward separation from anything Jewish was further enhanced by the desire to avoid any linkage between the church and the Jewish community after the disastrous Jewish revolt against the Roman imperial authorities (66–70 CE) that, besides the destruction of the Temple in Jerusalem, generated continued postwar pressure and retribution by Rome against the Jewish community.

Another factor contributing to the emergence of anti-Semitism in early Christianity may be the image of Jews that emerges from the New Testament itself. There are texts that remain open to anti-Judaic interpretation, and there is ample evidence that such interpretations emerged in the first centuries of Christian history.

Negative attitudes toward Jews in the New Testament were only the beginning of difficulties for the Jewish community. Unfortunately, there soon developed within the teachings of the early fathers of the church a strong tendency to regard Jews as entirely displaced from the covenantal relationship because of their unwillingness to accept Jesus as the Messiah, despite the clear teaching to the contrary on the part of Saint Paul in Romans 9 – 11, which served as a basis for the Second Vatican Council's renewed constructive theology of the Christian-Jewish relationship.

This belief, that the Jews had been totally rejected by God and replaced in the covenantal relationship by the "New Israel," led to the emergence of another widespread doctrine in patristic writings. I have in mind the so-called "perpetual wandering" theology that consigned Jews to a condition of permanent statelessness as a consequence of their displacement from the covenant as a punishment for murdering the Messiah. This condition of being permanently displaced persons was meant as an enduring sign of Jewish sinfulness and as a warning to others of what they could expect if they, too, failed to accept Christ. This theology became so deep-seated in popular culture that even a familiar houseplant — the "wandering Jew" — took on its name.

We can illustrate this theology of "perpetual wandering" with references from certain central figures in the patristic era. Eusebius of Caesarea (c. 265 – 339 CE), for example, speaks of how the royal metropolis of the Jews would be destroyed by fire and the city would become inhabited no longer by Jews "but by races of other stock, while they [the Jews] would be dispersed among the Gentiles throughout the whole world with never a hope of any cessation of evil or breathing space from troubles."[8] Saint Cyprian of Carthage (c. 210 – 258 CE), relying on various prophetic texts that suggest desolation and exile as a consequence of sin, envisioned Israel as having entered its final state of desolation and exile. Following in the same vein, Saint Hippolytus of Rome, who was born around 170 CE, insisted that, unlike the exilic experiences suffered by the Jews at the hands of the Egyptians and the Babylonians in earlier times, the post-biblical exile would continue throughout the course of human history. In the East, Saint John Chrysostom (344 – 407 CE) clearly linked the now permanent exilic condition of the Jews with the "killing of Christ." And Saint Augustine of Hippo (354 – 430 CE) in his classic work, *City of God,* speaks several times of the Jews as having "their back bend down always."

While the patristic writings were far more than an extended anti-Jewish treatise, Christians cannot ignore this "shadow side" of patristic theology, which in other aspects remains a continuing source of profound spiritual enrichment. Jews are very well aware of the "shadow side" of this theology; unfortunately, Christians generally are not. It has been omitted from basic Christian texts far too often. Yet, we cannot understand the treatment of Jews in subsequent centuries without some grasp of this theology. The history to which it gave rise is replete with persistent forms of social and religious discrimination and persecution, which brought on the Jewish community continual humiliation as well as political and civil inequality. On occasion, this further degenerated into outright physical suffering and even death, especially in such periods as that of the Crusades.

This legacy of anti-Semitism, with its profoundly negative social consequences for Jews as individuals and for the Jewish community as a whole, remained the dominant social pattern in Western Christian lands until the twentieth century. While we can point to some notable breaks in this pattern in such countries as Spain and Poland, as well as for individual Jews in the liberal democracies created in parts of Europe and North America, the respite was sometimes short-lived and, as in the case of Spain, followed by even more flagrant forms of attack on the Jewish community.

At the dawn of the twentieth century the theology of perpetual divine judgment on Jewish people did not vanish overnight. Rather, it continued to exercise a decisive role in shaping Catholicism's initial reactions, for example, to the proposal for restoring a Jewish national homeland in Palestine. It also was of central importance in shaping popular Christian attitudes toward the Nazis and their stated goal of eliminating all Jews from Europe and beyond through deliberate extermination. While I will return to this question of classical anti-Semitism and its role during that period, there is little doubt that this persistent tradition provided an indispensable seedbed for the Nazis' ability to succeed as far as they did in their master plan. They would not have secured the popular support they enjoyed were it not for the continuing influence of traditional Christian anti-Semitism on the masses of baptized believers in Europe.

Both Father Edward Flannery and the late Professor Uriel Tal have emphasized the significant impact of classical Christian anti-Semitism on the development of Nazism, despite their shared conviction that the philosophy of the Third Reich resulted primarily from distinctly modern forces. Flannery argues that the architects of the Shoah found their Jewish targets well-primed for the formulation of their racist theories:

> The degraded state of the Jews, brought about by centuries of opprobrium and oppression, gave support to the invidious comparisons with which the racists built their theories. And in their evil design, they were able to draw moral support from traditional views of Jews and Judaism.[9]

Professor Tal offered an analysis very similar to that of Father Flannery's in this regard. He insisted that Nazi racial anti-Semitism was not totally original when subjected to careful scrutiny. Rather, traditional Christian stereotypes of Jews and Judaism were clothed in new pseudoscientific jargon and applied to specific historical realities of the period. Tal insisted that racial anti-Semitism and the subsequent Nazi movement were not the result of mass hysteria or the work of single propagandists. The racial anti-Semites, despite their antagonism toward traditional Christianity, learned much from it, and succeeded in producing a well-prepared, systematic ideology with a logic of its own that reached its culmination in the Third Reich.[10]

CONTEMPORARY DEVELOPMENTS

Having traced the development of anti-Semitism within Christianity, we can turn to contemporary developments. In the three decades or so since the beginning of the Second Vatican Council, the negative theology of the Jewish people has lost its theological foundations. In chapter four of *Nostra Aetate,* the Council clearly asserted that there never existed a valid basis either for the charge of collective guilt against the Jewish community for supposedly "murdering the Messiah" or for the consequent theology of permanent Jewish suffering and displacement. With its positive affirmation of continued covenantal inclusion on the part of the Jewish people after the coming of Christ Jesus, following Saint Paul in Romans 9 – 11, the Council permanently removed all basis for the long-held "perpetual wandering" theology and the social deprivation and suffering that flowed from it.

The Second Vatican Council's removal of the classical "displacement/ perpetual wandering" theology from contemporary Catholic catechesis has been enhanced in subsequent documents from the Holy See and Pope John Paul ii. The Holy See's 1985 *Notes on the Correct Way to Present the Jews and Judaism in Preaching and Catechesis in the Roman Catholic Church,* issued to commemorate the twentieth anniversary of *Nostra Aetate,* make two very important constructive affirmations, especially when these are set over against the history of Catholicism's traditional approach to the question of Jewish existence. Both occur in paragraph 25 where the *Notes* maintain that "the history of Israel did not end in 70 AD [i.e., with the destruction of the Jerusalem Temple by the Romans]. . . . It continued, especially in a numerous Diaspora which allowed Israel to carry to the whole world a witness . . . while preserving the memory of the land of their forefathers at the heart of their hope" and, subsequently, that "the permanence of Israel (while so many ancient peoples have disappeared without a trace) is a historic fact and a sign to be interpreted within God's design." Both these statements clearly repudiate a "displacement" theology.

Pope John Paul II, who has contributed significantly to the development of the church's new theological outlook on Jews and Judaism,[11] wrote the following in his 1984 statement *Redemptionis Anno:*

> For the Jewish people who live in the State of Israel and who preserve in that land such precious testimonies of their history and their faith, we must ask for the desired security and due tranquillity that is the prerogative of every nation and condition of life and of progress of every society.[12]

This statement clearly exhibits on the part of the holy father a sense of the deep intertwining of faith and continued attachment to the land on the part of the Jewish people, a sense that further draws out the profound implications of the renewed theology of the Christian-Jewish relationship put forth by the Second Vatican Council.

Two recent documents of the Holy See further seal the coffin of the biblically unfounded "displacement" theology. The first is the text of the new *Catechism of the Catholic Church,* which reaffirms the two major points on which the Council built its new theological approach to the Jewish people. In paragraph 597 the *Catechism* rejects any idea that all Jews then or now can be charged with the responsibility for Jesus' death. It reminds Christians that their sins were largely the reason why Jesus died on the cross. And paragraph 849 speaks of the distinctiveness of Jewish faith as an authentic response to God's original revelation and underlines the permanence of the divine promise made to the people Israel.[13]

The second document is the *Holy See-Israeli Accords.* While this is fundamentally a political document that develops a framework for dealing with concrete issues, it has an underlying theological significance as well. Mindful of the long-standing theological approach to Jewish political sovereignty on the part of the Catholic tradition, the preamble to the *Accords* has set this essentially political document within the overall context of the process of Catholic-Jewish reconciliation underway in the church since the Second Vatican Council:

> . . . aware of the unique nature of the relationship between the Catholic Church and the Jewish people, and the historic process of reconciliation and growth in mutual understanding and friendship between Catholics and Jews.

So reads the opening part of the *Accords.*

We note that article 2 of the *Accords* contains a very strong and unequivocal condemnation by the Holy See of "hatred, persecution and all manifestations of anti-Semitism directed against the Jewish people and individual Jews." I welcome this forthright statement as well as the accompanying pledge by the Holy See and the State of Israel to cooperate in every possible way "in combating all forms of anti-Semitism and all kinds of racism and of religious intolerance, and in promoting mutual understanding among nations, tolerance among communities, and respect for human life and dignity" (1).

This statement makes concrete the renewed theological vision of the Christian-Jewish relationship developed at the Second Vatican Council. It also solidifies the notion that forms of racism, including anti-Semitism, are fundamentally sinful, as the 1989 Holy See document and the papal statements I cited earlier make clear.

The Holy See's action in formally recognizing Israel through the *Accords* represents a final seal on the process begun at the Second Vatican Council to rid Catholicism of all vestiges of "displacement theology" and the implied notion of perpetual Jewish homelessness. The *Accords* represent the Catholic Church's full and final acknowledgment of Jews as a people, not merely as individuals. I recognize that for the vast majority of Jews, Israel signifies their ultimate tie to Jewish peoplehood, their central point of self-identity. And, as the Holy See's 1974 guidelines on Catholic-Jewish relations pointed out, authentic dialogue requires that all partners come to understand and respect one another as they define themselves. As Arthur Hertzberg has shown very well in his classic work, *The French Enlightenment and the Jews*,[14] even democratic societies that were prepared to grant Jews a measure of personal freedom and political rights were unable to accept the idea of Jewish peoplehood.

Until now I have been speaking of developments that have already occurred. As we all know, much more needs to be done. In particular, there is need for continued scholarship and theological reflection, especially with regard to what many consider to be problematic New Testament texts. While it is not certain that any of these texts themselves can be legitimately termed "anti-Semitic," or even "anti-Judaic," scholars differ significantly on this point and will likely do so for the foreseeable future. I am aware that some scholars doing important research on this topic, including people here in Jerusalem, such as Malcolm Lowe, believe the problem is essentially one of mistranslation. Others interpret it primarily as an internal Jewish polemic, which was not an uncommon phenomenon in the period, as we know from certain Jewish documents, the Talmud included.[15] Retranslation (where scholarly consensus can be achieved) and reinterpretation certainly are to be included among the goals we pursue in the effort at eradicating anti-Semitism. But at this point, the requisite scholarly consensus on the especially problematic passages appears a long way off.

In the interim, as we await a scholarly resolution of the question of anti-Semitism in the New Testament, I would strongly urge that the church adopt a pastoral approach. Father Raymond Brown, a renowned Catholic scholar on the Gospel of John, has suggested the basis of such a pastoral approach, at least with respect to the Fourth Gospel, which is generally considered among the most problematic of all New Testament books in its outlook toward Jews and Judaism. In commenting on John's use of the term, "the Jews," Brown expresses his conviction that, by deliberately using this generic term (where other gospel writers refer to the Jewish authorities or the various Second Temple Jewish parties), John meant to extend to the synagogue of his own day blame that an earlier tradition had attributed to the Jewish authorities. Although John was not the first to engage in such extension, he is the most insistent New Testament author in this regard. Brown attributes this process in John to the persecution that Christians were experiencing during that time at the hands of the synagogue authorities. Jews who professed Jesus to be the Messiah had been officially expelled from Judaism, thus making them vulnerable to Roman investigation and punishment. Jews were tolerated by Rome, but who were these Christians whom the Jews disclaimed?

Father Brown maintains that this teaching of John about the Jews, which resulted from the historical conflict between church and synagogue in the latter part of the first century CE, can no longer be taught as authentic doctrine or used as catechesis by contemporary Christianity. This is the key pastoral point. Christians today must come to see that such teachings, while an acknowledged part of their biblical heritage, can no longer be regarded as definitive teaching in light of our improved understanding of developments in the relationship between early Christianity and the Jewish community of the time. As Brown says in his book, *The Community of the Beloved Disciple,* "It would be incredible for a twentieth-century Christian to share or justify the Johannine contention that 'the Jews' are the children of the Devil, an affirmation which is placed on the lips of Jesus (John 8:44)."[16]

Negative passages such as these must be reevaluated in light of the Second Vatican Council's strong affirmation in its *Declaration on the Relation of the Church to Non-Christian Religions (Nostra Aetate)* that Jews remain a covenanted people, revered by God. The teaching of recent popes has also emphasized this. Pope John Paul II, in particular, has often highlighted the intimate bond that exists between Jews and Christians who are united in one ongoing covenant.

NAZISM AND ANTI-SEMITISM

I would now like to return to the issue of Nazism and anti-Semitism, which continues to elicit considerable discussion today. I know it remains an important area of concern for this university, especially the Sassoon International Center for the Study of Anti-Semitism directed by Professor Yehuda Bauer. I am likewise aware of the many outstanding contributions made to our understanding of the Shoah by other members of your faculty, including Professors Israel Gutman and Emil Fackenheim.

During the past several decades, scholars throughout the world have advanced various perspectives on the relationship between the rise of Nazism and classical Christian hatred of the Jews. Some draw virtually a straight line from classical Christian thought regarding the Jewish people to the emergence of the Shoah. They point, for example, to Hitler's often-quoted remark to church leaders, who came to see him to protest his treatment of Jews, that he was merely putting into practice what the Christian churches had preached for nearly 2,000 years. These perspectives also highlight the close similarity between much of Nazi anti-Jewish legislation and laws against Jews in earlier Christian-dominated societies.

As I have already pointed out, relying on the research of Father Flannery and the late Professor Tal, there is little doubt that classical Christian presentations of Jews and Judaism were a central factor in generating popular support for the Nazi endeavor, along with economic greed, religious and political nationalism, and ordinary human fear. For many baptized Christians, traditional Christian beliefs about Jews and Judaism constituted the primary motivation for their support, active or tacit, of the Nazi movement. Some even went so far as to define the Nazi struggle against the Jews in explicitly religious and theological terms. In the church today, we must not minimize the extent of Christian collaboration with Hitler and his associates. It remains a profound moral challenge that we must continue to confront for our own integrity as a religious community.

Nevertheless, in the final analysis, I must side with the perspective of those scholars such as Yosef Yerushalmi who have insisted that "the Holocaust was the work of a thoroughly modern, neopagan state," not merely a "transformed" medieval anti-Semitism rooted in Christian teachings.[17] The Shoah cannot be seen as simply the final and most gruesome chapter in the long history of Christian anti-Semitism. Rather, it was a plan for the mass destruction of human lives, supposedly undertaken in the name of "healing" humanity, as the psychologist Robert J. Lifton has put it, rooted in modern theories of inherent biological and racial inferiority, coupled with the escalation of bureaucratic and technological capacities. At its depths, it was profoundly as anti-Christian as it was anti-Jewish, evidenced by the fact that at least one of its theoreticians attempted to rewrite the New Testament totally based on Nazi concepts. It coalesced several important modern strains of thought into its master plan for human extermination.

To bring this plan to realization required, as the Nazis envisioned it, the elimination of the "dregs" of society. These they defined as first and foremost the Jewish people, but the category also was extended to embrace the disabled, gypsies, the Polish leadership, homosexuals and certain other designated groups. Proper distinctions need to be maintained between the wholesale attack on the Jewish people, for whom there was absolutely no escape from Nazi fury, and the others subjected to systematic Nazi attack. But there is also a linkage with the victimization of these other groups whose suffering and death were integral, not peripheral, to the overall Nazi plan. This is what makes the Holocaust *sui generis,* even though the fate of its primary victims, the Jews, had important ties to classical Christian teachings.

FUTURE POSSIBILITIES

Let us turn now from the horrors of the past to the possibilities of the future. Confronting the legacy of anti-Semitism will not prove easy, but confront it we must. Allow me to discuss several ways in which this can be done.

DISCUSS HONESTLY THE HISTORY OF ANTI-JUDAISM IN CATHOLICISM. The history of anti-Semitism and of anti-Judaic theology must be restored to our

Catholic teaching materials. Innocence or ignorance is not a pathway to authentic virtue in this regard; courageous honesty is. In our religious education programs we should be prepared to tell the full story of the church's treatment of Jews over the centuries, ending with a rejection of the shadow side of that history and theology at the Second Vatican Council. We can and should highlight moments of relative tranquillity and constructive interaction when they occurred in such countries as Poland, Spain and the United States, but these stories should never obscure the more pronounced history of hostility and subjection.

UNDERSTAND THE HOLOCAUST. We also need an integral understanding of the Holocaust. In developing such an understanding, we have a responsibility to speak against unwarranted and generalized accusations directed at the church and church leaders. We need to reemphasize the protest statements and oppositional actions of Christian leaders and grassroots groups and individuals: The Fulda Declaration of the German Catholic Bishops, the Barmen Declaration of the Confessing Church (Lutheran) in Germany, the encyclical letter *Mit Brennender Sorge* issued in German by Pope Pius XI, the efforts of Archbishops Angelo Roncalli and Angelo Rotta, the Zegota movement in Poland, the many Catholic women religious whose communities hid Jews, the men and women of Le Chambon in France, Jan Karski of the Polish government-in-exile, the Austrian peasant Franz Jagerstatter — I could go on. To be sure, there were not enough. But these Christians preserved a measure of moral integrity in the church during these years of Nazi darkness.

Nevertheless, the witness of these courageous Christian leaders, groups and individuals should never be used to argue against the need for a full scrutiny of church activities by reputable scholars. We must be prepared to deal honestly and candidly with the genuine failures of some in the Christian churches during that critical period. To that end, I would repeat what I first said in my keynote address to those attending the meeting of the International Catholic-Jewish Liaison Committee held in Baltimore in May 1992. The Catholic Church must be prepared to submit its World War II record to a thorough scrutiny by respected scholars. The detailed investigation of diocesan records from the Nazi era undertaken that same year in Lyons, France, with the support of the cardinal archbishop, is a fine example of what I have in mind. Such efforts should avoid broad generalizations but instead focus in depth on specific geographic regions, as do, for example, the recent work on Poland by Dr. Ronald Modras[10] here at this university and the symposium papers collected by Professors Otto Dov Kulka and Paul Mendes-Flohr in the volume *Judaism and Christianity Under the Impact of National Socialism.*[19]

MAKE THE HOLOCAUST A SALIENT FEATURE OF CATHOLIC EDUCATION. Education about the Holocaust should become a prominent feature in Catholic education at every level. To assist in realizing this goal, Seton Hill College near Pittsburgh has established a program explicitly designed for Catholic teachers that works closely with both Yad Vashem and the U.S. Holocaust Memorial Museum. And in Chicago, I have instructed the archdiocesan school system to comply with the state mandate on Holocaust education even though it does not technically apply to our institutions.

DEVELOP A POSITIVE THEOLOGY OF RECONCILIATION AND BONDING. But we must go beyond merely teaching the failures of the past, as crucial as that task remains. *Nostra Aetate* and subsequent documents from the Holy See, as well as Pope John Paul II, have not merely removed the classical prejudices against Jews and Judaism from Catholic teaching. They have laid out the basis for a positive theology of reconciliation and bonding. This, too, must become part of our current effort in education.

In fact, several studies on Catholic religion materials undertaken by Sister Rose Thering at Saint Louis University,[20] Dr. Eugene J. Fisher at New York University,[21] and most recently, Dr. Philip Cunningham at Boston College,[22] have shown a steady development in the presentation of the Christian-Jewish relationship, from one marked by classical stereotypes to one focused on the bonding of Christians and Jews within the one covenanted family. Not all problems have been resolved, but the progress has been remarkable. In this connection, I wish to add that it is my hope that, at the same time as we seek to develop a positive Christian understanding, Jewish educators will also be able to rethink the Jewish community's understanding of its relationship with the church.

FOCUS ON THE LITURGY AND PREACHING. Liturgy and preaching are additional areas that require continued attention by the church. In 1988, the U.S. Bishops' Committee on the Liturgy released a set of guidelines for the presentation of Jews and Judaism in Catholic preaching.[23] They offer directions for implementing the vision of *Nostra Aetate* and subsequent documents of the Holy See in the church's ministry of the word during the various liturgical seasons. Especially highlighted are the seasons of Lent/Holy Week and Easter, whose texts can serve to reinforce classical Christian stereotypes of Jews and Judaism if not interpreted carefully. The great challenge of these liturgical seasons is that they become times of reconciliation between Jews and Christians rather than conflict and division, as they were in past centuries. Christians need to recognize their profound bonds with the Jewish people during these central periods of the liturgical year in accord with the vision expressed by the Second Vatican Council and Pope John Paul II.

PRAY FOR PEOPLE OF VISION AND RECONCILIATION. But education and preaching will not prove completely effective unless we also have women and men of vision and reconciliation who embody the new spirit of Jewish-Christian bonding. I especially honor all those Christians in this land who have embodied *Nostra Aetate* in their lives and work for many years. In a particular way, I would like to congratulate Father Marcel Dubois of the Dominican community on this his seventy-fifth birthday. Through his many years of service as a member of the faculty here at Hebrew University, and through his painstaking efforts as a consultant to the Holy See's Commission for Religious Relations with the Jews, he has helped to shape the face of contemporary Catholic-Jewish relations.

FOSTER A TRUE SPIRIT OF REPENTANCE. Above all, in light of the history of anti-Semitism and the Holocaust, the church needs to engage in public repentance. As I remembered the six million Jewish victims of the Shoah this morning at Yad Vashem, I was reminded of the holy father's call on the Christian community, in preparation for the celebration of the third millennium of Christianity, to foster a genuine spirit of repentance for "the acquiescence given, especially in certain centuries, to intolerance and even the use of violence in the service of truth." The church, he added, bears an obligation "to express profound regret for the weaknesses of so many of her sons and daughters who sullied her face, preventing her from fully mirroring the image of her crucified Lord, the supreme witness of patient love and of humble meekness."[24]

It is in this spirit that my brother bishops in Germany, on the occasion of the fiftieth anniversary of the liberation of Auschwitz-Birkenau, issued a statement in which they took responsibility for the failure of the Catholic community during the Shoah. While mindful of the exemplary behavior of certain individuals and groups, some of whom I have already named, the German bishops acknowledge that "Christians did not offer due resistance to racial anti-Semitism. Many times there was failure and guilt among Catholics." And they go on to add a point with which I wholeheartedly concur: "The practical sincerity of our will of renewal is also linked to the confession of this guilt and the willingness to painfully learn from this history of guilt."[25]

My friends, as I draw these reflections to a close, I cannot help but reflect on the fact that I have spoken to an often tragic past in the history of Christian-Jewish relations here in this city of Jerusalem, which both of our religious traditions have always envisioned as ultimately a city of peace. In this context, let me lift up the powerful words of the Nobel Prize winners, including Elie Wiesel, who gathered with President Lech Walesa of Poland at the fiftieth anniversary commemoration of Auschwitz-Birkenau. "To the victims of this crime, we owe a commitment to the memory both of their death and their life," they proclaimed in their appeal to the nations of the world. And they continued:

Their heritage must help mankind to build faith in a future free from racism, hatred and anti-Semitism. . . . In equal measure, we owe a duty to the living to safeguard peace, tolerance and fundamental human rights. . . . Let instruments of governance be created which will guarantee the peaceful resolution of all conflicts.

As we reflect today on the legacy of anti-Semitism, Jews and Christians need to recommit themselves to counter its disturbing resurgence in North America, Latin America and Europe, together with other forms of racism and intergroup violence. Here in Jerusalem, where the vision of peace may seem very far off at times, there is a need to find ways to cooperate for the development of a genuine peace among Christians, Jews, and Muslims, Arabs and Israelis, that includes living faith communities with full opportunity for economic justice. Jerusalem, my brothers and sisters, cannot become a mere monument to peace. It must be a true city of living communities of peace, a true *Neve Shalom.* That is my prayer. That is my hope. That is my dream!

[1] Pontifical Commission for Peace and Justice. *The Church and Racism: Towards a More Fraternal Society.* Washington, D.C.: U.S. Catholic Conference, 1988, 34 (#24).

[2] *The Church and Racism,* 23 (#15).

[3] Pope John Paul II. "The Sinfulness of Anti-Semitism," *Origins* 23:13 (September 5, 1991), 204.

[4] Pope John Paul II. *Crossing the Threshold of Hope,* ed. by Vittorio Messori. New York: Alfred A. Knopf, 1994, 96.

[5] Edward Flannery. *The Anguish of the Jews.* Revised edition. New York/Mahwah: Paulist Press, 1985.

[6] Wayne A. Meeks and Robert L. Wilken. *Jews and Christians in Antioch in the First Four Centuries.* Missoula MT: Scholars Press, 1978; and Robert L. Wilken. *John Chrysostom and the Jews: Rhetoric and Reality in the Late 4th Century.* Berkeley: University of California Press, 1983.

[7] Anthony J. Saldarini. "Jews and Christians in the First Two Centuries: The Changing Paradigm," *Shofar* 10 (1992), 34.

[8] *Demonstration of the Gospel,* I, I.

[9] Edward Flannery. "Anti-Zionism and the Christian Psyche," *Journal of Ecumenical Studies,* 6:2 (Spring 1969), 174–75.

[10] Uriel Tal. *Christians and Jews in Germany: Religion, Politics and Ideology in the Second Reich, 1870–1914.* Ithaca NY: Cornell University Press, 1975, 305.

[11] Cf. Eugene J. Fisher and Leon Klenicki, eds. *John Paul II on Jews and Judaism.* Washington DC: U.S. Catholic Conference, 1987.

[12] Cf. *The Pope Speaks,* 29:3 (1984), 219–20.

[13] Cf. *Catechism of the Catholic Church.* Collegeville MN: The Liturgical Press, 1994, #597; #839.

[14] Arthur Hertzberg. *The French Enlightenment and the Jews: The Origins of Modern Anti-Semitism.* New York: Schocken, 1968.

[15] Cf. John T. Pawlikowski. "New Testament Anti-Semitism: Fact or Fable?" in Michael Curtis, ed. *Anti-Semitism in the Contemporary World.* Boulder and London: Westview Press, 1986, 107–27.

[16] Raymond Brown. *The Community of the Beloved Disciple.* New York: Paulist Press, 1979, 41–42. Cf. also "The Passion According to John: Chapters 18 and 19," *Worship* 49 (March 1975), 130–31.

[17] Yosef Hayim Yerushalmi. "Response to Rosemary Ruether," in Eva Fleischner, ed., *Auschwitz: Beginning of a New Era?* New York: KTAV, the Cathedral Church of Saint John the Divine and the Anti-Defamation League, 1977, 103.

[18] Cf. Ronald Modras. *The Catholic Church and Anti-Semitism in Poland, 1933–1939.* Chur, Switzerland: Harwood Academic Publishers, 1994.

[19] Otto Dov Kulka and Paul R. Mendes-Flohr, eds. *Judaism and Christianity Under the Impact of National Socialism.* Jerusalem: The Historical Society of Israel and the Zalman Shazar Center for Jewish History, 1987.

[20] For a description and analysis of the Thering study, cf. John T. Pawlikowski, osm. *Catechetics & Prejudice: How Catholic Teaching Materials View Jews, Protestants and Racial Minorities.* New York/Paramus/Toronto: Paulist Press, 1973.

[21] Eugene J. Fisher. *Faith Without Prejudice: Rebuilding Christian Attitudes Toward Judaism.* Revised and expanded edition. New York: The American Interfaith Institute and Crossroad, 1993.

[22] Philip A. Cunningham. *Education for Shalom: Religion Textbooks and the Enhancement of the Catholic and Jewish Relationship.* Collegeville MN: The Liturgical Press, 1995.

[23] U.S. Catholic Bishops' Committee on the Liturgy. *God's Mercy Endures Forever: Guidelines on the Presentation of Jews and Judaism in Catholic Preaching.* Washington DC: U.S. Catholic Conference, 1988.

[24] Pope John Paul II. Apostolic letter, "As the Third Millennium Draws Near," *Origins* 24:24 (November 24, 1994), 411.

[25] "Statement of the German Bishops on the Occasion of the 50th Anniversary of the Liberation of the Extermination Camp of Auschwitz," January 27, 1995, 1–2.

CHURCH OF THE HOLY SEPULCHRE

PART OF THE DIALOGUE VISIT WAS A PILGRIMAGE BY THE CARDINAL AND THE CHRISTIAN
MEMBERS OF THE DELEGATION TO THE HOLY PLACES. THE CHURCH OF THE HOLY SEPULCHRE
IS BELIEVED TO COVER THE SITES OF CALVARY (WHERE THE CRUCIFIXION TOOK PLACE)
AND THE TOMB. THIS HOMILY WAS DELIVERED AT A MASS CELEBRATED AT THE SITE OF CALVARY.

THIS gospel reading is used throughout the universal Catholic Church on this Friday of the third week of Lent. But it is especially appropriate for our gathering this morning in this holiest of Christian sanctuaries, the Church of the Holy Sepulchre.

First, the event described in the gospel took place here in Jerusalem. Jesus was teaching in the Temple precincts, not very far from this holy place.

Second, the narrative describes one of the few discussions in the gospels in which Jesus and a scribe of the law have a fruitful dialogue and discover that they have much in common. That has also been the experience of the Chicago Catholic-Jewish Dialogue Group. While authentic dialogue is never easy, and there are many differences among us, mutual trust and honesty help us discover what we have in common.

Third, the dialogue in the gospel focuses on which is the most important law in the Torah. Jesus cites the Book of Deuteronomy, beginning with the Shema: "Hear, O Israel! The Lord our God is Lord alone! *Shema' yisra'el 'Adonay Elohenu, 'Adonay echad.* You shall love the Lord your God with all your heart, with all your soul, with all your mind and with all your strength." Then he immediately states the second most important commandment, quoting from the Book of Leviticus, "You shall love your neighbor as yourself."

My friends, we are in agreement about loving the one God, and we share that belief and commitment with Muslims, for whom Jerusalem is also a very holy city. But it is not easy to carry out the second commandment about loving our neighbor, and many interpretations of the law have sought to limit those whom we are to embrace as neighbors.

The question of who is our neighbor persists, at least below the surface of our consciousness. But through the Catholic-Jewish Dialogue Group, we have come to know one another as true neighbors. At the same time, from a Christian point of view, we cannot exclude anyone from the category of neighbor. That, of course, is much easier to say in theory than it is to carry out in practice. For Catholics, the neighbor includes our Orthodox brothers and sisters from whom we have been estranged for over a millennium, and our Jewish brothers and sisters with whom we have established a productive dialogue for nearly the first time in two millennia. And, for us, our neighbors include our Muslim brothers and sisters as well as Hindus and Buddhists. Indeed, no one is excluded. Unfortunately, our embrace is often not wide enough nor our commitment firm enough to love all our neighbors as we love ourselves. And for this, during this season of lenten repentance, we ask God's forgiveness and that of all our brothers and sisters throughout the world.

Jesus' teaching has remained credible for Christians through the centuries because he showed his love for his neighbors in so many ways — by healing the sick, consoling the bereaved, teaching the perplexed, welcoming the outcast. In Catholic teaching, he showed the depth of his great love for others by shedding his blood on the cross for the sins of the human family and by rising from the dead — both of which are remembered and celebrated in a very special way in this Church of the Holy Sepulchre in Jerusalem.

When we measure our lives against the standards of the Torah or Jesus' teaching, we always come up short. Many human pressures bombard us from all sides, alienating us from our neighbors and narrowing the scope of our concern and love.

For the differences and divisions that remain among us, and between us and the rest of our neighbors, let us listen again to the words of God spoken through the prophet Hosea and the psalmist: "Return to the Lord, your God . . . I am the Lord, your God: Hear my voice!"

My dear friends, my true neighbors, my beloved brothers and sisters, let us ask God to help us remove from our minds and hearts the obstacles that remain in our relationships so that we can more fully love God with all our being and our neighbor as ourself.

SAINT SAVIOR PARISH

SAINT SAVIOR IS THE ONLY PARISH CHURCH IN THE OLD CITY. AS A PARISH, ITS TERRITORY COVERS THE OLD CITY AND ALL OF EAST JERUSALEM. THE DELEGATION MET WITH THE PALESTINIAN CHRISTIANS THERE TO BETTER UNDERSTAND THEIR SITUATION. THEN THE CARDINAL CELEBRATED THE REGULARLY SCHEDULED SUNDAY MASS IN LATIN, ARABIC AND ENGLISH.

My dear brothers and sisters in the Lord, it is a great privilege to come to Jerusalem, the mother church of all the Christian communities throughout the world. I am very grateful for this opportunity to pray and visit with you. I bring you greetings from your brothers and sisters in the faith in the archdiocese of Chicago. They stand in solidarity with you.

Today's gospel recounts the wonderful parable about a loving father, a younger prodigal son and an older, hard-working son.

The younger son thought he was going to have a wonderful time! He would leave home with much money. He would be responsible for his own life. He thought he saw the light, but it turned out to be merely a faulty light bulb that burned out quickly. At first, he enjoyed himself, but then his fortunes changed quickly. He ended up feeding someone else's swine, and, even worse, they ate better than he did!

So, finally, he came to his senses and saw the light. And this time he faced reality. He decided to return home and humbly apologize to his father. He would ask his father for a job — not as a son but as a hired hand.

The father in the parable may seem a bit naive. Did he not know his son well enough to realize that he was irresponsible, that he would waste all his money? But the father in the parable symbolizes God — who lets us exercise the freedom he has given us but never abandons us.

When the father sees his son approaching in the distance, he runs out to greet him with an embrace. Before the son can finish his apology, his father announces that they will have a festive celebration because he wants to share with his family and friends the joy of the return of his son — not a hired hand!

The elder son, however, has rejected his younger brother. He is not happy to have him back home. We might well empathize with him; after all, from outward appearances, he had every reason to believe that his father favored his irresponsible brother. Moreover, the older son worked very hard and did not lead a dissolute life. He is very obedient. Yet, his father never hosted a party for him. So, he is hurt, angry and unhappy. He has no intention of going to his brother's party.

The elder son overlooks the fact that his father loves him, too. His father comes out and asks him to join the celebration. The father gently reminds him that the party is for his brother. Yes, his brother was lost, but now he is found. Yes, his brother was prodigal, but now he has seen the light. So, come to the celebration.

At that dramatic moment, the parable ends abruptly. Did the elder brother see the light and go to the party? Why did Jesus not bring the parable to a clearer conclusion? Because each of us who reads or hears the parable, and has identified with the elder son, must end the parable ourselves — by our own decisions, by the way we live our lives.

How do we act toward other members of our families, especially the ones who try to use us or outmaneuver us? How do we treat one another in our parish community? How do we act toward those who are different from ourselves? Do we recognize that all persons are the children of God — therefore, our brothers and sisters — and treat them accordingly?

It is much easier to ask such questions than to answer them in our hearts. The enormous divisions among the people of Jerusalem and the rest of the Holy Land have deep roots and will not easily be overcome. But we all know that peace and harmony is possible, and the road to peace is justice for all. Where injustice remains, where people are not treated fairly with all due respect for their human dignity, the path to peace will be long, indeed. And, ultimately, everyone will suffer even more.

My dear brothers and sisters, let us approach God, our heavenly Father, and ask him to give us all we need to walk in his ways — the ways of love, justice and peace.

MEETING WITH HONORABLE EHUD OLMERT, MAYOR OF JERUSALEM

❖

Mr. Mayor, thank you for receiving our Catholic-Jewish Dialogue Group from Chicago. Jerusalem is a unique city. Consequently, your role is quite different from that of other mayors throughout the world. We have come to express our respect for you.

As a Catholic bishop, I would also like to share with you the concerns of Christians regarding Jerusalem — not only the small community in Jerusalem itself but also Christians throughout the world. I have discussed these concerns with my Jewish friends who are with me.

As a Catholic bishop, it does not lie within my competence to address the political issues involving Jerusalem, which remain to be resolved through the peace process, namely the State of Israel and the Palestinians. We pray that there will be a successful and just resolution to that process.

As a churchman, however, I do have an interest in the religious status of Jerusalem, along with other Christian churches, as well as our Jewish and Muslim brothers and sisters. Jerusalem is the spiritual home of all Jews, Christians and Muslims. The resolution of the *religious* status of Jerusalem, therefore, is necessarily multilateral.

So, apart from the questions of sovereignty, which is a political question, the Catholic bishops of the United States, in their 1989 statement *Toward Peace in the Middle East,* called for a number of things that must be respected:

1) The sacred character of the holy city of the three Abrahamic faiths must be safeguarded.

2) Religious liberty should be ensured for individuals and groups, both in their private and public expression.

3) Religious communities must retain their acquired rights to shrines and holy places, as well as educational and social institutions.

4) There must be some kind of international guarantee protecting these rights.

Finally, Mr. Mayor, I believe with all my heart and soul, as do my colleagues here present, that the peace process offers the people of the Middle East, especially Israel, a truly historic opportunity. As we come to Jerusalem, we pray that this opportunity will be fully realized so that everyone may enjoy a just and lasting peace.

Cardinal Joseph Bernardin

WHERE DO WE GO FROM HERE?

In the 14 years that I have been archbishop of Chicago, I have spent a lot of time with my Jewish friends and colleagues. At our first meeting, when I spoke to the Chicago Board of Rabbis in 1982, I said to them, "I am Joseph, your brother." I sincerely believe this both from personal relationships and from theological truth. I have tried, as a brother, first to listen to my Jewish friends. From this I have deepened my appreciation for the Jewishness of Jesus, my Savior. And I have also been able to speak of the genuine love that the Catholic Church has for the Jewish community. If any of this has helped to heal past resentment and division, I am grateful.

When this project began, I asked to have the final word, to offer some perspective on "where we go from here." In one sense, the answer to that question is simple. We just keep going. On October 27, 1985, I presided at the twentieth anniversary of *Nostra Aetate*. By sharing that celebration with the Jewish community, I came to a new realization of the historic potential of the declaration of the Second Vatican Council. After that I resolved to seek every opportunity given to me as a local bishop to teach the message of *Nostra Aetate*.

We teach in a number of ways. A primary way is by our words. This book collects what I have said, and I will not try to summarize it here. But it has also been my conviction since I was the general secretary of the National Conference of Catholic Bishops, that another way we teach is by the programs and institutions we create. Ideas need some kind of mediating structure that both moves them out of the realm of idea and into the world of action. Structures are there to keep things moving. If there is a legacy of my teaching on *Nostra Aetate,* you will find it in the many joint programs that the archdiocesan Office for Ecumenical and Interreligious Affairs conducts with our partners, the American Jewish Committee, the Chicago Board of Rabbis, the Jewish Community Relations Council and the Spertus Institute of Jewish Studies. You will find it in the work of the Council of Religious Leaders of Metropolitan Chicago, which I am proud to have helped establish. And you will find it in two joint institutes: the Bernardin Center at Spertus and the Institute for Catholic-Jewish Education, which the archdiocese sponsors with the AJC and the Sisters of Sion. You will also find it in one relationship I have continued with Cincinnati in the R'fa-aye-nu Society.

Throughout my life as a bishop, I have learned over and over again that good relations need the support of an appropriate structure to insure implementation of ideas and continuity of effort. If I could offer one piece of advice on where you go from here it would be this: Continue to build the relationship between the two communities on friendship, and then be sure to support it with structures of implementation and continuity. Then just keep going.

I began this reflection with the question, "Where do *we* go from here?" Today, however, I find myself answering a different question, "Where do *you* go from here?" Just two weeks ago, I learned that the cancer I have been fighting for over a year has returned. It has spread to my liver and is inoperable. I have been told that it is terminal and that my life expectancy is a year or less. In light of that news, my prayer has been that I might use whatever time is left in a positive way; that is, a way that will be of benefit to the people I have been called to serve as archbishop of Chicago within the Catholic Church and in the wider community and to my own spiritual well-being.

When I traveled to Israel with leadership from the Catholic-Jewish Dialogue, one of the real blessings was for each of us to understand the religion of the other by sharing in sacred moments. I gained a profound interest in my Jewish friends' faith by our visit to Yad Vashem, in particular to the memorial to the children of the Holocaust. And I know that a similar experience happened for them accompanying me on the Way of the Cross. Both were special gifts.

I would like to end by sharing what I have said to my friends who have cancer and to the faithful of the archdiocese with whom I have celebrated the anointing of the sick. Because dialogue is sharing our faith experiences, I also want to share it with you. As a Christian, I believe that death is not the end, only a change. Death is the transition from earthly life to life eternal. We can look at death as an enemy or a friend. If we see it as an enemy, death causes anxiety. But if we see it as a friend, our attitude is totally different. In faith I want to say to you that I see my death as a friend.

As I conclude, I wish to tell you how much I love you and how much the Catholic-Jewish friendship has meant to me during the years I have been in Chicago. As we both go forward into the future God has planned for us, I want you to know that the dialogue has been a blessing for me. After 14 years I truly feel that you have accepted me as Joseph, your brother.

September 16, 1996

Mary Ellen Coombe and Sharon Morton

FOR REFLECTION AND DIALOGUE

CARDINAL BERNARDIN sees his reflections and actions as part of a great effort on the part of both the church and the Jewish people to foster mutual understanding and respect. He is always challenging us to find and take the next step.

Much depends on our willingness to meet each other in our neighborhoods and to grow in informed respect for one another even as we recognize our differences and problem areas. Cardinal Bernardin's efforts invite us to widen and deepen the dialogue. Thus we will enrich our own self-understanding and our understanding of the "other," leave stereotypes behind, and build bridges of trust and sensitivity.

These discussion questions are one way to begin or continue the dialogue. The questions pick up some of the main themes that Cardinal Bernardin has addressed over the years. We have tried to pose questions that can be addressed either by a group of Christians alone, a group of Jews alone, or a group of Jews and Christians together. There are enough questions for several different meetings. You may want to use them as they are presented in different sections or you may want to choose one question from each section.

In these questions, quotations from Cardinal Bernardin's addresses may be found in this book through the date on which the talk was given. The addresses are printed in chronological order.

THEOLOGICAL ISSUES

1. It was a *"monumental day in 1965 when . . . the Second Vatican Council, after careful deliberation, gave final approval to that document* [Nostra Aetate]*"* (September 28, 1988). What does this document say? What does it *not* say? Why is it so important for Jewish-Catholic relations? See the text of the document on page 189.

2. *". . . without deep immersion into the spirit and texts of the Hebrew Scriptures, Christians experience an emaciated version of Christian spirituality and know but a very truncated version of Jesus' full religious vision"* (September 28, 1988). Discuss.

3. Cardinal Bernardin speaks about the need for continued scholarship, especially with what many regard as "problematic texts" in the New Testament. What are some of these texts? In what ways are they problematic? Are there also problematic texts in the Hebrew Scriptures? How can our communities deal with these passages?

4. *". . . a dramatic shift in New Testament scholarship has begun to restore Jesus and his message to its original Jewish milieu"* (September 28, 1988). What do you know about Judaism in the first century? What can be done to make Christians aware of the Jewishness of Jesus? Why is this important? Does this make any difference to Jews?

5. Cardinal Bernardin discusses the emerging theology of the relationship between the church and the Jewish people. He says that theologians, church leaders and official documents are challenging the long-standing theology of displacement and working to replace it with a *"theology of covenantal partnership"* (September 28, 1988). How do you understand "displacement theology"? What are some of the ways in which this theology still finds expression? What are the building blocks for a new understanding of "covenantal partnership"? How can we begin to speak in a new way about the Jewish-Christian relationship? From a Catholic perspective? From a Jewish perspective?

ANTI-SEMITISM

1. Cardinal Bernardin traces the history of anti-Semitism in the church, which he says has *"deep roots . . . back to the earliest days of the church"* (March 23, 1995). And he says that *"there is little doubt that classical Christian presentations of Jews and Judaism were a central factor in generating popular support for the Nazi endeavor."* What do you think about this side of the church's history? Why do you think that the story of the church's treatment of the Jews over the centuries has been missing from many of the basic Catholic teaching resources?

2. The Holocaust *"was an attempt, Professor Emil Fackenheim has written, to wipe out the 'divine image' in history. 'The murder camp,' Fackenheim insists, 'was not an accidental by-product of the Nazi empire. It was its essence'"* (May 4, 1992). What questions does the Holocaust raise for Christians? For Jews? About God? About humanity? About institutions? What are the moral challenges for today?

3. Education at all levels about the Holocaust has increased over recent years. A recently passed Illinois law mandates Holocaust education in all public schools in that state. Cardinal Bernardin has asked that all Catholic schools do the same. How is learning about the Holocaust in the public arena and in a religious institution the same and how is it different?

4. In 1984, Cardinal Bernardin raises the issue of the "rhetoric of prejudice" and cites as examples remarks of Minister Farrakhan and Rabbi Kahane. What are more recent examples? What can Jews and Christians do together to oppose religious prejudice in all its forms?

5. *"Above all, in light of the history of anti-Semitism and the Holocaust, the church needs to engage in public repentance"* (March 23, 1995). What could public repentance of the church mean? For Christians? For Jews?

ISRAEL/PEACE

1. What is the connection to the land of Israel and to Jerusalem for Christians? For Jews? In what ways is this "connection" different or the same for Jews and Christians?

2. What are the concerns of the church about the situation in Israel? What are the concerns of the Jewish community? Do the American Catholic Church and the American Jewish community have a role to play in building peace in the Middle East? What is it?

3. For you, what was the important message of Cardinal Bernardin's trip to Israel with a delegation of Chicago Jews and Catholics? Do trips like this continue to be important? Why?

SOCIAL ISSUES

1. Where do our communities stand on the following issues? What are the values and teachings of our traditions that lead us to these positions? Sometimes we share common values and yet have diverse teachings and practices. Identify these areas and explore our different understandings.

   a) abortion
   b) euthanasia
   c) capital punishment
   d) the role of religion in the public arena
   e) the environment

   Add to this list.

2. Cardinal Bernardin is very quick to commend and recognize the Jewish community for its achievement and its commitment to social justice. He also addresses those issues that divide us. Why is it important to do both? How can we do the same in our lives in order to create understanding and dialogue?

3. Sometimes our two communities disagree about social and political issues. Is it possible to affirm our own position and at the same time understand and respect a different position? In what ways can we do this?

THE FUTURE

1. What is the basis of the "bond" between our two communities? Where does the pain remain? What must we do to strengthen our relationship so that we can participate together to "mend" our world?

2. *"When we dream alone, it is only a dream; when we dream together, it is the beginning of reality"* (May 4, 1992). What are our dreams? What is the reality we can reach together?

3. In Jerusalem, Cardinal Bernardin reflected together with a local Christian community on the parable of the prodigal son (March 26, 1995). Discuss the parable and his remarks.

C H R O N O L O G Y

✦

THE FOLLOWING INCLUDES ALL THE MATERIALS IN THIS BOOK AS WELL AS OTHER ADDRESSES
AND OTHER WORKS BY CARDINAL BERNARDIN FROM 1983 TO 1995.

May 7, 1983	Address to the Chicago Board of Rabbis
September 18, 1984	Address to the American Jewish Committee
December 2, 1984	Homily at a Prayer Serivce, Arab-Jewish-Christian Dialogue
June 20, 1985	Address to the Hyde Park-Kenwood Interfaith Council, Congregation Rodfei Zedek, Chicago
October 27, 1985	Address to *Nostra Aetate* Twentieth Anniversary Celebration, Mundelein College, Chicago
November 27, 1985	Homily at an Ecumenical Thanksgiving Service, Winnetka, Illinois
June 23, 1987	Response on Receiving the B'Nai B'rith International Humanitarian Award
July 22, 1987	Remarks at the Opening of the Joseph Cardinal Bernardin Center for the Study of Eastern European Jewry, Spertus College of Judaica, Chicago
April 14, 1989	Article: "A Wound That Remains Open," *The New World* newspaper, Chicago

April 15, 1988   Sermon at the Yom Hashoah Memorial Service, Emmanuel
                        Congregation, Chicago

September 28, 1988   Address at the Center for Jewish- Christian Learning, Saint
                        Thomas College, St. Paul, Minnesota

November 10, 1988   Address on the Fiftieth Anniversary of *Kristallnacht*

July 1, 1989   Address to the Seminar of Polish Seminary Professors, Joseph
                        Cardinal Bernardin Center for the Study of Eastern European
                        Jewry, Spertus College of Judaica, Chicago (originally
                        published in Polish by the Academy of Catholic Theology,
                        Warsaw, 1991)

September 29, 1989   Article: "A September Prayer," *The New World* newspaper,
                        Chicago

April 18, 1990   Address: "Together We Can Move Mountains: Reflections on
                        Catholic- Jewish Relations Today," Chicago Board of Rabbis

April 30, 1990   Invocation at the Benefit Luncheon for the U.S. Holocaust
                        Memorial Museum

May 7, 1990   Remarks at the Fundraising Luncheon for the Twelfth National
                        Workshop on Christian-Jewish Relations

May 8, 1990   Address: "The Religious Community's Role in Shaping Public
                        Values," Interfaith Conference of Greater Milwaukee

May 20, 1990   Reflections for a Prayer Service, Chicago Conference for Peace
                        in the Middle East, Saint James Cathedral, Chicago

November 5, 1990	Introduction of Jan Cardinal Willebrands, Twelfth National Workshop on Christian-Jewish Relations
November 6, 1990	Remarks at the Awards Banquet, Twelfth National Workshop on Christian-Jewish Relations
November 7, 1990	Address: "Religion and Power," Twelfth National Workshop on Christian-Jewish Relations
November 21, 1990	Prayer at the Interfaith Thanksgiving Service, National Conference of Christians and Jews, Chicago Temple United Methodist Church
January 11, 1991	Article: "Reconciling Church and Synagogue," *The New World* newspaper, Chicago
February 20, 1991	Invocation at the American Jewish Committee Dinner
June 3, 1991	Remarks on the Induction of Rabbi Herman Schaalman and Mr. Robert Adler into the Hall of Fame of the Jewish Community Centers of Chicago
June 7, 1991	Address: "The New Catholic Approach to Jews and Judaism," Jewish Reconstructionist Congregation, Evanston
November 1, 1991	Article: "Loud Cries and Quiet Whispers of Hope," *The New World* newspaper, Chicago
May 4, 1992	Address: "Preserving the Dignity of All Creation: Toward a Renewed Christian-Jewish Relationship," Jewish-Catholic International Liaison Committee, Baltimore, Maryland

June 1, 1992	Address to the Interfaith Clergy Institute, Chicago
September 24, 1993	Article: "Finding Hope for the Future in the Middle East," *The New World* newspaper, Chicago
November 9, 1993	Remarks and Benediction at the Dedication of the Zell Holocaust Memorial, Spertus College of Judaica, Chicago
April 15, 1994	Article: "Christians Must Refuse To Tolerate Even the Smallest Signs of Anti-Semitism," *The New World* newspaper, Chicago
June 28, 1994	Address to the Jewish National Fund, Tree of Life Banquet, Chicago
1995	"Anti-Semitism: A Catholic Critique" in *Toward Greater Understanding: Essays in Honor of John Cardinal O'Connor*, Anthony Cernera, ed., Sacred Heart University Press, Fairfield, Connecticut, 1995
March 22, 1995	Remarks for a Meeting with Patriarch Michael Sabbah, Latin Patriarch of Jerusalem
March 22, 1995	Remarks for a Meeting with Foreign Minister Shimon Peres
March 22, 1995	Remarks for a Meeting with Israel's President Ezer Weizman
March 22, 1995	Remarks for a Dinner Meeting with Intellectuals in Jerusalem
March 23, 1995	"Anti-Semitism: The Historical Legacy and the Continuing Challenge for Christians." Address on the occasion of receiving the Honorary Fellowship of the Hebrew University of Jerusalem, Mount Scopus, Israel

March 23, 1995	Remarks on the Visit to Yad Vashem
March 24, 1995	Homily at the Church of the Holy Sepulchre
March 24, 1995	Remarks at the Meeting with Mayor Freij of Bethlehem
March 24, 1995	Remarks on the Visit to Bethlehem University
March 25, 1995	Remarks for a Meeting with Patriarch Diodorus I of the Greek Orthodox Patriarchate of Jerusalem
March 25, 1995	Remarks after Kiddush at Hebrew Union College, Jerusalem
March 25, 1995	Remarks at the Meeting of Patriarchs and Heads of Christian Communities in Jerusalem
March 26, 1995	Homily at Saint Savior Parish, Jerusalem
March 26, 1995	Remarks at a Meeting with Mayor Olmert of Jerusalem
March 26, 1995	Remarks at a Meeting with Prime Minister Rabin
March 27, 1995	Homily at the Church of the Beatitudes
March 28, 1995	Remarks at a Meeting with Chairman Arafat
April 21, 1995	Article: "Anti-Semitism: Historical Legacy and Continuing Challenge for Christians," *The New World* newspaper, Chicago
April 28, 1995	Article: "Developments in Theology Move Church beyond Anti-Semitism," *The New World* newspaper, Chicago

May 12, 1995	Article: "Christian Anti-Semitism Helped Shape Popular Attitudes toward Nazis," *The New World* newspaper, Chicago
May 19, 1995	Article: "We Can Take Actions to Ensure Anti-Semitism Isn't Part of Future," *The New World* newspaper, Chicago
May 26, 1995	Article: "How Do We Interpret What the Gospel Says about Jews?" *The New World* newspaper, Chicago
June 2, June 9, 1995	Article: "Pray for the Peace of Jerusalem! May Those Who Love You Prosper!" *The New World* newspaper, Chicago
September 7, 1995	Address to the Jewish Federation of Metropolitan Chiago
November 9, 1995	Remarks on Reception of the International Leadership Award, Hebrew Union College/Jewish Institute of Religion, Chicago

GLOSSARY OF ORGANIZATIONS

THE COUNCIL OF RELIGIOUS LEADERS
OF METROPOLITAN CHICAGO

The Council of Religious Leaders of Metropolitan Chicago (CRLMC) is a roundtable of 40 chief executives of the Chicago area's Roman Catholic, Jewish, Orthodox and Protestant institutions. The Council serves as a clearinghouse for social issues and ideas affecting the people of Chicagoland, and strives to create a climate of understanding by focusing on the common ground among people of various religious faiths.

THE JEWISH COMMUNITY RELATIONS COUNCIL OF THE JEWISH
UNITED FUND OF METROPOLITAN CHICAGO

The Jewish Community Relations Council (JCRC) is the umbrella body for 39 major Jewish organizations in the Chicago area and is the community relations arm of the Jewish Federation/Jewish United Fund of Metropolitan Chicago. The JCRC interprets issues that are of concern to the Jewish community and advocates on behalf of Jewish community interests to representatives of other civic and community organizations, government officials and the media. Through its coordination of the Catholic-Jewish Scholars Dialogue and other frameworks, the JCRC works to advance intergroup and interfaith understanding and to enhance positive community relations.

SPERTUS INSTITUTE OF JEWISH STUDIES

The Spertus Institute of Jewish Studies, founded in 1924, is a center for Jewish scholarship, education and culture. The Institute consists of three major parts that work with integrated programs: Spertus College, an accredited graduate school offering masters and doctorate degrees, as well as continuing professional and public education; Asher Library, an extensive research library in Judaica that also serves as a learning resource center for the public; and the Spertus Museum, the largest Jewish museum in the Midwest, featuring exhibits, educational programs and collections reflecting all aspects of Jewish religious, cultural and historical experience. In addition, the Institute contains various programmatic centers, including the Zell Center for Holocaust Studies. Through its Joseph Cardinal Bernardin Center, the Institute expresses its commitment to and engagement in interreligious programs.

THE CHICAGO BOARD OF RABBIS

The Chicago Board of Rabbis (CBR) includes more than 220 Conservative, Orthodox, Reconstructionist, Reform and Traditional rabbis, making it the most comprehensive rabbinic organization in the region. Members serve in congregations, day schools and institutions of higher Jewish learning, hospitals and homes for the elderly, correctional facilities, Hillel chapters, and administrative positions. Because of its diversity, the CBR is recognized as the central address for Chicago's multifaceted rabbinate.

THE AMERICAN JEWISH COMMITTEE

The American Jewish Committee (AJC) is the nation's oldest human relations organization. It was founded in 1906 with the goal of protecting the civil and religious rights of Jews. The AJC works to ensure the security of Jews wherever they live, whether in the U.S., Israel or elsewhere. The organization also is committed to safeguarding the principles of American democracy by working to improve relations between all religious, racial and ethnic groups in the U.S. and through its advocacy of public policy positions. Finally, the AJC is dedicated to the enrichment of the quality of American Jewish life. Based in New York, the AJC has 32 offices throughout the U.S. with additional offices in Israel and Europe.

Vatican Council II

"DECLARATION ON THE RELATIONSHIP OF THE CHURCH TO NON-CHRISTIAN RELIGIONS," NOSTRA AETATE (NO. 4) OCTOBER 28, 1965

SOUNDING the depths of mystery which is the church, this sacred Council remembers the spiritual ties which link the people of the new covenant to the stock of Abraham.

The church of Christ acknowledges that in God's plan of salvation the beginnings of its faith and election are to be found in the patriarchs, Moses and the prophets. It professes that all Christ's faithful, who as people of faith are daughters and sons of Abraham (see Galatians 3:7), are included in the same patriarch's call and that the salvation of the church is mystically prefigured in the exodus of God's chosen people from the land of bondage. On this account the church cannot forget that it received the revelation of the Old Testament by way of that people with whom God in his inexpressible mercy established the ancient covenant. Nor can it forget that it draws nourishment from that good olive tree onto which the wild olive branches of the Gentiles have been grafted (see Romans 11:17-24). The church believes that Christ who is our peace has through his cross reconciled Jews and Gentiles and made them one in himself (see Ephesians 2:14-16).

Likewise, the church keeps ever before its mind the words of the apostle Paul about his kin: "they are Israelites, and it is for them to be sons and daughters, to them belong the glory, the covenants, the giving of the law, the worship and the promises; to them belong the patriarchs, and of their race according to the flesh, is the Christ" (Romans 9:4-5), the Son of the Virgin Mary. It is mindful, moreover, that the apostles, the pillars on which the church stands, are of Jewish descent, as are many of those early disciples who proclaimed the gospel of Christ to the world.

As holy scripture testifies, Jerusalem did not recognize God's moment when it came (see Luke 19:42). Jews for the most part did not accept the gospel; on the contrary, many opposed its spread (see Romans 11:28). Even so, the apostle Paul maintains that the Jews remain very dear to God, for the sake of the patriarchs, since God does not take back the gifts he bestowed or the choice he made. Together with the prophets and that same apostle, the church awaits the day, known to God alone, when all peoples will call on God with one voice and "serve him shoulder to shoulder" (Zephaniah 3:9; see Isaiah 66:23; Psalm 65:4; Romans 11:11–32).

Since Christians and Jews have such a common spiritual heritage, this sacred Council wishes to encourage and further mutual understanding and appreciation. This can be achieved, especially, by way of biblical and theological enquiry and through friendly discussions.

Even though the Jewish authorities and those who followed their lead pressed for the death of Christ (see John 19:6), neither all Jews indiscriminately at that time, nor Jews today, can be charged with the crimes committed during his passion. It is true that the church is the new people of God, yet the Jews should not be spoken of as rejected or accursed as if this followed from holy scripture. Consequently, all must take care, lest in catechizing or in preaching the word of God, they teach anything which is not in accord with the truth of the gospel message or the spirit of Christ.

Indeed, the church reproves every form of persecution against whomsoever it may be directed. Remembering, then, its common heritage with the Jews and moved not by political consideration but solely by the religious motivation of Christian charity, it deplores all hatreds, persecutions, displays of anti-Semitism leveled at any time or from any source against the Jews.

The church always held and continues to hold that Christ out of infinite love freely underwent suffering and death because of the sins of all, so that all might attain salvation. It is the duty of the church, therefore, in its preaching to proclaim the cross of Christ as the sign of God's universal love and the source of all grace.

Commission for Religious Relations with the Jews

GUIDELINES AND SUGGESTIONS FOR IMPLEMENTING THE CONCILIAR DECLARATION NOSTRA AETATE (NO. 4) DECEMBER 1, 1974

PREAMBLE

The declaration *Nostra Aetate,* issued by the Second Vatican Council on 28 October 1965, "on the relationship of the church to non-Christian religions" (4), marks an important milestone in the history of Jewish-Christian relations.

Moreover, the step taken by the Council finds its historical setting in circumstances deeply affected by the persecution and massacre of Jews which took place in Europe just before and during the Second World War.

Although Christianity sprang from Judaism, taking from it certain essential elements of its faith and divine cult, the gap dividing them was deepened more and more, to such an extent that Christian and Jew hardly knew each other.

After 2,000 years, too often marked by mutual ignorance and frequent confrontation, the declaration *Nostra Aetate* provides an opportunity to open or to continue a dialogue with a view to better mutual understanding. Over the past nine years, many steps in this direction have been taken in various countries. As a result, it is easier to distinguish the conditions under which a new relationship between Jews and Christians may be worked out and developed. This seems the right moment to propose, following the guidelines of the Council, some concrete suggestions born of experience, hoping that they will help to bring into actual existence in the life of the church the intentions expressed in the conciliar document.

While referring the reader back to the document, we may simply restate here that the spiritual bonds and historical links bonding the church to Judaism condemn (as opposed to the very spirit of Christianity) all forms of anti-Semitism and discrimination, which in any case the dignity of the human person alone would suffice to condemn. Further still, these links and relationships render obligatory a better mutual understanding and renewed mutual esteem. On the practical level in particular, Christians must therefore strive to acquire a better knowledge of the basic components of the religious tradition of Judaism; they must strive to learn by what essential traits the Jews define themselves in the light of their own religious experience.

With due respect for such matters of principle, we simply propose some first practical applications in different essential areas of the church's life, with a view to launching or developing sound relations between Catholics and their Jewish brothers and sisters.

I. DIALOGUE

To tell the truth, such relations as there have been between Jew and Christian have scarcely ever risen above the level of monologue. From now on, real dialogue must be established.

Dialogue presupposes that each side wishes to know the other, and wishes to increase and deepen its knowledge of the other. It constitutes a particularly suitable means of favoring a better mutual knowledge and, especially in the case of dialogue between Jews and Christians, of probing the riches of one's own tradition. Dialogue demands respect for others as they are and above all, respect for their faith and their religious convictions.

In virtue of her divine mission, and her very nature, the church must preach Jesus Christ to the world (*Ad Gentes,* 2). Lest the witness of Catholics to Jesus Christ should give offense to Jews, they must take care to live and spread their Christian faith while maintaining the strictest respect for religious liberty in line with the teaching of the Second Vatican Council (declaration *Dignitatis Humanae*). They will likewise strive to understand the difficulties which arise for the Jewish soul — rightly imbued with an extremely high, pure notion of the divine transcendence — when faced with the mystery of the incarnate Word.

While it is true that a widespread air of suspicion, inspired by an unfortunate past, is still dominant in this particular area, Christians, for their part, will be able to see to what extent the responsibility is theirs and deduce practical conclusions for the future.

In addition to friendly talks, competent people will be encouraged to meet and to study together the many problems deriving from the fundamental convictions of Judaism and of Christianity. In order not to hurt (even involuntarily) those taking part, it will be vital to guarantee not only tact but a great openness of spirit and diffidence with respect to one's own prejudices.

In whatever circumstances as shall prove possible and mutually acceptable, one might encourage a common meeting in the presence of God, in prayer and silent meditation, a highly efficacious way of finding the humility, that openness of heart and mind, necessary prerequisites for a deep knowledge of oneself and of others. In particular, that will be done in connection with great causes such as the struggle for peace and justice.

II. *LITURGY*

The existing links between the Christian liturgy and the Jewish liturgy will be borne in mind. The idea of a living community in the service of God, such as it is realized in the liturgy, is just as characteristic of the Jewish liturgy as it is of the Christian one. To improve Jewish-Christian relations, it is important to take cognizance of those common elements of the liturgical life (formulas, feasts, rites, etc.) in which the Bible holds an essential place.

An effort will be made to acquire a better understanding of whatever in the Old Testament retains its own perpetual value (cf. *Dei Verbum*, 14 – 15), since that has not been canceled by the later interpretation of the New Testament. Rather, the New Testament brings out the full meaning of the Old, while both Old and New illumine and explain each other (cf. ibid., 16). This is all the more important since liturgical reform is now bringing the text of the Old Testament ever more frequently to the attention of Christians.

When commenting on biblical texts, emphasis will be placed on the continuity of our faith with that of the earlier covenant, in perspective of the promises, without minimizing those elements of Christianity which are original. We believe that those promises were fulfilled with the first coming of Christ. But it is nonetheless true that we still await their perfect fulfillment in his glorious return at the end of time.

With respect to liturgical readings, care will be taken to see that homilies based on them will not distort their meaning, especially when it is a question of passages which seem to show the Jewish people, as such, in an unfavorable light. Efforts will be made to so instruct the Christian people that they will understand the true interpretation of all the texts and their meaning for the contemporary believer.

Commissions entrusted with the task of liturgical translation will pay particular attention to the way in which they express those phrases and passages which Christians, if not well informed, might misunderstand because of prejudice. Obviously, one cannot alter the text of the Bible. The point is that, with a version destined for liturgical use, there should be an overriding preoccupation to bring out explicitly the meaning of a text,[1] while taking spiritual studies into account.

The preceding remarks also apply to introductions to biblical readings, to the Prayer of the Faithful and to commentaries printed in missals used by the laity.

III. Teaching and Education

Although there is still a great deal of work to be done, a better understanding of Judaism itself and its relationship to Christianity has been achieved in recent years, thanks to the teaching of the church, the study and research of scholars, as also to the beginning of dialogue.

In this respect, the following facts deserve to be recalled:

▪ It is the same God, "inspirer and author of the books of both Testaments" (*Dei Verbum,* 16), who speaks both in the Old and New covenants.

- Judaism in the time of Christ and the apostles was a complex reality, embracing many different trends, many spiritual, religious, social and cultural values.

- The Old Testament and the Jewish tradition founded upon it must not be set against the New Testament in such a way that the former seems to constitute a religion of only justice, fear and legalism, with no appeal to the love of God and neighbor (cf. Deuteronomy 6:5; Leviticus 19:18; Matthew 22:34 – 40).

- Jesus was born of the Jewish people, as were his apostles and a large number of his first disciples. When he revealed himself as the Messiah and the Son of God (cf. Matthew 16:16), the bearer of the new gospel message, he did so as the fulfillment and perfection of the earlier revelation. And, although his teaching had a profoundly new character, Christ, nevertheless, in many instances, took his stand on the teaching of the Old Testament. The New Testament is profoundly marked by its relation to the Old. As the Second Vatican Council declared: "God, the inspirer and author of the books of both Testaments, wisely arranged that the New Testament be hidden in the Old and the Old be made manifest in the New" (*Dei Verbum*, 16). Jesus also used teaching methods similar to those used by the rabbis of his time.

- With regard to the trial and death of Jesus, the Council recalled that "what happened in his passion cannot be blamed on all the Jews then living, without distinction, nor upon the Jews of today" (*Nostra Aetate*, 4).

- The history of Judaism did not end with the destruction of Jerusalem, but rather went on to develop a religious tradition. And, although we believe that the importance and meaning of that tradition were deeply affected by the coming of Christ, it is still nonetheless rich in religious values.

- With the prophets and apostle Paul, "the church awaits the day, known to God alone, on which all peoples will address the Lord in a single voice and 'serve him with one accord' (Zephaniah 3:9) (*Nostra Aetate*, 4).

Information concerning these questions is important at all levels of Christian instruction and education. Among sources of information, special attention should be paid to the following:

- catechism and religious textbooks;
- history books;
- the mass media (press, radio, cinema, television).

The effective use of these means presupposes the thorough formation of instructors and educators in training schools, seminaries and universities.

Research into the problems bearing on Judaism and Jewish-Christian relations will be encouraged among specialists, particularly in the fields of exegesis, theology, history and sociology. Higher institutions of Catholic research, in association if possible with other similar Christian institutions and experts, are invited to contribute to the solution of such problems. Wherever possible, chairs of Jewish studies will be created and collaboration with Jewish scholars encouraged.

IV. *JOINT SOCIAL ACTION*

Jewish and Christian tradition, founded on the word of God, is aware of the value of the human person, the image of God. Love of the same God must show itself in effective action for the good of humankind. In the spirit of the prophets, Jews and Christians will work willingly together, seeking social justice and peace at every level — local, national and international. At the same time, such collaboration can do much to foster mutual understanding and esteem.

CONCLUSION

The Second Vatican Council has pointed out the path to follow in promoting deep fellowship between Jews and Christians. But there is still a long road ahead.

The problem of Jewish-Christian relations concerns the church as such, since it is when "pondering her own mystery" that she encounters the mystery of Israel. Therefore, even in areas where no Jewish communities exist, this remains an important problem. There is also an ecumenical aspect to the question: The very return of Christians to the sources and origins of their faith, grafted onto the earlier covenant, helps the search for unity in Christ, the cornerstone.

In this field, the bishops will know what best to do on a pastoral level, within the general disciplinary framework of the church and in line with common teaching of her magisterium. For example, they will create some suitable commissions or secretariats on a national or regional level, or appoint some competent person to promote the implementation of the conciliar directives and the suggestions made above.

On 22 October 1974 the holy father instituted the universal church for this Commission for Religious Relations with the Jews, joined to the Secretariat for Promoting Christian Unity. This special Commission, created to encourage and foster religious relations between Jews and Catholics — and to do so eventually in collaboration with other Christians — will be, within the limits of its competence, at the service of all interested organizations, providing information for them and helping them to pursue their task as in conformity with the instructions of the Holy See.

The Commission wishes to develop the collaboration in order to implement, correctly and effectively, the express intentions of the Council.

[1] Thus the formulas "the Jews", in Saint John, sometimes according to the context means "the leaders of the Jews," or "the adversaries of Jesus," terms which express better the thoughts of the evangelist and avoid appearing to arraign the Jewish people as such. Another example is the use of the words "pharisee" and "Pharisaism," which have taken on a largely pejorative meaning.

❖

National Conference of Catholic Bishops:
Secretariat for Catholic-Jewish Relations
Bishops' Committee on Ecumenical and Interreligious Affairs

GUIDELINES FOR
CATHOLIC-JEWISH RELATIONS
1985 REVISION

PERSPECTIVES

In its *Declaration on the Relationship of the Church to Non-Christian Religions* of 1965, the Second Vatican Council issued a historic statement on the Jews and summoned all Catholics to reappraise their attitude toward and relationship with the Jewish people. The statement was, in effect, a culminating point of initiatives and pronouncements of recent pontiffs and of numerous endeavors in the Church concerned with Catholic-Jewish harmony.

The call of the council to a dialogical encounter with Jews may be seen as one of the more important fruits of the spirit of renewal generated by the council in its deliberations and decrees. The council's call is an acknowledgment of the conflicts and tensions that have separated Christians and Jews through the centuries and of the Church's determination, as far as possible, to eliminate them. It serves both in word and action as a recognition of the manifold sufferings and injustices inflicted upon the Jewish people by Christians in our own times as well as in the past. It speaks from the highest level of the Church's authority to serve notice that injustices directed against the Jews at any time from any source can never receive Catholic sanction or support.

The message of the council's statement is clear. Recalling in moving terms the "spiritual bond that ties the people of the new covenant to

Abraham's stock," the Fathers of the council remind us of the special place Jews hold in the Christian perspective, for "now as before God holds them as the most dear for the sake of the patriarchs; he has not withdrawn his gifts or calling." Jews, therefore, the Fathers caution, are not "to be presented as rejected or accursed by God, as if this followed from Holy Scripture." The Passion of Jesus, moreover, "cannot be attributed without distinction to all Jews then alive, nor can it be attributed to Jews of today." The Church, the statement declares, "decries hatred, persecutions, displays of anti-Semitism directed against the Jews at any time and by anyone."

In light of these principles, the Fathers enjoin that "all see to it that nothing is taught, either in catechetical work or in the preaching of the word of God, that does not conform to the truth of the Gospel and the spirit of Christ." Rather, should Christians and Jews "further their mutual knowledge of and respect for one another, a knowledge and respect deriving primarily from biblical and theological studies and fraternal dialogues." The council's vision has been further specified and given urgency by subsequent pronouncements of the Holy See and of episcopal conferences and dioceses throughout the world. The 1975 Vatican guidelines, especially, detail catechetical, liturgical and social action steps that now need to be taken to implement the council's call for renewal. The statement of the American bishops of November 1975 refers to the task "as yet hardly begun, to explore the continuing relationship of the Jewish people with God and their spiritual bonds with the new covenant and the fulfillment of God's plan for both Church and Synagogue."

In a series of remarkable statements (see Sources), Pope John Paul II has sought to give positive direction to the dialogue, reminding us that "the links between the Church and the Jewish people are grounded in the design of the God of the Covenant" (March 6, 1982). The Holy Father has underscored, time and again, the vital importance of collaboration with the Jews for the working out of the Church's own mission in the world:

> Our common heritage impels us toward this, our common heritage of service to humanity and its immense spiritual and material needs. Through different but finally convergent ways we will be able to reach, with the help

of the Lord who has never ceased loving his people (cf. Romans 11:1), this true companionship in reconciliation and respect, and to contribute to a full implementation of God's plan in history (March 6, 1982).

The Roman Catholic Church in this country is provided with an historic opportunity to advance this cause — an opportunity to continue the leadership taken in that direction by our American bishops during the great debate on the declaration at the council. In the years since that time, much has been done in the United States to develop an atmosphere of mutual respect and spiritual kinship between Jews and Catholics.

The largest Jewish community in the world lives in the United States. In a land that has welcomed immigrants and refugees from persecution, our Church has committed itself without reserve to the ideal of equal opportunity and justice for all. In such a setting, the American Catholic community is providentially situated to distinguish itself in pursuit of the purposes of the council's mandate for the Church as a whole.

GENERAL PRINCIPLES

1. It is recommended that in each diocese a commission or secretariat, or member of an ecumenical commission, be assigned to Catholic-Jewish relations. "The question of Jewish-Christian relations concerns the Church as such, since it is when 'pondering her own mystery' that the Church encounters the mystery of Israel. Therefore, even in areas where no Jewish communities exist, this remains an important concern" *(Guidelines and Suggestions for Implementing the Conciliar Declaration).*

2. In keeping with the spirit of the Council's *Decree on Ecumenism and Declaration on the Relationship of the Church to Non-Christian Religions,* Catholics should take the initiative not only in Catholic-Protestant and Orthodox affairs but also in fostering Catholic-Jewish understanding. Public and formal projects, however, should have the approval of the ordinary of the diocese.

3. The general aim of all Catholic-Jewish meetings is to increase our understanding both of Judaism and the Catholic faith, eliminate sources

of tension and misunderstanding, initiate dialogues or conversations on different levels, multiply intergroup meetings between Catholics and Jews and promote cooperative social action.

4. These meetings should be marked by a genuine respect for the person and religious convictions, freedom of all participants, and a willingness to listen to and learn from the other party. They should be jointly planned and developed.

5. It is recommended that in order to maintain the dialogue on the highest possible level, its organization be accomplished in consultation with those experienced in the structural, doctrinal and interpersonal skills that the dialogue requires.

6. Proselytism, which does not respect human freedom, is carefully to be avoided. While the Christian, through the faith life of word and deed, will always witness to Jesus as the risen Christ, the dialogue is concerned with the permanent vocation of the Jews as God's people, the enduring values that Judaism shares with Christianity and that, together, the Church and the Jewish people are called upon to witness to the whole world.

7. Prayer in common with Jews should, when mutually acceptable, be encouraged, especially in matters of common concern, such as peace and the welfare of the community. Such prayer should meet the spiritual sensibilities of both parties, finding its inspiration in our common faith in the one God (cf. *Guidelines and Suggestions for Implementing the Conciliar Declaration,* 1).

8. Acknowledging the difficulties in interreligious marriages, preparation for them should expect each party to know well both religious traditions, so as to be cooperative with the religious duties of the spouse. Continuing pastoral care, as several diocesan interreligious guidelines already recognize, is also suggested.

9. A central principle of dialogue, cited by the 1975 Vatican guidelines, underlies all the above, namely, that Christians should "strive to learn by what essential traits the Jews define themselves in the light of their own religious experiences." Topics such as the Nazi attempt to annihilate the

Jewish people and the rebirth of a Jewish state in the land of Israel will obviously come up for discussion under this principle. While, as in the case of the latter, Christians may experience difficulties in sharing Jewish views on such questions, especially regarding specific, contemporary political controversies, an honest effort should be made "to understand the link between land and people which Jews have expressed in their writings and worship throughout two millennia as a longing for the homeland, holy Zion" (NCCB *Statement on Catholic-Jewish Relations*).

RECOMMENDED PROGRAMS

1. Catholic-Jewish relations should be advanced on all levels: clergy and lay, academic and popular, religious and social.

2. A favored instrument is the dialogue, a form of group conversation in which competent participants discuss assigned topics or themes in openness, candor and friendship. Those not well versed in interreligious affairs run the risk of unwittingly offending by inaccurate portrayal of each other's doctrine or way of life.

3. Diocesan and parochial organizations, schools, colleges, universities and especially seminaries should organize programs to implement the conciliar statement and subsequent official documents.

4. The pulpit should also be used for expounding these teachings and exhorting participation in programs fitted to the parochial level. Special care should be taken never to use the pulpit to portray Judaism as rejected by God or in any way unworthy of our love and esteem. (*Guidelines and Suggestions for Implementing the Conciliar Declaration*, 2).

5. School texts, prayerbooks and other media should, under competent auspices, continue to be examined in order to remove not only those materials that do not accord with the content and spirit of the Church's teaching but also those that fail to show Judaism's continuing role in salvation history in a positive light.

6. It is recommended that Catholic-Jewish understanding be fostered effectively at the popular level by means of so-called *open houses* in places of worship, mutual visits to schools, joint social events and *living room dialogues*.

7. Catholic-Jewish cooperation in the field of social action designed to promote public welfare and morality, and especially peace and justice, should be encouraged.

8. Orientation and resource material for the foregoing recommendations may be sought from the various Catholic and Jewish organizations that have been active in the field of Christian-Jewish relations. It is also suggested that contact be made with Protestant and Orthodox agencies and experts in this area of endeavor.

9. While parish and local programs to improve Catholic-Jewish relations must be pressed forward without delay, slower and deeper explorations of pertinent issues by Catholic and Jewish scholars must also be given a high priority. Since many of the problems in this area of Catholic-Jewish relations are intellectual in nature, research in history, psychology, sociology and the Bible by individual Catholic and Jewish scholars as well as collaborative scholarly enterprises are to be highly commended. Catholic seminaries and institutions of higher learning are especially important centers for such ongoing scholarly activity. The establishment of chairs of Jewish studies in Catholic institutions is encouraged, wherever possible.

10. The following themes, which, among others, are viewed by Christians and Jews involved in the dialogue as important issues affecting Christian Jewish relations, merit the attention and study of Catholic educators and scholars.

> a. Scholarly studies and education efforts should be undertaken to show the common historical, biblical, doctrinal and liturgical heritage shared by Catholics and Jews, as well as their differences. This involves not only

appreciation of the Hebrew Scriptures as a source of faith with their own perpetual value but also a recognition of Judaism as a living tradition that has had a strong and creative religious life through the centuries since the birth of Christianity from the common root.

b. As the council statement requires, the presentation of the Crucifixion story should be made in such a way so as not to implicate all Jews of Jesus' time or of today in a collective guilt for the crime. This is important for catechesis and homilies, especially during Lent and Holy Week, as well as for any dramatization of the events, such as passion plays.

c. In keeping with the Church's strong repudiation of anti-Semitism, a frank and honest treatment is needed in our history books, courses and seminary curricula of the history of Christian anti-Semitism, which climaxed in so much persecution, and of the Nazi attempt to destroy the Jewish population of Europe.

d. Continuing studies are needed of the life of Jesus and of the primitive church in the setting of the richly diverse and creative religious, social and cultural life of the Jewish community in the first century.

e. An explicit rejection should be made of the historically inaccurate notion that Judaism of that time, especially that of the Pharisaism, was a decadent formalism and hypocrisy. Scholars are increasingly aware of the closeness on many central doctrines between Jesus' teaching and that of the Pharisees. Many Jewish teachers adopted positions similar to those of Jesus on the critical religious and social issues of the time.

f. Catholic scholars need to assess the living and complex reality of Judaism after Christ, for example, in rabbinic literature and the permanent election of the Jewish people, alluded to by Saint Paul (Romans 9:29), and to incorporate the theological and spiritual results into Catholic teaching.

g. Further analysis of the use and implications for today of such expressions as "the Jews" by Saint John and other New Testament references that appear to place all Jews in a negative light is also called for. (These expressions and references should be fully and precisely clarified in accordance with the intent of the conciliar statement and subsequent teachings that Jews are not to be "presented as rejected or accursed by God as if this followed from Holy Scripture.")

11. Given the pluralistic and diverse character of both the American Catholic and American Jewish communities, interethnic and interracial group dialogue, e.g., Polish-Jewish, Hispanic-Jewish, Black-Jewish, etc., is to be encouraged where appropriate.

SOURCES

The Second Vatican Council, *Declaration on the Relationship of the Church to Non-Christian Religions (Nostra Aetate)*, October 28, 1965, U.S. Catholic Conference Office of Publishing and Promotion Services.

Vatican Commission for Religious Relations with the Jews, *Guidelines and Suggestions for Implementing the Conciliar Declaration* Nostra Aetate *(n. 4)*, December 1, 1974; *Notes on the Correct Way to Present the Jews and Judaism in Preaching and Catechesis of the Roman Catholic Church*, June 24, 1985; U.S. Catholic Conference Office of Publishing and Promotion Services.

Pope John Paul II, *Homily at Auschwitz*, June 7, 1979; *Address to the Jewish Community*, Mainz, Germany, November 17, 1980; *Address to Delegates of Episcopal Conferences on Relations with Judaism*, March 6, 1982; *Redemptionis Anno*, Good Friday, April 20, 1984; *Address to the International Council of Christians and Jews*, July 6, 1984.

National Conference of Catholic Bishops, *Statement on Catholic-Jewish Relations,* November 20, 1975, U.S. Catholic Conference Office of Publishing and Promotion Services.

Recent Statements of Presidents of the NCCB:

Archbishop Joseph Bernardin, "Address to the American Jewish Committee," May 14, 1975, earlier version excerpted in *Origins* 4 (March 13, 1975): 597– 98; "On Israel and the U.N.," September 3, 1975, and "On U.N. Vote on Zionism," November 11, 1975, in *Middle East Issues,* U.S. Catholic Conference Office of Publishing and Promotion Services, 1976.

Archbishop John R. Roach, "A Renewed Vision of Catholic-Jewish Relations," address to the executive committee of the Synagogue Council of America, March 12, 1981, *Origins* 10 (May 7, 1981): 751– 52.

Bishop James Malone, "The State of Jewish-Christian Relations," address to the Eighth National Workshop on Jewish-Christian Relations, October 29, 1984, *Origins* 14 (December 6, 1984): 406 – 9.

In addition, numerous dioceses and archdioceses in the United States have now issued their own local guidelines to implement these statements. These and other resources for programming can be obtained from:

> The Secretariat for Catholic-Jewish Relations
> National Conference of Catholic Bishops
> 3211 Fourth Street NE
> Washington DC 20017-1194

❀

National Conference of Catholic Bishops:
Bishops' Committee on the Liturgy

GOD'S MERCY ENDURES FOREVER:
GUIDELINES ON THE PRESENTATION OF JEWS
AND JUDAISM
IN CATHOLIC PREACHING
1988

PREFACE

Even in the twentieth century, the age of the Holocaust, the Shoah, the "Scouring Wind," God's mercy endures forever.

The Holocaust drew its fiery breath from the ancient, sometimes latent, but always persistent anti-Semitism which, over the centuries, found too large a place within the hearts of too many Christian men and women. Yet, since the Holocaust and since the Second Vatican Council, Christians have struggled to learn the reasons for such irrational and anti-Christian feelings against that special people for whom "God's mercy endures forever," to deal with those feelings, and to overcome them through knowledge, understanding, dialogue and love.

For the past 15 years, the Bishops' Committee on the Liturgy, and its Secretariat, have attempted to respond to the decree of *Nostra Aetate* and to the various documents issued by the Holy See's Commission for Religious Relations with the Jews, to see to it that our liturgical celebrations never again become occasions for that anti-Semitic or anti-Jewish sentiment that sometimes marred the liturgy in the past. Working with the Bishops' Committee for Ecumenical and Interreligious Affairs and the Anti-Defamation League of B'nai B'rith, the Committee on the Liturgy, and its Secretariat, have suggested pastoral ways to deal with such matters as Christians gathering for a seder in Holy Week, the proper understanding of the *Improperia* on Good Friday and the proclamation of the passion narratives in Holy Week, particularly on Good Friday.

The present statement and guidelines are also offered in response to *Nostra Aetate* and especially to the latest guidelines issued in 1985 by the Commission for Religious Relations with the Jews. These guidelines are intended to offer assistance to Catholic preachers so that Jews and Judaism are correctly and rightly presented in homilies and other forms of preaching. For preaching to be of the Spirit, the heart of the preacher must be converted. These guidelines are also meant to offer preachers assistance in their own understanding of Jews and Judaism and, if necessary, to be a help in their own conversion.

The preparation and publication of *God's Mercy Endures Forever* was made possible only because of the participation and insight of a number of men and women who are scholars of the Bible, of Christian and Jewish liturgy, or of Judaism. The Liturgy Committee and Secretariat owe a special debt of gratitude to the Anti-Defamation League of B'nai B'rith and to the NCCB Secretariat for Catholic-Jewish Relations for their support and assistance at every turn in the preparation of this document, which takes its title from that *hesed,* that enduring merciful love of God for all who are faithful to the law.

> Most Rev. Joseph P. Delaney
> Bishop of Fort Worth
> Chairman
> Bishops' Committee on the Liturgy

INTRODUCTION

On June 24, 1985, the solemnity of the Birth of John the Baptist, the Holy See's Commission for Religious Relations with the Jews issued its *Notes on the Correct Way to Present the Jews and Judaism in Preaching and Catechesis of the Roman Catholic Church* (hereafter, 1985 *Notes;* USCC Publications No. 970). The 1985 *Notes* rested on a foundation of previous Church statements, addressing the tasks given Catholic homilists by the Second

Vatican Council's *Declaration on the Relationship of the Church to Non-Christian Religions (Nostra Aetate)*, no. 4.

On December 1, 1974, for example, the Holy See had issued *Guidelines and Suggestions for Implementing the Conciliar Declaration* Nostra Aetate, no. 4 (hereafter, 1974 *Guidelines*). The second and third sections of this document placed central emphasis on the important and indispensable role of the homilist in ensuring that God's word be received without prejudice toward the Jewish people or their religious traditions, asking "with respect to liturgical readings," that "care be taken to see that homilies based on them will not distort their meaning, especially when it is a question of passages which seem to show the Jewish people as such in an unfavorable light" (1974 *Guidelines*, 2).

In this country, the National Conference of Catholic Bishops, in 1975, similarly urged catechists and homilists to work together to develop among Catholics increasing "appreciation of the Jewishness of that heritage and rich spirituality which we derive from Abraham, Moses, the prophets, the psalmists and other spiritual giants of the Hebrew Scriptures" (*Statement on Catholic-Jewish Relations*, November 20, 1975, 12).

Much progress has been made since then. As it continues, sensitivities will need even further sharpening, founded on the Church's growing understanding of biblical rabbinic Judaism.

It is the purpose of these present *Guidelines* to assist the homilist in these continuing efforts by indicating some of the major areas where challenges and opportunities occur and by offering perspectives and suggestions for dealing with them.

JEWISH ROOTS OF THE LITURGY

1. "Our common spiritual heritage [with Judaism] is considerable. To assess it carefully in itself and with due awareness of the faith and religious life of the Jewish people as they are professed and practiced still today can greatly help us to understand better certain aspects of the life of the church. Such is the case with the liturgy, whose Jewish roots remain still to be examined more deeply, and in any case should be better known and appreciated by the faithful" (Pope John Paul II, March 6, 1982).

2. Nowhere is the deep spiritual bond between Judaism and Christianity more apparent than in the liturgy. The very concepts of a liturgical cycle of feasts and the *lectio continua* principle of the lectionary that so mark Catholic tradition are adopted from Jewish liturgical practice. Easter and Pentecost have historical roots in the Jewish feasts of Passover and Shavuot. Though their Christian meaning is quite distinct, an awareness of their original context in the story of Israel is vital to their understanding, as the lectionary readings themselves suggest. Where appropriate, such relationships should be pointed out. The homilist, as a "mediator of meaning" (NCCB Committee on Priestly Life and Ministry, *Fulfilled in Your Hearing,* 1982), interprets for the liturgical assembly not only the Scriptures but their liturgical context as well.

3. The central action of Christian worship, the eucharistic celebration, is likewise linked historically with Jewish ritual. The term for Church, *ecclesia,* like the original sense of the word synagogue, is an equivalent for the Hebrew *keneset* or *keneddiyah* (assembly). The Christian understanding of ecclesia is based on the biblical understanding of *quahal* as the formal "gathering" of the people of God. The Christian *ordo* (order of worship) is an exact rendering of the earliest rabbinic idea of prayer, called a *seder,* that is, an "order" of service. Moreover, the Christian *ordo* takes its form and structure from the Jewish *seder:* the Liturgy of the Word, with its alternating biblical readings, doxologies and blessings; and the liturgical form of the Eucharist, rooted in Jewish meal liturgy, with its blessings over bread and wine. Theologically, the Christian concept of *anamnesis* coincides with the Jewish understanding of *zikkaron* (memorial reenactment). Applied to the Passover celebration, *zikkaron* refers to the fact that God's saving deed is not only recalled but actually relived through the ritual meal. The synoptic gospels present Jesus as instituting the Eucharist during a Passover *seder* celebrated with his followers, giving to it a new and distinctly Christian "memory."

4. In addition to the liturgical seasons and the Eucharist, numerous details of prayer forms and ritual exemplify the Church's continuing relationship with the Jewish people through the ages. The liturgy of the hours and the formulas of many of the Church's most memorable prayers, such

as the "Our Father," continue to resonate with rabbinic Judaism and contemporary synagogue prayers.

HISTORICAL PERSPECTIVES AND
CONTEMPORARY PROCLAMATION

5. The strongly Jewish character of Jesus' teaching and that of the primitive Church was culturally adapted by the growing Gentile majority and later blurred by controversies alienating Christianity from emerging rabbinic Judaism at the end of the first century. "By the third century, however, a de-Judaizing process had set in which tended to undervalue the Jewish origins of the Church, a tendency that has surfaced from time to time in devious ways throughout Christian history" (*Statement on Catholic-Jewish Relations,* 12).

6. This process has manifested itself in various ways in Christian history. In the second century, Marcion carried it to its absurd extreme, teaching a complete opposition between the Hebrew and Christian Scriptures and declaring that different Gods had inspired the two Testaments. Despite the Church's condemnations of Marcion's teachings, some Christians over the centuries continued to dichotomize the Bible into two mutually contradictory parts. They argued, for example, that the new covenant "abrogated" or "superseded" the old, and that the Sinai covenant was discarded by God and replaced with another. The Second Vatican Council, in *Dei Verbum* and *Nostra Aetate,* rejected these theories of the relationship between the scriptures. In a major address in 1980, Pope John Paul II linked the renewed understanding of Scripture with the Church's understanding of its relationship with the Jewish people, stating that the dialogue, as "the meeting between the people of God of the old covenant, never revoked by God, is at the same time a dialogue within our Church, that is to say, a dialogue between the first and second part of its Bible" (Pope John Paul II, Mainz, November 17, 1980).

7. Another misunderstanding rejected by the Second Vatican Council was the notion of collective guilt, which charged the Jewish people *as a whole* with responsibility for Jesus' death (cf. 21–25 below, on Holy Week). From

the theory of collective guilt, it followed for some that Jewish suffering over the ages reflected divine retribution on the Jews for alleged "deicide." While both rabbinic Judaism and early Christianity saw in the destruction of the Jerusalem Temple in 70 AD a sense of divine punishment (See Luke 19:42 – 44), the theory of collective guilt went well beyond Jesus' poignant expression of his love as a Jew for Jerusalem and the destruction it would face at the hands of imperial Rome. Collective guilt implied that because "the Jews" had rejected Jesus, God had rejected them. With direct reference to Luke 19:44, the Second Vatican Council reminded Catholics that "nevertheless, now as before, God holds the Jews most dear for the sake of their fathers; he does not repent of the gifts he makes or of the calls he issues," and established as an overriding hermeneutical principle for homilists dealing with such passages that "the Jews should not be represented as rejected by God or accursed, as if this followed from holy scripture" (*Nostra Aetate,* 4; cf. 1985 *Notes,* vi:33).

8. Reasons for the increased sensitivity to the ways in which Jews and Judaism are represented in homilies are multiple. First, understanding of the biblical readings and of the structure of Catholic liturgy will be enhanced by an appreciation of their ancient sources and their continuing spiritual links with Judaism. The Christian proclamation of the saving deeds of the one God through Jesus was formed in the context of Second Temple Judaism and cannot be understood thoroughly without that context. It is a proclamation that, at its heart, stands in solidarity with the continuing Jewish witness in affirming the one God as Lord of history. Further, false or demeaning portraits of repudiated Israel may undermine Christianity as well. How can one confidently affirm the truth of God's covenant with all humanity and creation in Christ (see Romans 8:21) without at the same time affirming God's faithfulness to the covenant with Israel that also lies at the heart of the biblical testimony?

9. As Catholic homilists know, the liturgical year presents both opportunities and challenges. One can show the parallels between the Jewish and Catholic liturgical cycles. And one can, with clarity, confront misinterpretations of the meaning of the lectionary readings, which have been too familiar in the past. Specifically, homilists can guide people away

from triumphalism that would equate the pilgrim Church with the reign of God, which is the Church's mission to herald and proclaim. Likewise, homilists can confront the unconscious transmission of anti-Judaism through clichés that derive from an unhistorical overgeneralization of the self-critical aspects of the story of Israel as told in the scriptures (e.g., "hardheartedness" of the Jews, "blindness," "legalism," "materialism," "rejection of Jesus," etc.). From Advent through Passover/Easter, to Yom Kippur and Rosh Hashana, the Catholic and Jewish liturgical cycles spiral around one another in a stately procession of challenges to God's people to repent, to remain faithful to God's call and to prepare the world for the coming of God's reign. While each is distinct and unique, they are related to one another. Christianity is engrafted on and continues to draw sustenance from the common root, biblical Israel (Romans 11:13 – 24).

10. In this respect, the 1985 *Notes,* stressing "the unity of the divine plan" (11), caution against the simplistic framing of the relationship of Christianity and Judaism as "two parallel ways of salvation" (7). The Church proclaims the universal salvific significance of the Christ-event and looks forward to the day when "there shall be one flock and one shepherd" (John 10:16; cf. Isaiah 66:2; Zephaniah 3:9; Jeremiah 23:3; Ezekiel 11:17; see also 31e below). So intimate is this relationship that the Church "encounters the mystery of Israel" when "pondering her own mystery" (1974 *Guidelines,* 5).

ADVENT: THE RELATIONSHIP BETWEEN THE SCRIPTURES

11. The lectionary readings from the prophets are selected to bring out the ancient Christian theme that Jesus is the "fulfillment" of the biblical message of hope and promise, the inauguration of the "days to come" described, for example, by the daily Advent Masses, and on Sundays by Isaiah in Cycle A and Jeremiah in Cycle C for the First Sunday of Advent. This truth needs to be framed very carefully. Christians believe that Jesus is the promised Messiah who has come (see Luke 4:22) but also know that his messianic kingdom is not yet fully realized. The ancient messianic prophesies are not merely temporal predictions but profound

expressions of eschatological hope. Since this dimension can be misunderstood or even missed altogether, the homilist needs to raise clearly the hope found in the prophets and heightened in the proclamation of Christ. This hope includes trust in what is promised but not yet seen. While the biblical prophesies of an age of universal *shalom* are "fulfilled" (i.e., irreversibly inaugurated) in Christ's coming, that fulfillment is not yet completely worked out in each person's life or perfected in the world at large (1974 *Guidelines,* 2). It is the mission of the church, as also that of the Jewish people, to proclaim and to work to prepare the world for the full flowering of God's reign, which is but is "not yet" (cf. 1974 *Guidelines,* II). Both the Christian "Our Father" and the Jewish *Kaddish* exemplify this message. Thus, both Christianity and Judaism seal their worship with a common hope: "Thy kingdom come!"

12. Christians proclaim that the Messiah has indeed come and that God's reign is "at hand." With the Jewish people, we await the complete realization of the messianic age.

> In underlining the eschatological dimensions of Christianity, we shall reach a greater awareness that the people of God of the Old and the New Testament are tending toward a like end in the future: the coming or return of the Messiah — even if they start from two different points of view (1985 *Notes,* 18–19).

13. Other difficulties may be less theologically momentous but can still be troublesome. For example, the reading from Baruch in Cycle C or from Isaiah in Cycle A for the Second Sunday of Advent can leave the impression that pre-Jesus Israel was wholly guilt-ridden and in mourning, and Judaism virtually moribund. In fact, in the original historical settings, such passages reveal Judaism's remarkable capacity for self-criticism. While Israel has periods of deep mourning (see Lamentations) and was justly accused of sinfulness (e.g., see Jeremiah), it also experiences periods of joy, return from Exile and continuing *teshuvah,* turning back to God in faithful repentance. Judaism was and is incredibly complex and

vital, with a wide variety of creative spiritual movements vying for the people's adherence.

14. The reform of the liturgy initiated by the Second Vatican Council re-introduced regular readings from the Old Testament into the lectionary. For Catholics, the Old Testament is that collection that contains the Hebrew Scriptures and the seven deuterocanonical books. Using post-biblical Jewish sources, with respect for the essential differences between Christian and Jewish traditions of biblical interpretation, can enliven the approach to the biblical text (cf. 31a and 31i below). The opportunity also presents a challenge for the homilist. Principles of selection of passages vary. Sometimes the readings are cyclic, providing a continuity of narrative over a period of time. At other times, especially during Advent and Lent, a reading from the prophets or one of the historical books of the Old Testament and a gospel pericope are "paired," based on such liturgical traditions as the *sensus plenior* (fuller meaning) or, as is especially the case in Ordinary Time, according to the principles of *typology*, in which biblical figures and events are seen as "types" prefiguring Jesus (see no. below).

15. Many of these pairings represent natural associations of similar events and teachings. Others rely on New Testament precedent and interpretation of the messianic psalms and prophetic passages. Matthew 1:23, for example, quotes the Septuagint, which translates the Hebrew *almah* (young woman) as the Greek for *virgin* in its rendering of Isaiah 7:14. The same biblical text, therefore, can have more than one valid hermeneutical interpretation, ranging from its original historical context and intent to traditional Christological applications. The 1985 *Notes* describe this phenomenon as flowing from the "unfathomable riches" and "inexhaustible content" of the Hebrew Bible. For Christians, the unity of the Bible depends on understanding all Scripture in the light of Christ. Typology is one form, rooted in the New Testament itself, of expressing this unity of Scripture and of the divine plan (see 31e below). As such, it "should not lead us to forget that it [the Hebrew Bible] retains its own value as revelation that the New Testament often does no more than resume" (1985 *Notes*, 15; cf. *Dei Verbum*, 14–18).

LENT: CONTROVERSIES AND CONFLICTS

16. The lenten lectionary presents just as many challenges. Prophetic texts such as Joel (Ash Wednesday), Jeremiah's "new covenant" (Cycle B, Fifth Sunday) and Isaiah (Cycle C, Fifth Sunday) call the assembly to proclaim Jesus as the Christ while avoiding negativism toward Judaism.

17. In addition, many of the New Testament texts, such as Matthew's references to "hypocrites in the synagogue" (Ash Wednesday), John's depiction of Jesus in the Temple (Cycle B, Third Sunday) and Jesus' conflicts with the Pharisees (e.g., Luke, Cycle C, Fourth Sunday) can give the impression that the Judaism of Jesus' day was devoid of spiritual depth and essentially at odds with Jesus' teaching. References to earlier divine punishments of the Jews (e.g., 1 Corinthians, Cycle C, Third Sunday) can further intensify a false image of Jews and Judaism as a people rejected by God.

18. In fact, however, as the 1985 *Notes* are at pains to clarify (sec. III and IV), Jesus was observant of the Torah (e.g., in the details of his circumcision and purification given in Luke 2:21–24), he extolled respect for it (see Matthew 5:17–20), and he invited obedience to it (see Matthew 8:4). Jesus taught in the synagogues (see Matthew 4:23 and 9:35; Luke 4:15–18; John 18:20) and in the Temple, which he frequented, as did the disciples even after the resurrection (see Acts 2:46; 3:1ff.). While Jesus showed uniqueness and authority in his interpretation of God's word in the Torah — in a manner that scandalized some Jews and impressed others — he did not oppose it, nor did he wish to abrogate it.

19. Jesus was perhaps closer to the Pharisees in his religious vision than to any other group of his time. The 1985 *Notes* suggest that this affinity with Pharisaism may be the reason for many of his apparent controversies with them (see 27). Jesus shared with the Pharisees a number of distinctive doctrines: the resurrection of the body; forms of piety such as almsgiving, daily prayer and fasting; the liturgical practice of addressing God as Father; and the priority of the love commandment (see 25). Many scholars are of the view that Jesus was not so much arguing against "the

Pharisees" as a group as he was condemning excesses of some Pharisees, excesses of a sort that can be found among some Christians as well. In some cases, Jesus appears to have been participating in internal Pharisaic debates on various points of interpretation of God's law. In the case of divorce (see Mark 10:2–12), an issue that was debated hotly between the Pharisaic schools of Hillel and Shammai, Jesus goes beyond even the more stringent position of the House of Shammai. In other cases, such as the rejection of a literal interpretation of the *lex talionis* ("An eye for an eye. . . . "), Jesus' interpretation of biblical law is similar to that found in some of the prophets and ultimately adopted by rabbinic tradition as can be seen in the Talmud.

20. After the Church had distanced itself from Judaism (cf. 5 above), it tended to telescope the long historical process whereby the gospels were set down some generations after Jesus' death. Thus, certain controversies that may actually have taken place between church leaders and rabbis toward the end of the first century were "read back" into the life of Jesus:

> Some [New Testament] references hostile or less than favorable to Jews have their historical context in conflicts between the nascent church and the Jewish community. Certain controversies reflect Christian-Jewish relations long after the time of Jesus. To establish this is of capital importance if we wish to bring out the meaning of certain gospel texts for the Christians of today. All this should be taken into account when preparing catechesis and homilies for the weeks of Lent and Holy Week (1985 *Notes*, 29; see 26 below).

HOLY WEEK: THE PASSION NARRATIVES

21. Because of the tragic history of the "Christ-killer" charge as providing a rallying cry for anti-Semites over the centuries, a strong and careful homiletic stance is necessary to combat its lingering effects today. Homilists and catechists should seek to provide a proper context for the proclamation of

the passion narratives. A particularly useful and detailed discussion of the theological and historical principles involved in presentations of the passions can be found in *Criteria for the Evaluation of Dramatizations of the Passion* issued by the Bishops' Committee for Ecumenical and Inter-religious Affairs (March 1988).

22. The message of the liturgy in proclaiming the passion narratives in full is to enable the assembly to see vividly the love of Christ for each person, despite their sins, a love that even death could not vanquish. "Christ in his boundless love freely underwent his passion and death because of the sins of all so that all might attain salvation" (*Nostra Aetate,* 4). To the extent that Christians over the centuries made Jews the scapegoat for Christ's death, they drew themselves away from the paschal mystery. For it is only by dying to one's sins that we can hope to rise with Christ to new life. This is a central truth of the Catholic faith stated by the *Catechism* of the Council of Trent in the sixteenth century and reaffirmed by the 1985 *Notes* (30).

23. It is necessary to remember that the passion narratives do not offer eyewitness accounts or a modern transcript of historical events. Rather, the events have had their meaning focused, as it were, through the four theological "lenses" of the gospels. By comparing what is shared and what distinguishes the various gospel accounts from each other, the homilist can discern the core from the particular optics of each. One can then better see the significant theological differences between the passion narratives. These differences also are part of the inspired word of God.

24. Certain historical essentials are shared by all four accounts: a growing hostility against Jesus on the part of some Jewish religious leaders (note that the Synoptic gospels do not mention the Pharisees as being involved in the events leading to Jesus' death but only the "chief priests, scribes and elders"); the Last Supper with the disciples; betrayal by Judas; arrest outside the city (an action conducted covertly by the Roman and Temple authorities because of Jesus' popularity among his fellow Jews); interrogation before a high priest (not necessarily a Sanhedrin trial); formal condemnation by Pontius Pilate (cf. the Apostles' and Nicene Creeds, which

mention *only* Pilate, even though some Jews were involved); crucifixion by Roman soldiers; affixing the title "King of the Jews" on the cross; death; burial; and resurrection. Many other elements, such as the crowds shouting, "His blood be on us and on our children" in Matthew, or the generic use of the term "the Jews" in John, are unique to a given author and must be understood within the context of that author's overall theological scheme. Often, these unique elements reflect the perceived needs and emphases of the author's particular community at the end of the first century, *after* the split between Jews and Christians was well underway. The bitterness toward synagogue Judaism seen in John's gospel (e.g., John 9:22;16:2) most likely reflects the bitterness felt by John's own community after its "parting of the ways" with the Jewish community, and the martyrdom of Saint Stephen illustrates that verbal disputes could, at times, lead to violence by Jews against fellow Jews who believed in Jesus.

25. Christian reflection on the passion should lead to a deep sense of the need for reconciliation with the Jewish community today. Pope John Paul II has said:

> Considering history in the light of the principles of faith in God, we must also reflect on the catastrophic event of the Shoah. . . .
>
> Considering this mystery of the suffering of Israel's children, their witness of hope, of faith and of humanity under dehumanizing outrages, the church experiences ever more deeply her common bond with the Jewish people and with their treasure of spiritual riches in the past and in the present (*Address to Jewish Leadership*, Miami, September 11, 1987).

THE EASTER SEASON

26. The readings of the Easter season, especially those from the book of Acts, which is used extensively throughout this liturgical period, require particular attention from the homilist in light of the enduring bond

between Jews and Christians. Some of these readings from Acts (e.g., Cycles A and B for the Third and Fourth Sundays of Easter) can leave an impression of collective Jewish responsibility for the crucifixion ("You put to death the author of life. . . ." Acts 3:15). In such cases, the homilist should put before the assembly the teachings of *Nostra Aetate* in this regard (see 22 above), as well as the fact noted in Acts 3:17 that what was done by some individual Jews was done "out of ignorance" so that no unwarranted conclusion about collective guilt is drawn by the hearers. The Acts may be dealing with a reflection of the Jewish-Christian relationship as it existed toward the end of the first century (when Acts was composed) rather than with the actual attitudes of the post-Easter Jerusalem Church. Homilists should desire to convey the spirit and enthusiasm of the early church that marks these Easter season readings. But in doing so, statements about Jewish responsibility have to be kept in context. This is part of the reconciliation between Jews and Christians to which we are all called.

PASTORAL ACTIVITY DURING HOLY WEEK
AND THE EASTER SEASON

27. Pope John Paul II's visit to the chief rabbi of Rome on Good Friday, 1987, gives a lead for pastoral activities during Holy Week in local churches. Some dioceses and parishes, for example, have begun traditions such as holding a "Service of Reconciliation" with Jews on Palm Sunday, or inviting Holocaust survivors to address their congregations during Lent.

28. It is becoming familiar in many parishes and Catholic homes to participate in a Passover Seder during Holy Week. This practice can have educational and spiritual value. It is wrong, however, to "baptize" the seder by ending it with New Testament readings about the Last Supper or, worse, turn it into a prologue to the eucharist. Such mergings distort both traditions. The following advice should prove useful:

> When Christians celebrate this sacred feast among themselves, the rites of the *haggadah* for the seder should be respected in all their integrity. The seder . . . should be

celebrated in a dignified manner and with sensitivity to those to whom the seder truly belongs. The primary reason why Christians may celebrate the festival of Passover should be to acknowledge common roots in the history of salvation. Any sense of "restaging" the Last Supper of the Lord Jesus should be avoided. . . . The rites of the Triduum are the [Church's] annual memorial of the events of Jesus' dying and rising (Bishops' Committee on the Liturgy *Newsletter,* March 1980, 12).

Seders arranged at or in cooperation with local synagogues are encouraged.

29. Also encouraged are joint memorial services commemorating the victims of the Shoah (Holocaust). These should be prepared for with catechetical and adult education programming to ensure a proper spirit of shared reverence. Addressing the Jewish community of Warsaw, Pope John Paul II stressed the uniqueness and significance of Jewish memory of the Shoah:

> More than anyone else, it is precisely you who have become this saving warning. I think that in this sense you continue your particular vocation, showing yourselves to be still the heirs of that election to which God is faithful. This is your mission in the contemporary world before . . . all of humanity (Warsaw, June 14, 1987).

On the Sunday closest to Yom Hashoah, Catholics should pray for the victims of the Holocaust and their survivors. The following serve as examples of petitions for the general intercessions at Mass:

> • For the victims of the Holocaust, their families and all our Jewish brothers and sisters, that the violence and hatred they experienced may never again be repeated, we pray to the Lord.

> • For the church, that the Holocaust may be a reminder to us that we can never be indifferent to the sufferings of others, we pray to the Lord.

- For our Jewish brothers and sisters, that their confidence in the face of long suffering may spur us on to a greater faith and trust in God, we pray to the Lord.

PRAYING THROUGHOUT THE YEAR

30. The challenges that peak in the seasons of Advent, Lent and Easter are present throughout the year in the juxtaposition of the lectionary readings. There are many occasions when it is difficult to avoid a reference either to Jews or Judaism in a homily based upon a text from the Scriptures. For all Scripture, including the New Testament, deals with Jews and Jewish themes.

31. Throughout the year, the following general principles will be helpful:

a.) Consistently affirm the value of the whole Bible. While "among all the scriptures, even those of the New Testament, the Gospels have a special preeminence" (*Dei Verbum,* 18), the Hebrew Scriptures are the word of God and have validity and dignity in and of themselves (ibid., 15). Keep in view the intentions of the biblical authors (ibid., 19).

b.) Place the typology inherent in the lectionary in a proper context, neither overemphasizing nor avoiding it. Show that the meaning of the Hebrew Scriptures for their original audience is not limited to nor diminished by New Testament applications (1985 *Notes,* II).

c.) Communicate a reverence for the Hebrew Scriptures, and avoid approaches that reduce them to a propaedeutic or background for the New Testament. It is God who speaks, communicating himself through divine revelation (*Dei Verbum,* 6).

d.) Show the connectedness between the Scriptures. The Hebrew Bible and the Jewish tradition founded on it must not be set against the New Testament in such a way that the former seems to constitute a religion of only retributive justice, fear and legalism, with no appeal to love of God or neighbor (cf. Deuteronomy 6:5; Leviticus 19:18, 32; Hosea 11:1–9; Matthew 22:34-40).

e.) Enliven the eschatological hope, the "not yet" aspect of the *kerygma*. The biblical promises are realized in Christ. But the Church awaits their perfect fulfillment in Christ's glorious return when all creation is made free (1974 *Guidelines*, II).

f.) Emphasize the Jewishness of Jesus and his teachings, and highlight the similarities of the teachings of the Pharisees with those of Christ (1985 *Notes*, III and IV).

g.) Respect the continuing validity of God's covenant with the Jewish people and their responsive faithfulness, despite centuries of suffering, to the divine call that is theirs (1985 *Notes*, VI).

h.) Frame homilies to show that Christians and Jews together are "trustees and witnesses of an ethic marked by the Ten Commandments, in the observance of which humanity finds its truth and freedom" (John Paul ii, Rome Synagogue, April 13, 1986).

i.) Be free to draw on Jewish sources (rabbinic, medieval, and modern) in expounding the meaning of the Hebrew Scriptures and the apostolic writings. The 1974 *Guidelines* observe that "the history of Judaism did not end with the destruction of Jerusalem but went on to develop a religious tradition . . . rich in religious values." The 1985 *Notes* (14) thus speak of Christians "profiting discerningly from the traditions of Jewish readings" of the sacred texts.

32. The 1985 *Notes* describe what is central to the role of the homilist: "Attentive to the same God who has spoken, hanging on the same word, we have to witness to one same memory and one common hope in him who is master of history. We must also accept our responsibility to prepare the world for the coming of the Messiah by working together for social justice, respect for the rights of persons and nations, and for social and international reconciliation. To this we are driven, Jews and Christians, by the command to love our neighbor, by a common hope for the kingdom of God, and by the great heritage of the prophets" (1985 *Notes*, 19; see also Leviticus 19:18, 32).

Cunningham, Philip A. *Education for Shalom* and *Proclaiming Shalom* (Collegeville MN: Liturgical Press, 1995). The first volume reports the author's study of current Catholic religious education materials, their strengths and weaknesses, and what primary and secondary teachers can do in the classroom to enhance the Catholic-Jewish relationship. The latter contains brief lectionary introductions for all three cycles as developed for the author's own parish.

Efroymson, David, Eugene J. Fisher and Leon Klenicki, eds. *Within Context: Essays on Jews and Judaism in the New Testament* (Collegeville MN: Liturgical Press, 1993). Seven Roman Catholic scholars and educators provide teachers and general readers with background and insights into how to read the New Testament with sensitivity to its Jewish milieu in the light of today's dialogue and scholarship.

Fisher, Eugene J., and Leon Klenicki, eds. *Spiritual Pilgrimage: Pope John Paul II, Texts on Jews and Judaism 1979 – 1995* (New York: Crossroad, 1995). All of the pope's statements, with introduction and thematic commentary by the editors.

Fisher, Eugene J. *Faith Without Prejudice* (Second edition. New York. Crossroad, 1993). A general introduction to the issues, with activities for parishes and schools and a selection of key Catholic documents.

Fisher, Eugene J., ed. *Interwoven Destinies* (New York: Paulist Press, 1993) and *Visions of the Other* (New York: Paulist Press, 1994). Six Christian and six Jewish scholars are paired in looking at the history and contemporary possibilities of two millennia of Jewish-Christian interrelations.

Jacobs, S. L., ed. *Contemporary Jewish and Christian Responses to the Shoah* (University Press of America, 1993). Two volumes of essays cover a wide range of historical and theological thinking.

Levine, Deborah J. *Teaching Christian Children about Judaism* (Chicago: Liturgy Training Publications, 1995). Seven lesson plans on Jewish life and ritual for use in Catholic schools and religious education classes.

Klenicki, Leon, and Geoffrey Wigoder. *A Dictionary of the Jewish-Christian Dialogue* (New York: Paulist Press, 1995). Brief descriptions of Jewish and Christian views on topics ranging from the afterlife to universalism.

Pawlikowski, John, and James Wilde. *When Catholics Speak about Jews* (Chicago: Liturgy Training Publications, 1987). Identifies difficulties in the lectionary and offers practical advice on how preachers can proclaim the gospel free of a negative portrait of Jews and Judaism.

Rudin, A. James. *Israel for Christians: Understanding Modern Israel* (Philadelphia: Fortress, 1983). Examines on a popular level the history of Zionism, the founding of the State of Israel and Christian reactions.

SIDIC is a journal published three times a year by the Sisters of Sion in Rome. It specializes in materials and articles on Jewish-Christian relations. Subscriptions are available through the Secretariat for Ecumenical and Interreligious Affairs, 3211 Fourth St., NE, Washington DC 20017. Two volumes have been edited into book form from SIDIC articles. Eugene Fisher, *The Jewish Roots of Christian Liturgy* (New York: Paulist Press, 1993). Katherine T. Hargrove, *Seeds of Reconciliation* (N. Richland Hills TX: BIBAL Press, 1996).

Contains seminal reflections on covenant and chosenness, family and Torah, the Holocaust and the catechism.

Willebrands, Cardinal Johannes. *Church and Jewish People: New considerations* (New York: Paulist Press, 1992). Collects the texts and addresses of the head of the Holy See's Commission for Religious Relations with the Jews from 1974 to 1990.

INDEX

Environmental crisis,
response to, 132–135

Evangelization,
32–34, 201

Fackenheim, Emil,
16, 119, 129, 131, 156

Federal Council of Churches,
126

Fisher, Eugene J.,
159

Flannery, Reverend Edward,
147, 150, 156

Fulda Declaration,
158

Gaudium et Spes.
See Pastoral Constitution on the
Church in the Modern World

Gibbons, James Cardinal,
125

Glemp, Jozef Cardinal,
96–97

Greenberg, Rabbi Irving,
116, 131

Guardini, Romano,
113

Hinduism,
and ecumenism, 120, 165

Holocaust,
6–7, 9, 39, 67, 114–115, 155–157, 191,
201
education about, 100, 158–160, 204,
221
impact on Catholic theology and
practice, 20–22, 49, 85–88, 121,
207–208
lessons of, 70–74, 115–119, 129–137,
143–144
non-Jewish victims of, 100–101, 130,
136, 157
roles of Catholics in, 31–32, 86, 88,
90–93, 128, 158–159, 161
See also Anti-Semitism; Nazism

Holy See-Israeli Accords,
152–153

Holy Week,
160, 217–219. *See also* Passion
narratives

Institute for Catholic-Jewish
Education,
12, 174

International Catholic-Jewish Liaison
Committee,
2, 32, 124, 129, 158

International Jewish Committee on
Interreligious Consultations,
129

Islam,
and ecumenism, 14, 41, 162, 164–66,
170–171. *See also* Nation of Islam

Israel
Bernardin's visit to (1995), 15–17,
143–171, 173–175
founding of, 9, 202
and idea of Jewish homeland, 17, 29–
31, 50, 67, 103, 148–149, 151–152
recent conflicts in, 21, 29–32, 40–41,
42, 49–51, 103–105, 109–112, 132,
135–136, 162, 170–171
recognition of by Holy See, 41, 49–51,
122–123, 153

Jacobs, Rabbi Louis,
11, 65

Jagerstatter, Franz,
158

Jerusalem,
contest for, 40–41, 104–105, 162,
164–66, 169, 170–171

Jerusalem Lecture,
16

Jesus,
Jewish background of, 18–19, 46, 48–
49, 78–80, 92, 164, 173, 189–190,
195, 204, 215–217, 222–223

Jewish Community Relations Council,
12, 174

John XXIII,
75, 121, 158

John Paul II,
1, 3, 18, 19, 25, 28–29, 31–32, 36, 41,
77, 80, 81–85, 104, 122–123, 128,
131, 133–4, 136, 140–41, 149,
151–155, 159–161, 199–200, 209,
211

Joseph Cardinal Bernardin Center for
the Study of Eastern European Jewry,
13, 69, 137, 174

Kahane, Rabbi Meir,
40, 47

Kristallnacht,
89–93

Ku Klux Klan,
125

Laborem Exercens,
77, 134

Lent,
215–217

Life,
respect for, 42–44, 53, 105–107.
See also Abortion

Liturgy,
relationship between Catholic and
Jewish, 193–194, 209–223

Lonergan, Reverend Bernard,
139

Lumen Gentium,
84

Marcion,
211

Marriage,
interfaith, 13

Middle East,
recent conflicts in, 21, 29–32, 40–41,
42, 49–51, 103–105, 109–112, 132,
135–136, 162, 170–171. *See also*
Israel

Mit Brennender Sorge,
158

National Catholic Welfare Conference,
126

National Conference of Catholic
Bishops,
29, 40, 42, 45, 50, 128, 173, 209

National Conference of Christians
and Jews,
14

National Interreligious Task Force
on Soviet Jewry,
33, 47

Nation of Islam,
40, 47

Nazism,
5–7, 20–22, 47, 70–74, 81, 85–88,
89–97, 114–116, 119, 121, 129–
137, 150–151, 155–157, 201.
See also Holocaust

New Testament.
See Scripture

Nietzsche, Friedrich,
115

PUBLICATIONS RELATED TO THE JEWISH-CATHOLIC DIALOGUE

The following are available from book stores or from Liturgy Training Publications (1-800-933-1800).

From Desolation to Hope: An Interreligious Holocaust Memorial Service. The texts in this book were gathered by Dr. Eugene Fisher and Rabbi Leon Klenicki for interfaith prayer on Yom Hashoah. ($2.95)

Jews and Christians: A Dialogue Service about Prayer. This script for an interfaith conversation was created by Rev. Bruce Robbins and Rabbi Leon Klenicki and is copublished with the Anti-Defamation League of B'nai B'rith and the General Commission on Interreligious Concerns of the United Methodist Church. ($4)

The Passover Celebration: A Haggadah for the Seder. This participation book for the seder meal was prepared by Rabbi Leon Klenicki especially for interfaith gatherings. ($2.95) *Songs for the Seder* is an audiocassette with music for all the songs in the Passover book. ($5.95)

Teaching Christian Children about Judaism. Deborah Levine has created seven lessons for children in Catholic grade school or religious education: the liturgical year, Rosh Hashanah, Hanukkah, Passover, scripture, the Sabbath, the synagogue. In addition to the teachers' materials there are take-home pages to be copied and an audiocassette.

Thank God: Prayers of Jews and Christians Together. A resource for the household or for any gathering where Christians and Jews are to work or dialogue together. The materials were gathered by Carol Frances Jegen, BVM, and Rabbi Byron Sherwin. ($6.50)

When Catholics Speak about Jews: Notes for Homilists and Catechists. John Pawlikowski and James Wilde discuss the continuing danger of anti-Semitism, even if unconscious, in Catholic preaching and teaching. ($5.95)